LINUX
MULTIMEDIA
HACKS™

Other resources from O'Reilly

Related titles

Skype Hacks™
Linux Desktop Hacks™
GIMP Pocket Reference
Knoppix Hacks™
Linux in a Nutshell
Linux in a Windows
    World

Linux Pocket Guide
Test Driving Linux
Knoppix Pocket
    Reference
Linux Cookbook™
Linux Server Hacks™
Running Linux

Hacks Series Home

hacks.oreilly.com is a community site for developers and power users of all stripes. Readers learn from each other as they share their favorite tips and tools for Mac OS X, Linux, Google, Windows XP, and more.

---

oreilly.com

oreilly.com is more than a complete catalog of O'Reilly books. You'll also find links to news, events, articles, weblogs, sample chapters, and code examples.

---

oreillynet.com is the essential portal for developers interested in open and emerging technologies, including new platforms, programming languages, and operating systems.

Conferences

O'Reilly brings diverse innovators together to nurture the ideas that spark revolutionary industries. We specialize in documenting the latest tools and systems, translating the innovator's knowledge into useful skills for those in the trenches. Visit *conferences.oreilly.com* for our upcoming events.

Safari Bookshelf (*safari.oreilly.com*) is the premier online reference library for programmers and IT professionals. Conduct searches across more than 1,000 books. Subscribers can zero in on answers to time-critical questions in a matter of seconds. Read the books on your Bookshelf from cover to cover or simply flip to the page you need. Try it today for free.

LINUX
MULTIMEDIA
HACKS™

Kyle Rankin

O'REILLY®

Beijing · Cambridge · Farnham · Köln · Paris · Sebastopol · Taipei · Tokyo

Linux Multimedia Hacks™
by Kyle Rankin

Copyright © 2006 O'Reilly Media, Inc. All rights reserved.
Printed in the United States of America.

Published by O'Reilly Media, Inc., 1005 Gravenstein Highway North, Sebastopol, CA 95472.

O'Reilly books may be purchased for educational, business, or sales promotional use. Online editions are also available for most titles (*safari.oreilly.com*). For more information, contact our corporate/institutional sales department: (800) 998-9938 or *corporate@oreilly.com*.

Editor:	David Brickner	**Production Editor:**	Jamie Peppard
Series Editor:	Rael Dornfest	**Cover Designer:**	Marcia Friedman
Executive Editor:	Dale Dougherty	**Interior Designer:**	David Futato

Printing History:

November 2005: First Edition.

 This book uses RepKover™, a durable and flexible lay-flat binding.

ISBN: 0-596-10076-0

[M]

Contents

Credits

About the Author

Kyle Rankin is a system administrator who enjoys troubleshooting, problem solving, and system recovery. He has been using Linux in many different forms for over seven years. Kyle is currently the president of the North Bay Linux Users Group in California (*http://nblug.org*). He is the author of *Knoppix Hacks* and *Knoppix Pocket Reference* for O'Reilly Media, a contributing writer for *Linux Desktop Hacks* and *Windows XP Hacks*, and has written for a number of print and web publications.

Contributors

The following people contributed their writing, code, and inspiration to *Linux Multimedia Hacks*:

- Jono Bacon [Hack #43] is an established writer, developer, and musician. Jono has been working as a full-time writer and technology consultant/developer since 2000 for a variety of publishers and companies and is a coauthor of *Linux Desktop Hacks* (O'Reilly), in which this hack originally appeared.

- Robert Bernier [Hacks #12 and #72] works as a consultant for SRA America, *http://sraapowergres.com*, as the PostgreSQL Business Intelligence Analyst and is the creator of *pg_live*, a live CD distribution designed to profile PostgreSQL. Robert teaches, and also writes for numerous publications including O'Reilly's onlamp.com and hard-copy magazines in Europe and North America.

- David Brickner [Hacks #14 and #53] is a Linux desktop enthusiast and an editor at O'Reilly. He authored *Test Driving Linux* and the *Linux Desktop Pocket Guide*.

- Jorge Castro [Hack #7] is a network administrator at the Oakland University School of Engineering and Computer Science. He has written for Ars Technica and the GNOME Journal. He is currently serving as a board member for the michigan!/usr/group LUG in the metropolitan Detroit area.

- Bill Childers [Hacks #45 and #66] is Director of Enterprise Systems for Quinstreet, Inc. He's been working with Linux and UNIX since before it was cool, and previously worked for Sun Microsystems and Set Engineering.

- Jerome Couderc [Hack #29] is a 29-year-old computer engineer at a French insurance company. His hobbies are developing EasyTAG and mountain biking.

- Alan Donovan [Hack #42] is a researcher in the field of programming languages and program analysis. He holds degrees from the University of Cambridge and MIT, where he currently works in the Computer Science and Artificial Intelligence Laboratory. His hack can also be found in *iPod and iTunes Hacks* (O'Reilly).

- Edd Dumbill [Hack #87] is a free software hacker, writer, and entrepreneur. He has a weblog at *http://usefulinc.com/edd/blog*.

- Michael Grigoriev [Hack #19] recently completed his undergraduate degree in Computer Science at the University of Waterloo and will be starting work at Google shortly. He spends most of his free time reading, watching movies, or hacking on various open source projects.

- Robert Kaye [Hacks #27, #30, #31, #32, #83, and #84] is the Mayhem & Chaos Coordinator and creator of MusicBrainz, the music metadata commons. For more information about him, visit *http://mayhem-chaos.net* or read his blog at *http://mayhem-chaos.net/blog*.

- Alexander Koenig [Hack #41] started the terminatorX project while studying computer science in Stuttgart and Esslingen, Germany. He is now working as a system architect in the Stuttgart area and continues to maintain terminatorX in his spare time.

- Nicholas Petreley [Hack #23] is a writer, consultant, and editor-in-chief of Tux, the online Linux magazine for the desktop (*http://www.tuxmagazine.com*). He is a coauthor of *Linux Desktop Hacks* (O'Reilly), where this particular hack first appeared.

- Ted Wallingford [Hack #99] believes that VoIP and the Internet are today's revolution in distance communication. Ted's writing habit led him to write marketing and technical white papers for Gateway Computer and the former Amiga, Inc., where he served as webmaster in 1999. Ted is the author of the O'Reilly books *Switching to VoIP* and *VoIP Hacks* (from which this hack is borrowed).

- Jarod Wilson [Hacks #77, #78, and #79] is a relatively long-time Linux user (dating back to 1997), on both a personal and professional level. He currently works for Linux Networx as an HPC cluster jockey and spends a good chunk of his nonexistent spare time working on various things related to the MythTV project (open source Linux PVR).

Acknowledgments

I couldn't start the acknowledgments section without thanking my wife Joy for supporting me through this whole process yet again and helping me not only manage my work time, but also my free time. Thanks for keeping me motivated, caffeinated, and for generally removing outside stresses so I could get this done.

A big thank you to all of the contributing writers for your hard work, sometimes under tight schedules, and to the tech reviewers Robert Kaye, Seb Ruiz, and Robert Kulagowski for your valuable feedback. Thanks also to Adam Israel for your image hacking tips.

Extra thanks to my editor, David Brickner, for thinking of me for this book in the first place and helping me every step of the way until it was finished. Thanks also to the production editor Jamie Peppard, who managed the book in its final stages and prepared it for the printer; Nancy Reinhardt, who copyedited the text; Marcia Friedman, who designed the cover; and Ellen Troutman Zaig, for her work on the index.

Preface

If you ask most people to name the most powerful platform for multimedia, you probably won't hear Linux as their answer. Dealing with images, audio, and video, with all their different formats and requirements, is never easy. Since Linux has a—in many ways undeserved—reputation for being complicated anyway, many people likely figure that multimedia programs under Linux add an extra level of complication.

The fact is that Linux has a number of very powerful and versatile tools, both graphical and command-line, for viewing and editing just about any multimedia content. I admit that I've been intimidated by some of these programs in the past, but as I've gotten more comfortable with the tools, and as they have become more user-friendly over the years, I've come to the conclusion that Linux multimedia tools are not just on par with programs on other platforms in terms of both ease of use and power, in many cases the Linux tools are just plain better.

Compatibility with proprietary media formats has long been an issue under Linux. I remember the days when sites that posted videos in anything but MPEG-1 or -2 were horribly flamed by Linux users in Slashdot threads (not that it takes much to be flamed in a Slashdot thread). I admit I grumbled to myself sometimes as I waited for someone to post a link to a video in a format I could play under Linux. Of course, this was over five years ago. Today Linux enjoys compatibility with just about any media format you run into, even despite the proprietary nature of many video and audio codecs. I've found that these days I end up taking for granted that a video—whether downloaded or streamed—will play on my system.

In some cases, Linux has a definite advantage over other platforms in the multimedia realm. The Web contains a number of really useful tools for media management, from Audioscrobbler to manage music recommendations and chart your listening habits, to MusicBrainz, CDDB databases, cover art, song lyric services, TV listings, and many other web-based services. Nowhere have all of these services been used all together like they have under Linux.

Finally, the free and open nature of most Linux multimedia applications creates an environment where one great tool spawns another great tool. Most Linux multimedia programs are built from a foundation of powerful command line utilities and add either ease of use or integration with other command line tools. Any improvement to the base tools therefore gets incorporated upstream. This means that for most applications you can get your work done whether you prefer a GUI or the command line. In this book, I cover how to access the power of Linux multimedia tools for both environments.

Why Linux Multimedia Hacks?

The term *hacking* has a bad reputation in the press, where it is often to refer to someone who breaks into systems or wreaks havoc, with computers as their weapon. Among people who write code, though, the term *hack* refers to a "quick-and-dirty" solution to a problem, or a clever way to get something done. And the term *hacker* is taken very much as a compliment, referring to someone as being *creative*, having the technical chops to get things done. The Hacks series is an attempt to reclaim the word, document the good ways people are hacking, and pass the hacker ethic of creative participation on to the uninitiated. Seeing how others approach systems and problems is often the quickest way to learn about a new technology.

Multimedia programs under Linux are incredibly powerful and lend themselves to all sorts of clever hacks. That said, these programs often mystify people, so *Linux Multimedia Hacks* takes the best of Linux's multimedia tools and shows you step by step how to use these tools to do cool things you not have thought possible with images, audio, and video.

How to Use This Book

You can read this book from cover to cover if you like, but each hack stands on its own, so feel free to browse and jump to the different sections that interest you most. If there's a prerequisite you need to know about, a cross-reference will guide you to the right hack.

For the most part you can look for hacks based on the multimedia type. Image hacks have their own chapter, audio hacks have their own chapter, and so on. Some topics or programs (such as MPlayer) are too broad to fit in a single hack, so these topics start out with a more general-purpose hack and follow up with hacks that draw on that and add more specific information.

I do make the assumption that you feel comfortable using the command line, editing text files, or installing programs from source or using your distribution's package manager. If you are very new to Linux and find these basic tasks daunting, I suggest you also pick up a thorough introduction to Linux books such as O'Reilly's *Running Linux*.

How This Book Is Organized

The book is divided into several chapters, organized by subject:

Chapter 1, *Images*
> This chapter contains hacks specifically for images. Here you'll find tips ranging from basic image edits to automated image manipulation.

Chapter 2, *Audio*
> Here you will find hacks for all things audio. There are a number of hacks that cover useful audio playing tools so you can compare and contrast the features of some of the best. You will also find many hacks that deal with audio manipulation from audio format conversion to tweaking metadata within your audio files.

Chapter 3, *Video*
> The video tools under Linux are some of the best, and this chapter shows you how to get the most out of them. Anything from playing just about any video format to extracting and converting between different video formats, to creating your own VCDs and DVDs is covered here.

Chapter 4, *Broadcast Media*
> When you want your multimedia content to reach a lot of people, one of the best ways is through broadcasting. Hacks to turn your computer into an open source Tivo as well as tips for accessing and creating your own web broadcasts can be found here.

Chapter 5, *Web*
> The Web is a great place to combine many different types of media all at once. In this chapter, you will find hacks to help you tweak your web browser under Linux so it can get the most out of the multimedia Web.

Conventions Used in This Book

The following is a list of the typographical conventions used in this book:

Italics

    Indicates Linux pathnames, filenames, commands, packages, and program names; URLs; and new terms where they are defined.

`Constant width`

    Shows code examples, the contents of files, and console output, as well as the names of options and variables.

`Constant width bold`

    Used to show commands or other text that should be typed literally by the user.

`Constant width italic`

    Used in code examples and tables to show sample text to be replaced with your own values.

Gray type

    Used to indicate a cross-reference within the text.

You should pay special attention to notes set apart from the text with the following icons:

This is a tip, suggestion, or general note. It contains useful supplementary information about the topic at hand.

This is a warning or note of caution, often indicating that your data or your privacy might be at risk.

The thermometer icons found next to each hack indicate the relative complexity of the hack:

beginner   moderate   expert

Using Code Examples

This book is here to help you get your job done. In general, you may use the code in this book in your programs and documentation. You do not need to contact us for permission unless you're reproducing a significant portion of the code. For example, writing a program that uses several chunks of code from this book does not require permission. Selling or distributing a CD-ROM of examples from O'Reilly books *does* require permission. Answering a question by citing this book and quoting example code does not require permission. Incorporating a significant amount of example code from this book into your product's documentation *does* require permission.

We appreciate, but do not require, attribution. An attribution usually includes the title, author, publisher, and ISBN. For example: "*Linux Multimedia Hacks* by Kyle Rankin. Copyright © 2006 O'Reilly Media, Inc., 0-596-10076-0."

If you feel your use of code examples falls outside fair use or the permission given above, feel free to contact us at *permissions@oreilly.com*.

How to Contact Us

We have tested and verified the information in this book to the best of our ability, but you may find that features have changed (or even that we have made mistakes!). As a reader of this book, you can help us to improve future editions by sending us your feedback. Please let us know about any errors, inaccuracies, bugs, misleading or confusing statements, and typos that you find anywhere in this book.

Please also let us know what we can do to make this book more useful to you. We take your comments seriously and will try to incorporate reasonable suggestions into future editions. You can write to us at:

O'Reilly Media, Inc.
1005 Gravenstein Highway North
Sebastopol, CA 95472
(800) 998-9938 (in the U.S. or Canada)
(707) 829-0515 (international/local)
(707) 829-0104 (fax)

To ask technical questions or to comment on the book, send email to:

bookquestions@oreilly.com

The web site for *Linux Multimedia Hacks* lists examples, errata, and plans for future editions. You can find this page at:

http://www.oreilly.com/catalog/linuxmmhks

For more information about this book and others, see the O'Reilly web site:

http://www.oreilly.com

Safari Enabled

 When you see a Safari® Enabled icon on the cover of your favorite technology book, that means the book is available online through the O'Reilly Network Safari Bookshelf.

Safari offers a solution that's better than e-books. It's a virtual library that lets you easily search thousands of top tech books, cut and paste code samples, download chapters, and find quick answers when you need the most accurate, current information. Try it for free at *http://safari.oreilly.com*.

Got a Hack?

To explore Hacks books online or to contribute a hack for future titles, visit:

  http://hacks.oreilly.com

## CHAPTER ONE

Images
Hacks 1–12

Ever since the GIMP emerged as a killer app for image editing, Linux has held a unique place when it comes to image tweaking. On one hand, a number of great tools allow you to perform all sorts of manipulation on an image both in a GUI and in an automated command-line form. What's more, all these utilities are free. On the other hand, Linux is not popular with professionals, because some notable commercial image-editing applications aren't natively available on Linux. However, even without commercial support, the free tools available on a Linux machine provide a great deal of image-editing power, whether you are a pro or a novice.

The hacks in this chapter provide you with the tools and know-how to perform standard changes to your images, from cropping to resizing to creating thumbnails to adding watermarks. I have also included a whole series of hacks that delve into the power of the ImageMagick suite of tools. This command-line suite lets you perform all sorts of functions on your images and the command-line interface makes it simple to write scripts that automatically modify your images. I've even included some sample scripts to get you started.

If you take a lot of digital photos, you will find a number of hacks to help you through the full process of using a digital camera with Linux. Some of the hacks include tips to access your camera under Linux, automatically sync it with your computer, tweak your photos, and even remove red eye. I also cover some tools that help you create slideshows and manage even large directories full of years of photographs.

HACK
#1

Take a Screenshot

Use command-line or GUI tools to take screenshots in a variety of formats.

If you spend any time changing the look of your desktop with fancy themes and icons, what fun is it if you don't post your new cool desktop for everyone to see? The final proof of any successful desktop tweaking is a screenshot you can show off to your friends. You can use a number of methods to take screenshots, and this hack introduces you to some of the most common ones.

From the Command Line

One of the simplest and most universal ways to take a screenshot is with the *import* command from the ImageMagick suite of utilities. This is a very common tool, and chances are that ImageMagick is already installed by your distribution; if not, packages should be readily available. *import* has two major screenshot modes. To take a picture of the entire screen, type:

```
$ import -window root screenshot.png
```

The `-window root` argument tells *import* to take a picture of the entire screen. If you type:

```
$ import screenshot.png
```

Your cursor turns into crosshairs, allowing you to drag across the section of screen you want to copy. Once you release the mouse button, the part of the screen that is selected becomes the part *import* will put into your image. *import* supports all common image formats used for screenshots, including JPEG, PNG, and BMP (useful for lossless screenshots). All you have to do is name your output file with the file extension you want—*import* will figure out the rest.

If you want to set a time delay so you can arrange your windows or possibly hide the terminal containing the *import* command, just preface your *import* command with *sleep*. To allow five seconds before a screenshot is taken, type:

```
$ sleep 5; import -window root screenshot.png
```

I like to timestamp my screenshots because it makes it easy to tell when they were taken, and prevents me from overwriting other screenshots. To name a screenshot after today's date, encapsulate the date command you want to use inside backticks. The following command will create a screenshot named *YYYY-MM-DD.png* with YYYY, MM, and DD filled in with the year, month, and day respectively:

```
$ import -window root `date +%Y-%m-%d`.png
```

From Within GNOME

GNOME uses its own screenshot program called *gnome-panel-screenshot*. This program can be accessed a number of ways, but probably the easiest is to press the Print Screen key on your keyboard. This immediately takes a screenshot of the entire screen and displays a dialog you can use to name and save the screenshot file. To take a picture of the current window, just press Alt–Print Screen instead. This program is also accessible in the panel menu. Click Actions → Take Screenshot. You can even access this program directly from the command line with:

```
$ gnome-panel-screenshot --delay 5
```

This command causes GNOME to pause five seconds before taking a screenshot. GNOME then presents you with a dialog so you can choose the filename to save to.

From Within KDE

If you use the KDE desktop, *ksnapshot* is the KDE alternative to *gnome-panel-screenshot* and can usually be found within the K Menu → Graphics menu. The GUI allows you to choose a delay, take a screenshot, and choose whether to take the screenshot of the entire desktop or just the current window. You can, of course, also start *ksnapshot* just by typing ksnapshot in a terminal window or in the Run Command window, which you can access by pressing Alt-F2.

HACK #2 Convert from One Image Format to Another

Use the ImageMagick convert tool to change between image formats.

When you deal with images on a regular basis, it's often useful to convert them to different image formats. You can use graphical tools such as the GIMP to open files and save them into different formats, but if you deal with a lot of images you might find that process a bit cumbersome. The ImageMagick tool *convert* solves this problem by providing a command-line interface to image conversion. With *convert* you can change any ImageMagick-supported image format to any other ImageMagick-supported image format. The full list of supported formats is rather large—you can view the full list in the ImageMagick man page (the man page is ImageMagick, not imagemagick)—but among the supported formats are BMP, CMYK, GIF, JPEG, PBM, PNG, RGB, SVG, TIFF, and XPM.

The ImageMagick tools are commonly used by a number of other frontends, so you are likely to find the *convert* tool already packaged for your distribution with the rest of the ImageMagick tools. The standard usage of *convert* is simple: provide an input file and an output file as arguments, and *convert* will figure out the format based on the file extension. So, to convert a BMP to a PNG, type:

```
$ convert image.bmp image.png
```

One of the advantages to a command line image conversion tool is that it lends itself really well to scripting. For instance, the following command converts an entire directory of BMP files to JPEG—the bit of *sed* in the command preserves the filenames but changes the extension to *.jpg*, and the results are fed to *convert*, which knows from the extension what format to make the new files:

```
$ for i in *.bmp; do j=`echo $i | sed -e 's/\.bmp/\.jpg/'`;          \
convert $i $j; done;
```

The backslash at the end of the first line denotes a line break in this book—you can enter everything as one entry.

Tile Images

convert also supports a wide range of image processing functions it can perform as it is converting an image. Even if you don't want to convert from one image format to another, you can still use *convert* to process the image into a new file. For instance, the tile argument tells *convert* to tile the input image into an output image of a size you specify with the -size argument. To take a 16×16 JPEG image and tile it across a new 640×480 JPEG image, you would type:

```
$ convert -size 640x480 tile:image.jpg tiledimage.jpg
```

Replace *image.jpg* and *tiledimage.jpg* with the input file and output files, respectively.

Add a Border to an Image

The -border and -bordercolor arguments let you add a border of specified width and height to an image. The width you specify applies to the left and right of the image, while the height applies to the top and bottom of the image. You can pass a color either in text (red, blue, white, etc.) or as an RGB value. To add a white border around an image (so it looks like a photographic print), type:

```
$ convert -border 15x18 -bordercolor white image.jpg image2.jpg
```

The first border measurement sets the width of the top and bottom border edges; the second measurement sets the width for the left and right borders.

The color names come from X's *rgb.txt* file. To view the contents of this file without having to locate it, use this command:

```
$ showrgb
255 250 250        snow
248 248 255        ghost white
248 248 255        GhostWhite
245 245 245        white smoke
245 245 245        WhiteSmoke
...¶
```

You can also surround your image with a beveled frame with the -frame and accompanying -mattecolor options. The -frame argument accepts a width and height for the frame itself, plus an optional width for a beveled edge on the outer and inner edge of the frame, respectively. The mattecolor option accepts a hexadecimal RGB value. So, to add a red 25 × 25-pixel red frame to an image with a 5-pixel outer bevel, type:

```
$ convert -frame 25x25+5x5 -mattecolor "#FF0000" image.jpg framedimage.jpg
```

Flip and Flop Images

The -flip and -flop arguments allow you to flip an image up and down or left and right, respectively. The -flop argument will convert the image so it looks like it would in a mirror, and the -flip argument flips it upside down. You can also combine the arguments .

> There are a large number of more advanced imaging effects you can perform using the *convert* tool. To see all of them, check out the *convert* man page or type **convert** **--help** in the command line.

HACK #3 Make Image Thumbnails

Use a simple script to create thumbnails from any number of images.

[Hack #2] introduced the *convert* utility as a means to convert between different image formats and perform basic image processing from the command line. *convert* also has resizing options that make it perfect for creating image thumbnails.

The primary argument used to create an image thumbnail is -thumbnail. This argument tells *convert* to create a thumbnail of the input image with the specified geometry. Thumbnails are scaled-down versions of the original, which means the height-to-width ratio is automatically preserved, so you need to specify only one dimension for the conversion. For instance, to create a thumbnail that has a *width* of 160 pixels, type:

```
$ convert -thumbnail 160 image.jpg thumbnail.jpg
```

To create a thumbnail with a *height* of 160 pixels, precede the geometry with x:

```
$ convert -thumbnail x160 image.jpg thumbnail.jpg
```

This command comes in particularly handy if you plan to upload a lot of digital photos to a web gallery, because you can script the entire operation. To create a thumbnail with a width of 160 pixels from every JPEG image in a directory, type

```
$ for i in *.jpg; do convert -thumbnail 160 $i thumb-$i; done;
```

Each image in the directory will have a thumbnail with *thumb-* at the beginning of the filename. This command also works well to create a series of thumbnails of different sizes—just run two different convert commands in the script. So, to create a mid-sized thumbnail with a width of 400 pixels and a small thumbnail with a width of 160 pixels, type:

```
$ for i in *.jpg; do convert -thumbnail 400 $i mid-$i; \
convert -thumbnail 160 $i thumb-$i; done;
```

You can even get fancy and combine other convert arguments with your commands. For instance, to add a 10-pixel beveled grey frame around the mid-size image, and a 2-pixel grey frame around the small thumbnail, type:

```
$ for i in *.jpg; do convert -thumbnail 400 -frame 10x10+2x2 \
-mattecolor "#999999" $i mid-$i; convert -thumbnail 160 -frame 2x2 \
-mattecolor "#999999" $i thumb-$i; done;
```

HACK #4   Animate Images

Pass arguments to the convert tool to turn a directory of images into an animated GIF—all without opening a GUI tool.

The *convert* utility has plenty of tricks up its sleeve. One of the tricks is the simple conversion of a series of images into a single animated GIF file. Since *convert* can handle a large variety of image formats, you don't even need to start out with a directory of GIF-only images.

When it comes to image processing, *convert* does a lot of the heavy lifting on its own. In fact, the only option you need to concern yourself with is the -delay option, which specifies, in milliseconds, how long to wait between each image change. You can use the *animate* tool from the ImageMagick suite to test your animation. To see what your animation would look like with a one-second delay on a directory full of GIF images, type:

```
$ animate -delay 100 *.gif
```

This command displays each image in alphabetical order, one after the other. If you want to display them in a different order, specify the images in that order on the command line. Once you are satisfied with your delay rate you can use the same number with the convert command. To convert a directory of GIF files into a single animated GIF with one second between frames, type:

```
$ convert -delay 100 *.gif animated.gif
```

Because I used a file glob here, I assumed the images were in alphabetical sequence. If they aren't in order, either specify each file on the command line (with the animated GIF specified last) or rename the files so that they are sequential. To see your newly created animated GIF, type:

```
$ display animated.gif
```

This tool can be particularly useful if you take periodic images with a webcam, even if they are JPEGs. Simply put all the webcam images you want to animate into a directory and type:

```
$ convert -delay 100 *.jpg animated.gif
```

Replace *.jpg with a file glob that matches your image format.

HACK #5 Leave a Watermark

Use the composite tool from ImageMagick to add custom watermarks to your images.

Copy protection, particularly digital copy protection, is a topic that has been discussed more and more over recent years. In the case of protecting graphical content, often what you want the most is simply to prevent people from taking your images and using them as their own. To protect against redistribution, many online image galleries have taken to adding watermarks—logos or text that identify the owners of the content—to their images (see Figure 1-1). The watermark labels the owner of the content kind of like your mom writing your name on your underwear before you went to camp. If someone decides to take your image and host it on their site, they must cut out your watermark and leave an easily identifiable hole in the image. This hack will describe how to use the ImageMagick tool *composite* to add your own custom watermark to your image gallery.

Before you watermark your images, you must first create the image you will use as a watermark. How the watermark is designed is mostly a matter of taste, but there are a few conventions you can use to make a good watermark:

- Your watermark should have relatively small dimensions as compared to the image you will watermark. This might seem to go without saying, but if a watermark is too big, not only will it prohibit people from copying your image, it will also prohibiting people from *seeing* your image. Try your watermark on a couple of representative images to see just how much of the image it obscures.

- A watermark should have a transparent background. This convention follows the thinking of the previous one. The goal is to display the watermark but not obscure the image, so a transparent background ensures your logo will be seen but the large borders around the watermark won't.

- Consider a monochromatic watermark. It might be tempting to create a colorful and fancy watermark for your images, but the watermark will be combined with images of various colors, so a colorful watermark may clash with some of your images.

Once your watermark has been created, the next step is to decide the ideal placement on your images. This can be tough. After all, images come in lots of shapes and sizes, and—again—you don't want to obscure a crucial part of the image. A common convention is to place watermarks near the bottom right-hand corner of an image. You could certainly place a watermark in the center of your image, but you run the chance of obscuring the part of the image people most want to see.

composite has a number of advanced options, but for watermarking there are only a couple you absolutely need: -gravity and -watermark. The -gravity option defines a number of locations for a watermark. The supported locations are north, east, south, west, northeast, southeast, southwest, northwest, and center. The -watermark option takes as its argument a percentage that defines how translucent to make the watermark (which will determine how much your image will show through). To add a 35% translucent watermark in the bottom right-hand corner of an image (Figure 1-1), type:

```
$ composite -watermark 35% -gravity southeast watermark.gif image.jpg \
image-watermarked.jpg
```

In this example, **watermark.gif** is the watermark (with a transparent background), **image.jpg** is the image to watermark, and **image-watermarked.jpg** is the newly created combination of the two. Once you have created the image, view it to make sure that the transparency level is acceptable and the watermark is in the correct location.

> *composite* adds no padding to the watermark, so if you type **-gravity southeast**, it puts the watermark exactly in the bottom righthand corner of the image. If you want to add padding, go into the watermark image itself and increase the size of your canvas. Since the background of the watermark is transparent, the larger canvas will act as padding.

Since this is a command-line program, it lends itself rather well to scripts. To add your watermark to all JPEG images in your current directory, type:

```
$ for i in *.jpg; do j=`echo $i | sed -e 's/\.jpg/-wm.jpg/'`; \
composite -watermark 35% -gravity southeast watermark.gif $i $j; done;
```

Figure 1-1. Image with a watermark in the bottom righthand corner

All the watermarked images will have -wm added to the image name. To avoid accidentally renaming the files, you might want to store all your watermarked files in a separate directory. In that case, assuming the directory is called ~/watermarked, you would type:

```
$ for i in *.jpg; do composite -watermark 35% -gravity southeast \
watermark.gif $i ~/watermarked/$i; done;
```

HACK #6 Pull Images from a Digital Camera

Get the images from your camera with either standard USB storage device support or gphoto.

So you have a digital camera full of pictures, and you have a Linux machine with the GIMP raring to go, but you need to get the pictures from the camera to the computer under Linux. As this hack illustrates, using your digital camera under Linux is not much of a headache, particularly with newer distributions and newer cameras.

Although there are many ways to categorize digital cameras, when it comes to using them under Linux there are only two categories: cameras that act as USB storage devices and cameras that don't. Generally, newer cameras act like USB storage devices (such as a USB thumb drive) when plugged into a computer, but many older cameras use proprietary communication standards even though they use standard USBs or serial ports. The easiest way to tell which type of camera you have is to plug it into a non-Linux system. If it shows up as a regular hard drive, under Linux you can treat it like a USB storage device. Otherwise you may have to go the *gtkam* route, which I describe later, in the section, "Non-USB Storage Devices."

USB Storage Devices

Most modern desktop Linux distributions offer automatic management of USB storage devices—just plug in a USB key or other device, and KDE or Gnome will automatically create a new icon on your desktop that you can click to access the device. If you have such a distribution, then using your digital camera is easy: plug in the camera, click on the icon that appears on the desktop, and browse it like you would any other hard drive. You can copy and paste images to your desktop or another folder, and when you are done you can close the window, right-click on the icon, unmount the camera, and unplug it.

If you don't have such a desktop environment, it still isn't too difficult—you just have to go through an extra step or two. In order to mount your camera, you need to determine which SCSI drive Linux has assigned it. To do this, run tail on your */var/log/syslog* or */var/log/messages* log file as root, and then plug in the device. You should see output something like this:

```
# tail -f /var/log/messages
Jul 19 20:44:36 moses kernel: SCSI device sda: 58605120 512-byte hdwr
sectors (30006 MB)
Jul 19 20:44:36 moses scsi.agent[30251]:       sd_mod: loaded sucessfully
(for disk)
Jul 19 20:44:36 moses kernel:  /dev/scsi/host0/bus0/target0/lun0: p1
Jul 19 20:44:36 moses kernel: Attached scsi disk sda at scsi0, channel 0, id
0, lun 0
Jul 19 20:49:16 moses kernel: usb 4-1: USB disconnect, address 4
Jul 19 21:03:26 moses -- MARK --
Jul 19 21:23:26 moses -- MARK --
Jul 19 21:35:19 moses kernel: usb 1-1: new full speed USB device using uhci_
hcd and address 3
Jul 19 21:35:19 moses kernel: scsi1 : SCSI emulation for USB Mass Storage
devices
Jul 19 21:35:22 moses usb.agent[4679]:       usb-storage: already loaded
```

In the output you can see that Linux assigned my digital camera the *sda* device in this line:

```
Jul 19 20:44:36 moses kernel: SCSI device sda: 58605120 512-byte hdwr
sectors (30006 MB)
```

To access the files on the camera, I become root, create a mount point under */mnt*, and then use the *mount* command to access it:

```
# mkdir /mnt/camera
# mount -t vfat /dev/sda1 /mnt/camera
```

Now I can browse to */mnt/camera* either in the terminal or with a file manager and copy files from the camera. I specified a filesystem type of vfat because almost all digital camera media (indeed all flash media) are formatted as vfat. When I'm finished, I unmount the drive and unplug it:

```
# umount /dev/sda1
```

Like with all USB storage devices, remember to unmount the camera before unplugging it from the computer or powering it off. This ensures that all changed files have been completely written to the camera. Unplugging any USB drive while files are being written almost guarantees file damage.

Non-USB Storage Devices

Not all digital cameras operate as generic USB storage devices, even if they have a USB port. This is particularly true of older digital cameras. To use one of these cameras you must use *gtkam*, digiKam, gphoto2, or another program that uses the *libgphoto* libraries to provide basic access to the files on your digital camera.

Most major desktop distributions have packages for *gtkam* and *libgphoto* so you can use your standard packaging tool to install them. Otherwise download the source from the official *gtkam* page at *http://www.gphoto.org/proj/gtkam* and compile it according to the installation instructions.

Before you run *gtkam*, connect the camera to the computer by the USB or serial port. Then start *gtkam* through your application menu or type **gtkam** in a terminal. The main window appears fairly blank by default, and the first step is to click Camera → Add Camera to open a dialog that displays the full list of cameras *gtkam* supports.

Click Detect for *gtkam* to probe the USB ports for your camera, or select it from the list of camera models and click OK. You are dropped back to the main window that then presents you with thumbnails of all your photos. *gtkam* doesn't provide a lot of photo-editing features; basically you can zoom in and out on your photos and select some or all to save for later editing. Once you are finished, be sure to close *gtkam* before you unplug your digital camera from the computer.

HACK
#7

Manage Photos with f-spot

Install f-spot and get an iPhoto-like photo organization tool under Linux.

Digital cameras have become so cheap and ubiquitous that every moment is a picture opportunity because there is always a camera—or camera phone—

within reach. And with the ever-declining cost of flash storage media, the expense of taking just one more picture is so close to free that it hardly counts. These days, even casual photographers have thousands of images they need to keep track of and, because the photos are digital, they need to keep track of them on their computer. *f-spot* is a tool that aims to bring ease of use and power to photo management in Linux. It has a tag-based system of classifying groups of photos, as well as an integrated timeline feature that lets the user manage large collections by the date the picture was taken. *f-spot* also features good "touch up" tools that allow you to resize, crop, adjust color, and rotate groups of photos quickly without having to resort to larger tools such as the GIMP. *f-spot* is currently maintained by Larry Ewing, who, coincidentally, designed Tux the Penguin.

Install f-spot

f-spot is built on the Mono platform and, as such, requires the runtime to be installed. This is usually handled by your Linux distributor, but might require the installation of Mono and GTK# by the end user. You can find Mono and GTK# at *http:/www.go-mono.com*. The latest source code to *f-spot* can be found at its homepage at *http://www.gnome.org/projects/f-spot*. *f-spot* is still relatively young, so updates are common. But even at its young age, *f-spot* already has some powerful features.

Import Your Pictures to f-spot

When you first launch *f-spot*, you are met by an import dialog box. From here you can choose a folder to import your pictures from. (You can also search recursively inside folders and assign tags to the pictures. I'll go into tagging later.) After selecting the folder and clicking OK, *f-spot* begins importing your photos. The graphical thumbnails in the progress screen let you monitor your photos as they're being imported. When importing is complete, your photos will be thumbnailed in the main *f-spot* window, ready to be managed.

View Your Pictures

f-spot starts out in Browse mode, which allows you to scroll through your pictures visually. At the top of the browse window is a timeline. Many digital cameras attach EXIF metadata to the photos they take. To view this data, click on a picture and press Ctrl-I. Some of this data (such as when the date the photo was taken) is extremely useful for organizing photos. *f-spot* parses this information and allows you to browse your collection by date. Click on the box in the timeline and drag it to different points in the timeline. When you release the box, the focus switches to the first picture taken on that date, and the thumbnail "throbs" just a little to get your attention.

To view a picture in fullscreen mode, click on it to select it, and then click on the fullscreen button on the toolbar. A slideshow view is also available on the toolbar.

Edit Your Pictures

Some of the newer, more expensive cameras keep track of their orientation and adjust automatically, but those of us with older, cheaper cameras still need to manually rotate our pictures so they look right. Click on a picture, and then click on Rotate Left or Rotate Right to correct the picture's orientation. To select multiple pictures hold down Ctrl while clicking. This allows you to select a group of pictures and rotate them all at once.

Double clicking on a photo puts *f-spot* into edit mode; this is useful for cropping pictures or applying other touch-ups. In this mode you can press Ctrl-M to zoom in, and Ctrl-Shift-M to zoom out. Scrolling the mouse wheel up or down also zooms in and out, respectively. When you're in this mode, a new toolbar appears on the bottom. From this toolbar you'll be able to do more advanced editing such as cropping, red-eye reduction, and color adjustment. The dropdown list is used in conjunction with the crop tool. Clicking and dragging on the image draws a box on the image. This is how you'll measure a crop. Once you've drawn a box around the area you want to crop, click on the crop icon. This crops the image according to the box you just drew. The dropdown list has a selection of pre-made crop adjustments—for example 8×10. Selecting 8×10 in this dropdown list will restrict your crop to that ratio. This allows you, for example, to edit an entire batch of shots to be 8 ×10 portraits.

Before you go too crazy with the crop tool, you should familiarize yourself with *f-spot*'s undo function. *f-spot* doesn't have an "undo" function like typical programs; instead it keeps track of each version of a photo you edit and allows you to select which version to view. This information is available at the bottom of the sidebar. Since *f-spot* keeps track of the versions of the photo, if you are overzealous with the crop tool, you can always click back to the original and start again. *f-spot* is also smart enough to put this modified version as a separate file on disk so that modifications you make won't affect the original.

f-spot also has some rudimentary red-eye correction. You can select the "red area" via the selection tool, but instead of using the crop button, click on the red eye button and *f-spot* will correct the picture the best it can. For best results, select each eye separately, because applying this effect to a large area can have unintended results.

The last editing button in the bottom toolbar is the color adjustment, which enables you to edit the exposure and color temperature of the photo. At the bottom right in this mode are also left and right arrows that allow you to move throughout your collection to do mass cropping without having to switch back to browse mode.

Organize Your Pictures with Tags

Small touchups are easy in *f-spot*, but the real killer feature is the tag functionality. *f-spot* comes out of the box with some individual pre-made tags, such as Favorites, and some tag categories, such as People, Places, and Events. You can assign any number of tags to any of your photos, as well as make your own tags and tag categories (see Figure 1-2).

Figure 1-2. f-spot with tags displayed

Tagging photos is easy. Select the photo you want to tag and then drag it to proper tag and drop. Ctrl-click on multiple pictures to select more than one, and then drag and drop them onto tags. You can also drag and drop the tag onto a group of pictures or right-click on an individual picture and select the tag via the context menu. Right-clicking on a blank area in the sidebar will give you an opportunity to create your own tags and categories. Checking the box next to a tag or tag group will make *f-spot* show only pictures tagged with those tags.

So why use tags? They allow you to group your pictures in whatever kind of album you want. For example, I can tag a set of pictures as *Beagles*, a tag in the category of *Dogs*. I can then classify my other dog pictures according to breeds. A picture of a beagle can be tagged as both Dogs and as Beagles, whereas a picture of a boxer would be tagged Dogs and Boxers. To view all my pictures of dogs, I check just the box next to the category Dogs; to view pictures of only beagles, I check only the Beagles tag. Of course, making a bunch of tags can create clutter, which is why *f-spot* automatically thumbnails your tags in the sidebar with a picture from its group, allowing you to visually browse your tags. When you first import your pictures into *f-spot*, you have the option of tagging a set of photos. This allows you to mass tag a bunch of photos that you might want classified under one event or place.

Tags are extremely flexible and are limited only by the resourcefulness of the user. When combined with the timeline feature, tags allow you to view your groups of pictures in entirely new ways—for example "pictures of our beagle that were taken in 2005." Tags become even more useful as your photo collection grows.

Export Photographs

Now that you've categorized and meticulously tagged your photos, it's time to share them with the world. *f-spot*'s export capabilities make this very easy. First, select a set of pictures to export. Tags help in the selection, as you can just click on the tag for the album you want to see and then individually select the pictures from there. In the File menu you'll notice an entry for Send Mail. This will launch your mail client and automatically attach the selected pictures to an email message. Although this is sufficient for one or two pictures, it doesn't scale very well.

In the File menu, under export, you'll notice options to export to Flickr, VFS, Web Gallery, Original, and CD. The simplest is CD. This allows you to burn any group of selected pictures right to CD-R/RW from within *f-spot*. When the CD-burning option is selected, a dialog pops up showing you which pictures will be burnt onto CD. Click OK to launch your CD-burning tool.

f-spot also has support for the popular flickr (*http://www.flickr.com*) photo hosting service. Select flickr and fill in your flickr account information to export your photos directly into your flickr account. There is also an option for exporting the tags and categories from *f-spot* right into flickr, which means that your collection will retain its classification. The Web Gallery option is similar to the flickr export, except it allows you to export to the popular Gallery software that is common on the Web **[Hack #100]**. Both the flickr and Web Gallery options allow for resizing your photos before upload if you have bandwidth limitations. flickr exports your selected pictures into a static HTML album, suitable for uploading to any web host.

See Also

- *http://www.gnomejournal.org/article/23/an-introduction-to-f-spot*

—Jorge Castro

HACK #8 Edit Images
Use the GIMP to crop, scale, and otherwise edit your photos.

[Hack #6] discusses different ways under Linux to access the photos from a digital camera, but what tools do you use once the photos are on your computer? Sometimes you might be fine with a picture, but other times you may want to crop out something, resize the photo, or rotate it so it has the right orientation. While there are a number of programs that can do all these things—even some that run from the command line—the GIMP is the de facto standard when you want to edit images graphically. In this hack, I cover how to perform some of the common changes you might want to make to a photo or other image. The GIMP can do a number of pretty advanced things, but this hack sticks to the basics.

The first step is to install the GIMP. Installation is made easy by the fact that this is a very popular program that has been around for a long time. Any major Linux distribution should offer the GIMP in its packages, and some even install it by default, so check your application menu. If it isn't installed, just use your standard packaging tool to install it.

To start the GIMP, select it from your desktop's menu or, alternatively, type **gimp** in a terminal. The first time the GIMP runs, it goes through a basic configuration wizard; the defaults should be suitable for most users. The default interface might seem daunting at first if you aren't experienced with image editing tools, but for basic editing you only need to be concerned with a few of the widgets you see. After the GIMP has loaded, click File → Open and select the image you want to edit.

The GIMP will open the image into its own window and depending on the size of the image, the GIMP might scale down the image to fit on the screen. To zoom in, hit the + key on the keyboard or click the magnifying glass button on the toolbar and then click on the image. To zoom out, hit the − key or click the magnifying glass button, and then hold Ctrl when you click on the image.

One common image-editing function is image cropping. Cropping lets you select the part of the image that you want to keep and removes everything else. This can be useful if a picture is a bit off-center, or if you want to focus on a particular subject in a photo. To crop an image, first click the crop tool on the toolbar (it's the one with the knife icon), right-click on your image and select Tools → Transform Tools → Crop & Resize, or press Shift-C. Next move your mouse to the top corner of the area you want to crop; then click and drag the cursor down to the opposite corner. As you move the cursor, use the location of the cursor shown at the bottom left-hand corner of the window to gauge the cursor location. Use the Crop & Resize window that appears to fine-tune the coordinates (Figure 1-3). Then click the Crop button in the Crop & Resize window to complete the crop.

Figure 1-3. GIMP Crop & Resize window

> If you want to undo a change, just press Ctrl-Z or right-click
> on the image and select Edit → Undo.

When dealing with photos, another common need is to rotate them to the correct orientation. The GIMP can do this for you without any quality loss, provided the images are rotated 90, 180, or 270 degrees. To rotate a photo 90 degrees clockwise, right-click the image, and select Image → Transform → Rotate 90 degrees CW. The menu also provides options to rotate the image 90 degrees counterclockwise, 180 degrees, and even to flip the image horizontally or vertically.

You can also use the GIMP to scale images, so they are smaller or larger than normal. [Hack #3] covers creating thumbnails from the command line, but you can also use the GIMP to make thumbnails. To scale an image, right-click on the image and select Image → Scale Image. Enter the new dimensions in the Width and Height fields. Click the widget just to the right of the Width and Height fields to change the proportion of width to height. Then click the Scale button to finish the operation.

> There are a number of advanced image manipulation tools in
> the GIMP that you can use to edit saturation, hue, bright-
> ness, contrast, color, and similar settings. To access these
> options right-click on the image and go to the Layer → Col-
> ors menu.

HACK #9   Remove Red Eye from Photos

Follow a few basic steps with the GIMP to remove red eye from photos.

Red eye happens to the best of us. Nowadays many cameras have red-eye reduction features, but whether you are dealing with older scanned-in photos, or you just forgot to turn on that feature, sometimes you get digital photos that have red eye in them. Since red eye seemingly turns even the sweetest child into demon spawn, you generally want to remove it from your photos before you send them out to relatives. Although it might seem as if you need extensive experience and expensive tools to edit your photos, with the GIMP you can take out red eye in a few simple steps.

The basic steps in this procedure are to select the red area of the eye and then open the channel mixer and change the red, green, and blue values until the red eye looks like a normal pupil. The specifics of these steps are a bit more involved, but as you'll see, they mostly require a bit of time and tinkering.

Select the Red Eye

First you need to select the red eye. Zoom in your image (hit the + key) until the part of the picture with the red eye is mostly filling the window. There are a number of ways to select the red part of the eye, but the fuzzy selection tool is the easiest to use.

The simplest way to select the red part of the eye is to go into the different color channels and disable all but either the green or the blue color channel. Click File → Dialogues → Channels, and click both the red and blue channels so that only the green channel is selected (alternatively, you can select only the blue channel). Now click the eye icon next to the red channel so that you see only the blue and green channels in the image.

Change to the fuzzy selection tool (hit the Z key or select the tool from the toolbar) and click on a red portion of the eye. The first time you do this, you probably won't select all the red, so cancel the selection with Ctrl-Shift-A. Then go to the fuzzy selection tool settings window, make sure feather edges is turned on, increase the threshold, and try again. This part of the process probably requires the most tinkering, so just try different threshold values until you select all of the red. Once you have it right, hold down the shift key and click on a red section of the other eye to select it, too. Now you can go back to your channels and turn on visibility for the red channel and make sure that all three color channels are on. With both eyes selected, you can move on to taking out the red.

Take the Red Out

To take the red out of the selected area, right click on the image and select Filters → Colors → Channel Mixer. The channel mixer lets you adjust the levels of red, green, and blue in the image. You'll definitely want to move the red levels down, and then move the green and blue levels up. Turn on the preview and experiment with the settings until the eye in the preview looks normal. You'll likely want to turn up green the most, then blue, then red. When the eye looks right, click OK to see the changes applied to the image. If it isn't quite how you want, hit Ctrl-Z to undo the change, go back, and try again until it's right. Once you are satisfied with the change, click File → Save.

If the "marching ants" of the selection tool are making it difficult to see your change, hit Ctrl-T to toggle the display of the selection.

Create a Slideshow

Use Kuickshow or gThumb to turn a directory of photos into a slideshow.

For just about every vacation, there is a vacation slide presentation. After all, most people don't just take vacation pictures for themselves, they take them for their friends and family to see as well. In the past, to set up a slide presentation you had to take your film to get developed into slides, and then arrange them into your slide projector. Today with a digital camera, you can quickly, easily, and inexpensively set up a slideshow with open source tools.

There are a number of open source slideshow tools, but for the purposes of this hack I discuss two: KuickShow and gThumb. These slideshow programs are parts of the GNOME and KDE desktop environments respectively, but you can run them on either environment. In addition, one of the programs most likely will be prepackaged by most major Linux distributions.

KuickShow is a simple slideshow program for KDE. You can launch it from the Graphics programs menu for your desktop environment, or you can type kuickshow from the command line. The KuickShow interface is relatively simple. The toolbar along the top provides you with file system navigation tools and buttons to launch the slideshow and configure KuickShow itself (see Figure 1-4). The main section of the window along the bottom is a basic file system browser that lets you navigate to the section of the file system containing your images. Navigate to your images directory and then click the Start Slideshow icon on the toolbar, click File → Start Slideshow, or hit F2 to start your slideshow. KuickShow will display the images one by one, with a delay between images. Hit Esc to exit the slideshow.

KuickShow is pretty configurable. Click Settings → Configure KuickShow to open the configuration window. Here you can configure the background color that displays behind images, apply brightness, contrast, and gamma adjustments, toggle whether to switch to full screen, configure the delay between slides, and change the default key bindings.

gThumb is a GTK application that is more photo management program than slideshow tool. Select gThumb from the Graphics programs menu for your desktop environment or type gthumb at the command line. The gThumb interface is split into three main sections and a toolbar (see Figure 1-5). The toolbar gives you quick access to common gThumb functions. The rest of the interface is split up into panes that display directory information, individual image previews, and thumbnails of all of the images in the current directory. The layout of these three panes can be configured within the gThumb preferences page.

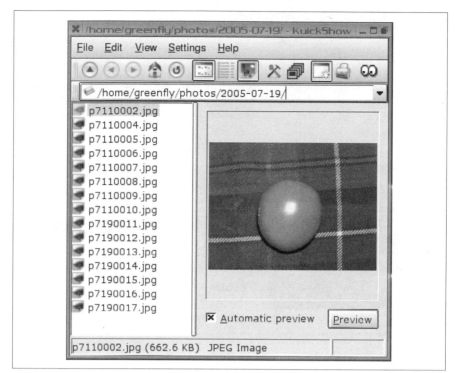

Figure 1-4. Default KuickShow window

Browse to the directory that contains your slideshow photos to see thumb-nails of the images. Click on any individual thumbnail to make a larger version appear in the preview pane, and double-click to switch to a single-paned window displaying an even larger version of your image. Right click an image to access a number of options, including the ability to open the image with another tool such as the GIMP. You don't necessarily have to resort to a tool like the GIMP just to rotate the images, though, because gThumb supports 90-, 180-, and 270-degree rotation as well as the ability to flip the image horizontally or vertically. This makes it easy to ensure that all of your images have the proper orientation before you start the slideshow.

To start the slideshow, click the Slideshow button on the toolbar, choose View → Slideshow, or type s. gThumb will display each image and pause for a few seconds before it moves to the next image. When the slideshow is fin-ished gThumb will return to the folder view, or you can hit Esc during the slideshow to do so immediately.

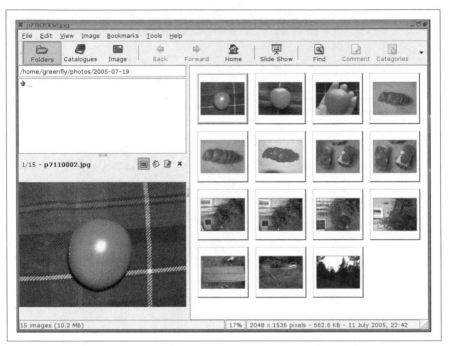

Figure 1-5. Default gThumb window

HACK #11   Automatically Synchronize Your Camera and Computer

With a custom *hotplug* script, you can automatically synchronize your computer and USB storage device camera just by plugging in the camera.

On a particular vacation where I brought both my laptop and my digital camera, I noticed I was offloading the day's pictures onto my laptop each night. The manual process was to plug in the camera, mount it as a USB storage device, create a new directory for the images, copy the images to the new directory, and, finally, unmount the camera. With a few tweaks to *hotplug* and a little detective work, I was able to make the entire process hands free: I now plug in the camera, and it automatically synchronizes everything for me. In this hack I describe the tweaks to *hotplug*, along with tips for creating your own custom synchronization script.

Configure Hotplug

Hotplug is a program under Linux that manages hot-pluggable devices. For the most part it is a program you don't have to think about—just plug in your USB mouse, for instance, and *hotplug* will make sure the applicable drivers are loaded. *Hotplug* is very powerful, however, in that it allows you to customize what to do when a certain device is plugged in. The first step to configuring *hotplug* is to plug in a camera and scan the system logs to make sure the camera is recognized. In the case of my camera, *hotplug* recognized that it was a USB storage device and made sure my *usb-storage* module was already loaded:

```
Jan 19 15:46:27 clover kernel: hub.c: new USB device 00:02.0-1, assigned
address 4
Jan 19 15:46:27 clover kernel: WARNING: USB Mass Storage data integrity not
assured
Jan 19 15:46:27 clover kernel: USB Mass Storage device found at 4
Jan 19 15:46:31 clover usb.agent[10819]: kernel driver usb-storage already
loaded
```

USB drives (and in this case cameras that function as USB drives) work as regular SCSI hard drives in this situation and require the *sd_mod* module to be loaded. You could just mount the device that is created (*/dev/sda1* typically, unless multiple drives are plugged in simultaneously), copy files, and be finished with the camera. But if you want to automatically synchronize this camera to your computer, you must perform special commands just for this drive, and not for any other USB storage device. To set up automatic synchronization, you first need some information from */proc*. The */proc/bus/usb/devices* file will show information about the various USB devices on the system. For instance, here is a snip from the file when my digital camera is plugged in:

```
T:  Bus=01 Lev=01 Prnt=01 Port=00 Cnt=01 Dev#=  2 Spd=12  MxCh= 0
D:  Ver= 1.10 Cls=00(>ifc ) Sub=00 Prot=00 MxPS= 8 #Cfgs=  1
P:  Vendor=07b4 ProdID=0105 Rev= 0.01
S:  Manufacturer=OLYMPUS
S:  Product=C740UZ
S:  SerialNumber=000255534644
C:* #Ifs= 1 Cfg#= 1 Atr=c0 MxPwr=  0mA
I:  If#= 0 Alt= 0 #EPs= 2 Cls=08(stor.) Sub=06 Prot=50 Driver=usb-storage
E:  Ad=04(0) Atr=02(Bulk) MxPS=  64 Ivl=0ms
E:  Ad=83(I) Atr=02(Bulk) MxPS=  64 Ivl=0ms
```

Yeah, it's a lot of gibberish, but there is information in there that is useful for setting up *hotplug*. The parts that are of interest to you are Vendor=07b4, ProdID=0105, Product=C740UZ, and Driver=usb-storage. You can use these sections to configure *hotplug* to do certain things when this device is plugged in. Generally *hotplug* will detect that a device is a USB storage device automatically. In case your drive isn't automatically detected, you will have to add a configuration line for it in */etc/hotplug/usb/usb.usermap*. The first four columns of *usb.usermap* are all that should concern you, and the information you need for those columns can be found in those special sections of the */proc/bus/usb/devices* file. The first column contains the USB module to associate with the device, or what follows the Driver option (Driver=usb-storage). The second column uses 0x00f for all USB storage devices. The third and fourth options contain the hex code for the Vendor and Product ID respectively. The rest of the fields don't matter—the first three fields are enough to match this device—so put in 0x00 for those. For my camera, the file would look like this:

```
# usb.usermap file
# This is autogenerated by update-usb.usermap program
# Note: you may use /etc/hotplug/usb/*.usermap
# usb module          match_flags idVendor idProduct bcdDevice_lo bcdDevice_
hi bDeviceClass bDeviceSubClass
#bDeviceProtocol bInterfaceClass bInterfaceSubClass bInterfaceProtocol
driver_info
usb-storage     0x00f  0x07b4 0x0105 0x00    0x00    0x00    0x00    0x00
0x00    0x00    0x00
```

This line in *usb.usermap* tells *hotplug* to run the */etc/hotplug/usb/usb-storage* script whenever it sees that this device is plugged in. That script can then load modules or run other programs (including setting up programs to run when the drive is removed). The next step is to create this file and add an entry that matches your camera based on the PRODUCT environment variable the *hotplug* script generates. Then create the directory in which the camera will be mounted (in this example */mnt/camera*). The */etc/hotplug/usb/usb-storage* script for my camera would look like this (replace *username* with your user's name):

```
#!/bin/sh
DEVICE=`grep "kernel: Attached scsi .*disk" /var/log/syslog | tail -n 1 |
cut -f 10 -d " "`
case "$PRODUCT" in
# Olympus C750 camera
    7b4/105/1)
    /bin/mount -t vfat /dev/${DEVICE}1 /mnt/camera
    echo -e '#!/bin/sh\n/bin/umount /mnt/camera' > $REMOVER
    chmod a+x $REMOVER
    export DISPLAY=":0.0"
    #su username -c /home/username/bin/camera_sync
    ;;
esac
```

The second line needs some explanation. USB drives are assigned SCSI drive designations on the fly starting from *sda* and going up. While I could just say */dev/sda1*, if more than one USB device were plugged in at the time, the wrong device might get mounted. With the standard Linux device system, there isn't an easy way to determine what SCSI drive letter was assigned to the USB drive. A kludge around this fact is to simply grab the last mention of a USB SCSI drive assignment out of the system log and cut out the device information. Based on your kernel version, your system might log this information slightly differently, so you may have to compare the *grep* pattern to your *syslog* file and possibly adjust the -f 10 value to match the field that contains the SCSI device entry.

The PRODUCT environment variable specifies the Vendor and Product IDs for the current USB device. To see what kind of environment variables are present when this script is run, you can insert a set > /tmp/settings line above the case statement. Read through that file to see how PRODUCT is set for your product. In my case it was set to 7b4/105/1. Then set up the case statement to mount this camera when that device is actually plugged in to /mnt/camera. This method is a bit brittle, as you will see below, but it does work. Another environment variable, REMOVER, specifies the name of a script that is run after the device is removed. This script is empty by default, so I echoed in the umount command I wanted to use when I removed the drive.

Next make the script executable with this command:

```
$ chmod a+x /etc/hotplug/usb/usb-storage
```

Then restart the *hotplug* service:

```
$ /etc/init.d/hotplug restart
```

Now plug the camera and type **df** to confirm that /mnt/camera is mounted. After you unplug the drive, the drive will be umounted.

Use autofs Instead of Mounting Manually

There are some problems with the previous method. For one, the drive isn't unmounted until it already has been removed. This could result in file system corruption over time if the device failed to sync before being removed. The solution is to use *autofs* to mount the device on demand and then unmount when idle.

First, install the *autofs* system with your distribution's package manager. Then modify /etc/auto.master and add a line for your removable drives:

```
# $Id: ch01,v 1.18 2005/11/01 16:22:02 andrews Exp jamie $
# Sample auto.master file
# Format of this file:
# mountpoint map options
# For details of the format look at autofs(5).
/var/autofs/misc        /etc/auto.misc
/var/autofs/net         /etc/auto.net
/var/autofs/removable   /etc/auto.removable     --timeout=2
```

That last line tells *autofs* to mount any removable devices specified in /etc/auto.removable under /var/autofs/removable, and to unmount them after two seconds of idling. Now create the /etc/auto.removable file:

```
sda     -fstype=vfat,umask=002      :/dev/sda1
sdb     -fstype=vfat,umask=002      :/dev/sdb1
sdc     -fstype=vfat,umask=002      :/dev/sdc1
sdd     -fstype=vfat,umask=002      :/dev/sdd1
```

This file sets up mount points under */var/autofs/removable/*, the mounting options to use, and indicates which device to mount. All of this happens outside */etc/fstab* or any other mounting, so remove the */mnt/camera* mount point. Instead, have the USB-storage *hotplug* script you created make a symlink to the *autofs* mount point when the drive is inserted, and then remove the symlink when the drive is removed. That way, you can deal only with */mnt/camera* and not worry about */var/autofs* directories. The new and improved */etc/hotplug/usb/usb-storage* follows:

```
#!/bin/sh
DEVICE=`grep "kernel: Attached scsi .*disk" /var/log/syslog | tail -n 1 |
cut -f 10 -d " "`
case "$PRODUCT" in
# Olympus C750 camera
    7b4/105/1)
    ln -s /var/autofs/usb/$DEVICE/dcim/100olymp /mnt/camera
    echo -e '#!/bin/sh\nrm /mnt/camera' > $REMOVER
    chmod a+x $REMOVER
    export DISPLAY=":0.0"
    #su username -c /home/username/bin/camera_sync
    ;;
esac
```

Now, plug in the camera and confirm that */mnt/camera* was created. In my case, I created the symlink to dig into the camera's directory structure and take me directly to the images (*/dcim/100olymp*). Change this directory path to match the path your camera uses. Because you are using *autofs*, the camera will not be mounted unless you access */mnt/camera*. After two seconds, *autofs* will unmount the drive. You can monitor */var/log/syslog* to watch this happening:

```
Jan 19 16:24:35 clover automount[14059]: mount(generic): calling mkdir_path
/var/autofs/removable/sda
Jan 19 16:24:35 clover automount[14059]: mount(generic): calling mount -t
vfat -s -o umask=002
/dev/sda1 /var/autofs/removable/sda
Jan 19 16:24:36 clover automount[14059]: mount(generic): mounted /dev/sda1
type vfat
on /var/autofs/removable/sda
Jan 19 16:24:39 clover automount[14066]: running expiration on path
/var/autofs/removable/sda
Jan 19 16:24:39 clover automount[14066]: expired /var/autofs/removable/sda
```

As you can see, the drive unmounted seconds after the command finished since it had been idling. It would now be safe to remove the camera.

Make a Synchronization Script

Until now, the */etc/hotplug/usb/usb-storage* script had the following line commented out:

```
su username -c /home/username/bin/camera_sync
```

This line executes a custom camera syncing script as the normal user. This way you can change the script and add features without having to be root. Use *su* to change to your user from the root user so all of the images will be accessible by your normal user. The synchronization script relies on *rsync* to perform the synchronization logic, and the complete script looks like this:

```
#!/bin/sh
$DATE=`date +%Y-%m-%d`
mkdir -p ~/photos/$DATE
rsync -r --size-only -b --suffix="-1.jpg" /mnt/camera/ ~/photos/$DATE/
```

This script creates a new directory, named with today's date, under a photos directory I created in my home directory. Then *rsync* synchronizes the images with that directory according to their file sizes (since other Unix-style file data isn't present on the FAT32 drives most cameras use). The --suffix argument handles any potential duplicate files that may occur, in case your camera doesn't create unique-enough filenames across multiple flash cards. You can also launch a slideshow tool such as gThumb with this script and immediately look at thumbnails of all your photos. Once this script is created, uncomment the corresponding line from */etc/hotplug/usb/usb-storage* and plug in your camera to test the synchronization. Any pictures on the camera will appear in a new directory under *~/photos*.

If you don't clear your photos off the camera between syncs, plugging in the camera on a different day will cause this script to create a new directory containing the same photos.

Make a Screen-Capture Movie

HACK
#12

Create animated screen-capture movies as the ultimate aid in a presentation or tutorial.

If a picture is worth a thousand words, then how about a thousand pictures—or a graphical animation? Getting your message across depends a lot on the tools you have at hand, the environment you'll be presenting to, and the audience. It's one thing to stand in front of a classroom with a blackboard, a projector, and a room full of PCs, but it's quite another to describe a set of ideas to multiple people standing in front of a kiosk, in a hall filled with competing noises and distractions. Wouldn't it be great to create an animated presentation complete with screenshots and textual notes without first taking a course in multimedia and purchasing expensive development applications? Of course it would!

Let's set the stage: the objective is to create a screen-shot movie that demonstrates how to use a feature in an application. In addition, you should be able to provide commentary within the movie to explain what's going on.

Ideally, you can make a movie with tools that don't take long to learn and use. The technique demonstrated here shows how to capture screenshots in rapid succession. These screenshots are then converted into a single file that can be read by nothing more complicated than a browser.

The Tools

For this hack you'll need the following tools:

- The *ImageMagick* command-line utilities to create, edit, and convert images from one format to another
- *xwininfo*, the window information utility for X
- A small bash script to record multiple screen captures

How to Use the Tools

Launch the application you want to record. Use *xwininfo* to obtain the target window's hexadecimal ID number. When you run the command, your cursor changes to a crosshair—just click on the window whose information you want to capture. In this example, the ID number, 0x140001d, comes from the fifth line in the output below:

```
$ xwininfo

xwininfo: Please select the window about which you
          would like information by clicking the
          mouse in that window.
xwininfo: Window id: 0x140001d "making movies.sxw - OpenOffice.org 1.1.0 "
  Absolute upper-left X:  4
  Absolute upper-left Y:  18
  Relative upper-left X:  0
  Relative upper-left Y:  0
  Width: 920
  Height: 630
  Depth: 16
  Visual Class: TrueColor
  Border width: 0
  Class: InputOutput
  Colormap: 0x1400001 (installed)
  Bit Gravity State: ForgetGravity
  Window Gravity State: StaticGravity
  Backing Store State: NotUseful
  Save Under State: no
  Map State: IsViewable
  Override Redirect State: no
  Corners:  +4+18   -100+18  -100-120  +4-120
  -geometry 920x630+4+18
```

Use the ID number with the *import* command to capture the window. If this succeeds, you'll hear two beeps from the PC's speaker. If you want a frame around the screencapture, add the -frame switch. By the way, the *import* command can capture screens to any file format, but the MIFF format is very fast:

```
$ import -window 0x140001d openoffice.miff
```

View the screencapture with *display*:

```
$ display openoffice.miff
```

If you prefer a different format, use *convert* to, well, convert the image:

```
$ convert openoffice.miff openoffice.png
```

Now that you know how to take a single screenshot, here's a simple *bash* script to collect multiple screencaptures for use in your movie. It takes two command-line arguments: the window ID and the number of shots to capture:

```
#!/bin/sh
# A simple bash script to screen capture
#
# Supply two arguments, the window id and number of captures

let x=1

# loop until it has captured the number of captures requested
while [ "$x" -le "$2" ]
do
    import -window $1 "capture$x.miff"
    # uncomment the line below
    # if you want more time in between screen captures
# sleep 2s
    let x+=1
done
```

Invoking the script is straightforward. Make it executable, then type:

```
$ ./capture.sh w_idno_capt
```

w_id is the hexadecimal ID obtained from *xwininfo*, and no_capt is the number of screenshots to record. Every two seconds the capture script will "snap" a screenshot and label it as *capture.miff*, with a number that indicates the order in which the images were taken. You can, of course, modify the script to capture in other image formats (replace the extension of capture$x.miff with the extension of your desired format) or to increase the time delay between snapshots (uncomment # sleep 2s and increase the value to the desired number or seconds).

Use animate to display a slideshow of your captured images:

```
$animate -delay 20 *.miff
```

The *delay* number controls how much time to wait between displays of the individual screencaptures. The units are in hundredths of a second.

Finally, converting the animated images to a more convenient, single-file format is accomplished by using the convert utility. There are several likely formats:

- MNG is a license-free, multi-image file format similar to PNG, but with more bells and whistles. This format is not yet widely used, but it is very neat, and there are plug-ins for all the major browsers. The convert command is:

    ```
    $ convert -delay 20 *.miff capture.mng
    ```

- GIF, you should know.

    ```
    $ convert -delay 20 *.miff capture.gif
    ```

- MPEG encoding requires you to download and compile the *mpeg2encode utility source code*, but it does allow you to add sound.

    ```
    $ convert -delay 20 *.miff capture.mpg
    ```

Enhancing a Screencapture

It's not always enough to replicate a series of keystrokes and pop-up menus. Sometimes you need details that help better explain what's going on. For that matter, it's nice to make a plain screen look fantastic with all sorts of graphical special effects. That's where *mogrify* comes in.

```
$ mogrify -fill blue -pointsize 25 -draw 'text 10,20 "Hello World" ' \
capture1.miff
```

This command adds the phrase "Hello World" to the *capture1.miff* image. The words will be colored blue, with a point size of 25. The words are placed relative to the top left corner of the image in terms of *x* (10 pixels to the right) and *y* (20 pixels down) coordinates.

The *montage* command makes its additions on a copy of the original. Remember to use the -geometry switch with the current window size (for example, -geometry 920x630); otherwise, the copy will have a size of 120×120 pixels:

```
$ montage -fill black -pointsize 50 -draw 'text 100,300 \
```

Drawing a box behind the words will make them stand out:

```
$ montage -fill yellow -draw 'Rectangle 80,250 400,400' -fill black \
    -pointsize 20 -draw 'text 100,300 "@instruction1.txt"' \
    -geometry 920x630 capture1.miff capture1a.miff
```

Remember that you read the switches from left to right. Why? Because each set of options can be changed by the next option to its right. For example, you won't be able to see the words in the following example because the yellow box covers them since drawing text precedes drawing the colored box:

```
$ montage -fill black -pointsize 20 -draw 'text 100,300 "@instruction1.txt"' \
-fill yellow -draw 'Rectangle 80,250 400,400' -geometry 920x630 \
capture1.miff capture1a.miff
```

 Did you notice the @instruction1.txt? The @ token instructs the utility to place the contents of a text file, *instruction1.txt* in this case, into the image.

Screen Capture Tips

The best way to figure out what looks good is by experimentation. Here are a few things I've learned that may save you some time:

- The more instructions and options on the *import* command, the longer the capture will take.

- Do the screen captures using the MIFF file format. Capturing to any other format can slow down the capture process. You can always convert the images to another format at a later time.

- The screenshot capture rate depends on the window size.

- Listen to the beeps; this will give you an idea how quickly or slowly you should navigate through your window.

- Use the root flag to capture the entire screen of your desktop:

  ```
  import -window root capture.miff
  ```

- Identify and rehearse the steps you want to record. This is known as a making a *storyboard*. The screen-capturing process will save every action, good and bad, so practice the steps before invoking the bash script.

- Inserting a *sleep* command inside the bash script can give you much-needed time to prepare the application for the next screenshot without feeling rushed.

- Reviewing each shot after capture helps identify the good and bad images. Simplify this tedious operation by using *display* to load and edit an entire series of images with one command.

- You may have noticed that listing files with numbers doesn't always sort the way you want. Here's a shell trick to ensure that the files are never out of sequence:

  ```
  display capture?.miff capture??.miff
  ```

- Clicking once on a displayed image will put the ImageMagick program into editing mode, and clicking the image again will make the menu disappear. The editing tools have many of the same options that are available on the command line. Pressing the space bar advances to the next image.

- Improve the flow of your presentation by adjusting the speed and duration of the frame rates of your animation. You can do this while converting the individual images.

- Add comments and special effects to the images only after you've established their respective animation frame rates. Make a backup of your animation first.

You should exercise discretion when choosing your file format. I experimented with GIFs, MPEGs, and MNGs. For example, the resulting uncompressed GIF was 14 MB. (ImageMagick binaries do not use the proprietary compression algorithm unless you enable that option and recompile.) The MPEG was 4.6 MB. The MNG was the smallest at 500 K. The *fancy screen-capture demo* was substantially larger, with the GIF at 26 MB, the MPEG at 6. 7 MB, and the MNG again the smallest at 4.7 MB. However, it was interesting to note that converting the fancy movie MNG to PCX files and then converting it back reduced the size to 1.6 MB, 65% smaller.

The MNG format is clearly superior to GIF, but it is not very well supported, and takes quite a long time to decompress before it's ready to play. Mozilla's MNG plug-in failed to bring up the small demo. The ImageMagick utility *animate* worked fine. KDE's Konqueror could only run the small demo, where an HTML tag embedded the MNG file with the <src> tag. The GIF version of the demos played well in *animate*, Mozilla, and Konqueror.

Another factor to consider is that file formats such as GIF and MNG don't really stream, so players need to load the entire file into RAM before you can see it. Large graphics may consume too much RAM, crashing your application. One easy solution is to enlarge the virtual memory by using a swap file. This issue may also come up when using *convert*.

MPEG is a good choice when resources are at a premium and it's not possible to add a swap file. You may need to experiment with the *convert* options to prevent color loss, though.

animate is a good option because the presentation is so exact and easy to control. Viewing GIF format guarantees that any browser can read the file quickly. Beware, though—both formats are RAM hungry.

Conclusion

ImageMagick is a very sophisticated graphics-manipulation package. This hack has covered only its barest capabilities. Anybody who decides to use it as a development platform can increase his productivity by using scripts. *ImageMagick* has an API with a complete set of language bindings for over 16 languages, including Perl, Java, C, C++, and Cold Fusion.

—Robert Bernier

## CHAPTER TWO

Audio
Hacks 13–46

Many people in the Linux community believe that choice is good. Perhaps second only to text editors, audio applications under Linux truly embody this philosophy. Even if you limit yourself to strictly audio players, you don't have enough fingers and toes to count all the programs out there. XMMS, Rhythmbox, amaroK, juK, and others are on the GUI end; hybrid programs can play both audio and video files; and command-line tools such as *mpg123* and *mpg321*, may also have GUI frontends.

Everyone listens to music differently. Some people listen to a single CD or album, every track in sequence. Others put their entire music collection on shuffle. Some people like minimalist audio players while others want every option and effect under the sun. With all the audio choices under Linux, no matter how you like to listen to your music, Linux has an application that fits. Beyond simply listening to music, Linux also has a number of tools to help you rip, mix, manage, and burn your audio—even "scratching" your digital audio is possible.

In this chapter, I highlight some of the best Linux audio applications. There are also hacks in this chapter that take you through the full audio extraction process from ripping CDs to encoding them to tagging the resulting files. Linux has a number of amazing audio tools to automate common tasks, and I've tried to include some of the most useful. At the end of the chapter, I also cover how to access a number of different portable media players under Linux so your music can follow you wherever you go. So put on some music, crank the volume up to 11, and let Linux handle the rest.

Mix Your Audio for Perfect Sound

Use the mixer to understand and tweak the different volume levels your sound card provides.

Almost every audio device you encounter has some way to control the volume, whether through a volume knob on a radio, the remote control on a television, or the series of controls on a sophisticated sound board. To control the sound on a Linux system, you use a mixer program. Even though the purpose of the mixer—to change the volume—is simple, often the sheer number of options the mixer provides can prove daunting to new users: it's not as simple as adjusting a single master volume control. Also, Linux has two different systems for sound, OSS and ALSA, so there is additional complexity that is not immediately obvious. In this hack, I cover a few mixer programs and describe the differences among Master, PCM, and the other major volume controls.

You can launch a mixer program a few different ways. If you use the GNOME or KDE desktop environments, the quickest way to access the mixer is to click the speaker icon on the desktop panel. Windows users will find this applet similar to the speaker on the Windows taskbar. A single click on the icon lets you change the master volume (see Figure 2-1); a right-click shows you various options for the mixer applet. For common volume control, you may only need to access the master volume. To access all of the advanced volume controls, double-click on the applet to launch a complete mixer.

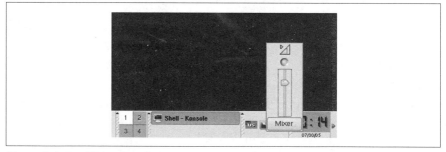

Figure 2-1. Panel Mixer applet

Whether you use OSS or ALSA sound drivers, you will find a base set of volume controls in a mixer application that are based on the default volume controls on the OSS mixer (*/dev/mixer*). OSS is the older of the two sound systems. As such, it is often more stable than ALSA, although a number of newer sound cards are only partially supported in their OSS drivers, if at all. OSS is still present in the latest Linux kernels, but ALSA is the preferred sound system, as it often provides more complete support for newer sound cards—something you will notice in the different options you have in an

ALSA-ready mixer. Whichever sound system you use, when you launch the mixer applet, you will see at least these basic volume controls:

Master

This option controls the master volume for the sound card. The master volume overrides the volume levels for all of the other controls, and muting it or moving it to the lowest level will effectively mute all other sound controls.

PCM

You will likely use this control as often if not more often than the master volume control. The PCM (Pulse Coded Modulation) control sets the volume level for the */dev/dsp* device on the system, which most audio programs output to. You would use this control if you wanted to change the volume for your media player, for instance. Use PCM instead of the master volume to control the volume for these devices so you don't inadvertently change the volume for the other controls on your sound card. For example, you might want to keep your microphone at the same volume, but increase the volume of your speaker. Changing PCM leaves the mic levels where they were before, but changing the master volume affects both the speaker and the microphone.

Speaker

This controls the volume for the speaker built into the PC. On a Linux system, you might want to use this control to change the volume of the system beep your terminal makes.

Line

The Line works as the master volume for the line-out port(s) on your sound card. Each line-out port also has its own volume control that is numbered starting from one, so a sound card with a single line out would also have a Line1 control.

Mic

The mic control manages the volume of your microphone and will often be muted by default so that any noise it picks up will not interfere with any other sound output on the system.

CD

On systems with CD-ROM drives that have been connected to the sound card with the audio-out cable, this control will manage the volume of the CD player.

PhoneIn/PhoneOut

These controls allow you to change the volume for the phone-in and phone-out ports (often RCA jacks on the back of computer) on your sound card. Fancier sound cards sometimes have these jacks available to connect to other AV equipment.

In addition to the above options, if you use ALSA you will find a number of other controls in an ALSA-capable mixer applet such as *alsamixer*. These controls let you access more advanced features of your sound card, but note that the presence of a control in the mixer doesn't necessarily indicate that the feature actually works! Here are some of the common options you might see:

Master Mono
> This option is muted by default, but if it is enabled, it will make all audio monaural instead of stereo and control the volume of that mono-audio source.

Headphone
> Present on some laptops, this option allows you to control the volume level on the headphone jack without affecting the volume of the speakers.

3D Control
> This option is muted by default, but allows you to enable surround sound if your card supports it.

> You do not necessarily have to use an ALSA-compatible mixer if you use ALSA, provided you enable the ALSA OSS compatibility layer, specifically OSS mixer compatibility. With OSS mixer compatibility, OSS mixers will still have access to the basic volume control options, but will not be able to change some of the more advanced options your sound card may provide.

Command-Line Mixer Applications

In addition to whatever mixer program your desktop environment provides, there are some basic command-line mixer programs you can use to access the same volume controls without using a mouse. Two common command-line mixers are *aumix* and *alsamixer*. *aumix* is an OSS mixer with some particularly useful features for scripting, and *alsamixer* is the default command-line mixer program for ALSA.

aumix provides you with access to the standard OSS mixer controls completely from the command line. If you type **aumix** at the command line with no arguments, you will enter its interactive mode, where you can use the up- and down-arrow keys to switch between mixer controls and the left- and right-arrow keys to change the volume of the selected control. Hit the *m* key to toggle mute on a control, and press Tab or Enter to switch between the volume and balance controls for a device.

aumix really becomes useful with command-line arguments. All the different mixer controls are assigned an argument as listed in Table 2-1.

Table 2-1. Common aumix command-line arguments

Argument	Function
-v	Main volume
-b	Bass
-c	CD
-i	Igain
-l	Line
-m	Microphone
-o	Line out
-p	PC speaker
-s	Synthesizer
-t	Trebel
-w	PCM
-x	Imix
-1	Line 1
-2	Line 2
-3	Line 3

Each of these arguments can accept a number of options such as q to query the current level for the device, and + and - to increment and decrement the volume by a single level. You can also specify a particular volume level by using a number instead of + or -, or you can even follow + or - with a number to control how much to increment or decrement. For example, to set the master volume to 50%, increase PCM by ten and increase the line out by one, type:

```
$ aumix -v 50 -w+10 -o+
```

This functionality is particularly useful to bind *aumix* commands to key sequences so that you can mute your sound with a quick keypress, instead of mousing to a mixer applet. You might also find *aumix* handy if you schedule any audio programs with *cron*. *aumix* solves the problem of making sure that no one changes the volume on the computer between the time you set it and time your script runs. You can run an *aumix* command immediately before your command executes.

HACK #14 Surround Yourself with Sound

Get theater-quality sound out of your multi-speaker setup.

When you've invested a lot of money in your audio and speaker setup, you want to make sure you get the most out of it. Don't settle for basic stereo sound—make your bass go boom boom, your center channel speak, and your rear speakers provide ambience. Under Windows, configuring this is often quite easy, as the soundcard manufacturer usually provides a program to enable surround sound, but no such software exists for Linux, so you need to go a more manual route. This hack will show you how to enable surround sound, test it, and use it with MPlayer [Hack #48].

For this hack to work, you need a soundcard that supports more than just stereo output and, of course, multiple speakers. The ideal setup, and the one I am targeting in this hack, is what is known as "5.1 surround sound." This means you have a pair of front speakers, a pair of rear speakers, a center channel speaker, and a subwoofer. As you can see, this is 5 speakers plus a .1 for the subwoofer. (Just to confuse things, some settings will call this a 6 channel configuration.) Here is what you can expect out of each speaker:

Front right and left

These two speakers provide basic stereo output. Most music CDs are designed to output stereo sound, which means these two speakers are all that is required to have an enjoyable music listening experience. Though adequate for listening to a DVD, you'll miss out on many positional effects (the placement of sounds so that it seems as if they are coming from specific places, both on and off screen). When your system is configured for 5.1 surround sound, these speakers will provide the bulk of your nonspeaking sound.

Subwoofer

The job of the subwoofer is to output low frequency sound—just how low depends upon the quality of your subwoofer. With a subwoofer added to your setup, your other speakers are relieved of the duty of producing low bass sounds. This is good, because those speakers aren't really designed for that type of output, and they'll sound better because they will only be playing the audio they can handle well. Bass output is nondirectional, so it doesn't matter where you place the subwoofer: you should still be able to hear and feel its effects. When the subwoofer is combined with just the front right and left speakers, it is known as 2.1 surround sound.

Center

This speaker mostly outputs the dialogue track from a DVD. Having speech come from a speaker underneath or on top of the monitor "centers" the voices to the images and prevents the odd effect in which dialogue doesn't seem to be coming from the actors' mouths, but rather someplace offstage. During loud action sequences with no speech, the center is sometimes used to enhance the overall fullness of the sound to further immerse you in the action.

Rear right and left

These speakers are used for off-stage and ambient sound. For example, if the movie scene has an actor being chased by a car, these speakers output the sounds of the car when it is behind the actor. Or if it is raining outside, these speakers output the rain audio to make you feel as if it is raining all around you instead of just in front of you. Scene music is often sent to these speakers as well, to more fully immerse you in the action. It may seem as if these speakers only have a supporting role in your audio setup, but think about it this way: is a movie itself any good without a supporting cast?

I tested this using nForce4 integrated sound and Logitech X-530 5.1 speaker set. The nForce4 sound is provided by the *Intel8x0* Alsa driver, which is commonly used in many integrated solutions, so the instructions I give here should work without modification on many setups. I'm going to assume you already have basic audio working. (This is typically not a problem with most modern Linux distributions.) You'll also need to follow your speaker installation instructions and make sure you have each of the cables plugged into the correct outputs.

Configuring Your Mixer

[Hack #13] provided a basic introduction to the concept of audio mixers that control the volume levels of your audio outputs. For this hack you are going to use the *alsamixer* command-line mixer, because it is very straightforward to use. You should find each of the options I'll describe here in the KDE (*kmix*) and GNOME (*gnome-alsamixer*) equivalents, but the settings may be in non-obvious places in the program. To get started, run this command inside a terminal:

```
$ alsamixer
```

This opens an ncurses-based mixer program that you can control with your keyboard. The left and right arrows will move you to the different options, the up and down arrows control the volume or settings of that option, pressing M toggles the muting of that channel, and Esc quits and saves your changes. If you already have basic sound working, then your Master and PCM channels are already unmuted and their volume set.

In this program you need to set volume levels for the other speaker channels as well as tell the mixer how you want audio sent to the various speakers.

Using the *alsamixer* options for my nForce4 Intel8x0 based soundcard as a basis, here are the settings you want to configure:

Center and LFE

Unmute and set volumes levels for these two channels. Center obviously controls your center channel speakers, whereas LFE controls your low frequencies, so it determines output levels to your subwoofer.

Surround

There are two options for this. The first sets the volume levels for the rear speakers. The second controls how independently the center and rear speakers work. By default this set to Shared, but for movie watching, you should set it to Independent.

Channels

This option, which you have to scroll to the right to see, tells Alsa how many speakers you have. Set to 6 for 5.1. Most programs I use still need to be explicitly told how many speakers I have, so I've not found this option to be particularly meaningful. Perhaps in the future.

Duplicate front

When this option is unmuted, it duplicates the output sent to the front pair of speakers to the rear. This is useful when listening to stereo music if you want output from all of your speakers, but it is not desirable when movie watching. Keep this muted to ensure the rear speakers receive independent audio signals.

These settings provide the basic foundation for 5.1 audio. These settings should exist for any soundcard that supports surround sound, but I can't guarantee the option labels will remain the same.

Testing Surround Sound

When first playing with surround sound, it's useful to test speaker output using an audio file that sends audio to each speaker in turn. You can obtain such a file from *ftp://ling.lll.hawaii.edu/pub/greg/Surround-SDL-testfiles.tgz*. Download and unpack this file:

```
$ wget ftp://ling.lll.hawaii.edu/pub/greg/Surround-SDL-testfiles.tgz
$ tar -xvzf Surround-SDL-testfiles.tgz
```

In the expanded directory you'll find a few WAV files that have multichannel output. My personal favorite is *chan-id.wav*, which when played speaks the name of each channel in the appropriate speaker—provided, of course, that everything is configured correctly. To test, use this command:

```
$ aplay -Dsurround51 chan-id.wav
```

This command uses the Alsa *aplay* player to send output to each channel in turn. If you don't specify -Dsurround51, you will only get stereo output. You know everything is working correctly if you hear a woman's voice announcing each speaker channel in the appropriate speaker. If this doesn't happen for you, then go back to *alsamixer* and see if you missed anything.

I've noticed a few oddities with this test. For example, when I run it on my Mandriva machine with the previous command, everything works correctly— except my subwoofer delivers a muffled and jumbled "rear rear left right," and the rear channel speakers then give their identification correctly. The command's text output suggests that I run the command this way:

```
$ aplay -Dplug:surround51 chan-id.wav
```

When I do this, the front and center speakers work as they should, but I get no other output from my other speakers except for the rear right, which states the jumbled "rear rear left right." None of this turns out to matter. As long as you do get the front and center speakers to announce themselves correctly, and you hear *something* out of the rear speakers, surround sound should work with MPlayer.

Movie Watching

The real reason for surround sound is to create a near theater experience when movie watching. This section covers configuring MPlayer for surround sound. As you may recall from "Use MPlayer" [Hack #48], the *mplayer* command for viewing a DVD is simply:

```
$ mplayer dvd://
```

Go to a scene with dialogue. Pay careful attention to which speaker the dialogue is coming out of. It will most likely be the left and right front speakers. Is any background sound coming from the rear speakers? Probably not. When you launch *mplayer* this way, the center and rear speakers remain silent. You have to tell *mplayer* that you have a multi-speaker setup like this:

```
$ mplayer -channels 6 dvd://
```

Again, listen to a scene with dialogue and listen for background sound from the rear speakers. In my setup, my center channel is still muted, but I hear sound and dialogue from my rear speakers. The problem here is that we haven't told *mplayer* what sound system to use. This is done with a simple addition to the command:

```
$ mplayer -ao alsa -channels 6 dvd://
```

Now, go to the same scenes as before. If everything is configured correctly in *alsamixer*, you should hear most of your sound coming from the front left and right speakers, dialogue coming from the center speaker, ambient sounds from the rear speakers, and, if you're watching explosions, then a nice boom boom from your subwoofer.

> While performing your tests, you may find it useful to add
> the -ss nn option to your *mplayer* command. This skips for-
> ward the specified number of seconds so you can always
> start playing at a scene that lets you test both the rear- and
> center-channel speakers.

Specifying these settings each time you run MPlayer can be annoying. To get
around this, add the options to your ~/.mplayer/config file like so:

```
# Write your default config options here!
ao=alsa
channels=6
```

As you can see, each option is identical to what you type at the command
line, minus the preceding dash and converting the space to an equal sign.

If you use a GUI frontend to *mplayer*, it will probably provide its own preference option to enable surround sound, so check those settings if the ones
in your configuration file don't work.

—*David Brickner*

HACK #15   Play Multiple Sounds at the Same Time

Play audio from multiple sources—even if your sound card doesn't support it.

Most Linux users don't think too much about exactly how sound is mixed.
On many sound cards, you can send only a single sound at a time. So, for
instance, if you are playing an MP3, you won't be able to hear any desktop
sounds you have configured, and your instant messenger won't audibly alert
you to incoming messages. Although some sound cards can support mixing
from multiple sources, many less-expensive cards and those integrated on
motherboards don't, so as a result you need to use a sound server. A sound
server, in effect, sits between your applications and the sound card, mixes
the different sound sources, and presents a single source for output. The
default sound server under KDE is aRts, and the default under GNOME is
EsounD. This hack covers how to use and configure aRts and EsounD.

aRts (Analog Real-Time Synthesizer) is a system of modules used to synthesize
audio. These modules can perform various audio tasks, such as adding audio
effects, mixing, filtering, and a number of other things. The *artsd* sound server
uses this system to mix audio from multiple sources in real time. Because it sits
between the sound card and applications, an application must have aRts support to directly take advantage of the *artsd* server (there's a workaround if it
doesn't, which I will talk about in just a bit). aRts is a core component of KDE
(at least for the time being), so it is fully supported there, and a number of
other media applications can use aRts as well, through the use of plug-ins.

EsounD (or Enlightened Sound Daemon) is a sound server like *artsd*. It sits between the sound card and programs accessing the sound card so that it can mix sounds and pass them along as output. Because of this, an application needs EsounD support to work with *esd* properly. Since GNOME defaults to using EsounD as its sound server, GNOME applications generally have EsounD support. EsounD has been around for some time, so there's a good chance that recent media applications (again, particularly those for GNOME) support EsounD either directly or through a plug-in.

Since KDE uses aRts by default, if your distribution packages KDE it should package aRts and, specifically, *artsd*. In fact, if KDE is already installed, you already have *artsd* installed (and it is probably running). Likewise, EsounD is packaged by most major distributions, particularly if they include GNOME, and the EsounD package should already be installed if GNOME is installed. You don't have to run KDE to use *artsd* or GNOME to use *esd*. Simply install the *artsd* or EsounD package included with your distribution to use it with your window manager or desktop application.

Generally, *artsd* and *esd* do not start when the computer starts. Instead they are launched by the desktop environment when it starts. If you use KDE or GNOME, this is taken care of for you; otherwise you will need to consult with the documentation for your window manager or desktop environment to learn how to start applications when the window manager is launched.

Configure aRts

aRts can be configured directly from the KDE Control Center, so launch the Control Center from the K Menu or, alternatively, type **kcontrol** in a terminal. Inside the Control Center click Sound & Multimedia → Sound System to access the aRts configuration (see Figure 2-2). The first clue that *artsd* is running is the first checkbox, labeled "Enable the sound system." If it is checked, *artsd* is running; if not, it isn't. That means if you do need to completely bypass *artsd*, you can disable it here. If you find that sound skips during playback, you might need to check the next option, Run, with the highest possible priority (realtime priority) and, optionally, increase the size of the sound buffer until the skipping stops.

I previously mentioned that *artsd* sits between the sound card and programs, so if you have it running, programs that directly access */dev/dsp* won't work. The next option in the control center lets you automatically suspend *artsd* when it's idle. That way other programs can use the sound card directly once the timeout period has elapsed.

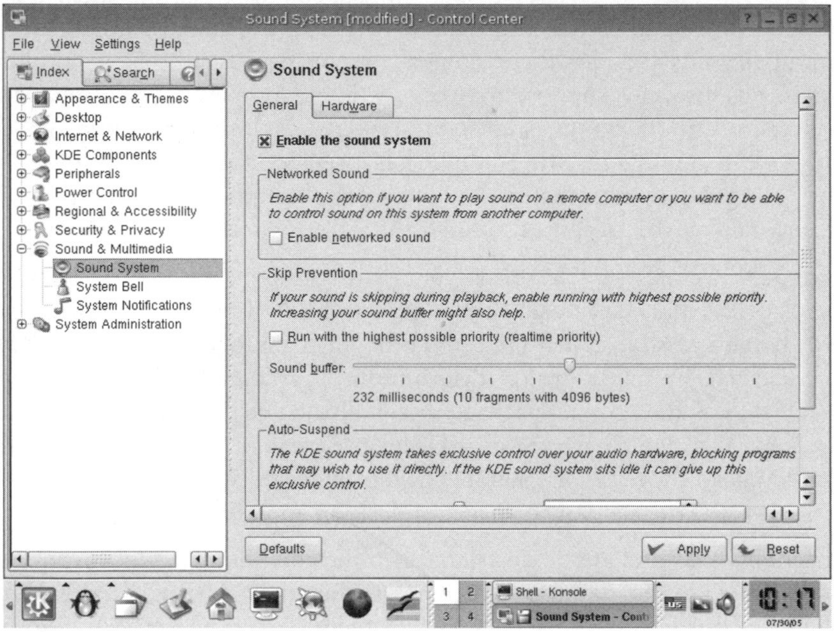

Figure 2-2. KDE Control Center aRts configuration

Configure EsounD

There isn't much configuration to be done with EsounD: essentially, you just need to be concerned with whether or not GNOME uses it. To check, launch the GNOME Control Center from a menu, or type **gnome-control-center** in a terminal. Then go to the sound section and check whether the sound server checkbox is checked.

Legacy Compatibility

Both aRts and EsounD provide another method of compatibility with legacy programs through *artsdsp* and *esddsp*, respectively. Certain programs, such as *Quake*, were programmed to access OSS and know nothing of Linux sound servers. What's more, games like this are no longer being developed, so it's unlikely support is going to be added in. The *artsdsp* and *esddsp* programs basically act as a wrapper around a program and intercept and process any sound card calls. The standard way to use *artsdsp* is:

```
$ artsdsp programname option1 option2 ...
```

Some programs, such as *Quake*, want to do direct memory mapping for sound, which *artsdsp* can emulate with the --mmap option To play *Quake* run:

```
$ artsdsp --mmap quake
```

The *esddsp* program acts in basically the same way, just type *esddsp*, then whatever program you wish to run, followed by its arguments:

```
$ esddsp programname option1 option2 ...
```

artsdsp and *esddsp* don't work for every program. For *artsdsp*, experiment with and without the --mmap options to see what provides the best results.

Get MP3 Libraries for Red Hat–Based Distributions

Enable MP3 support on Red Hat–based distributions with a simple addition to yum.

Software licenses, particularly licenses for multimedia libraries, have always been a touchy point for Linux. There are a number of proprietary media formats out there competing for our eye and ear. Many of these media formats have restrictions in their licensing that require either the user or, more often, the developer of multimedia software to pay a licensing fee to use their library. One such media format is MP3.

Many people consider MP3 to be a "free" format simply because it doesn't have DRM functionality built-in but, in fact, the company Fraunhofer Gesellschaft owns a number of patents on parts of the technology that creates MP3s and requires that MP3 encoders and possibly MP3 decoders pay licensing fees. Most Linux distributions manage the MP3 encoder licensing simply by not including MP3 encoding libraries directly into their distribution. Instead you must download the encoder from a third-party source to limit the distribution's liability (**[Hack #24]** will provide more information about MP3 encoders under Linux). For the most part, Linux distributions have historically ignored the liability for shipping MP3 decoding libraries—that is, until Red Hat 8. Starting with this version, Red Hat dstopped shipping MP3 libraries with the OS (*http://www.redhat.com/advice/speaks_80mm.html*). As a result, if you use Red Hat or a derivative such as Fedora or CentOS, you will need to go through an additional step to install MP3 support.

To install MP3 support on Red Hat–based systems, you will first need to add a third-party package repository to your package manager. Although there are several repositories that provide the package you need, for this example, I use the Dag software repository (*http://dag.wieers.com/home-made/apt*) for everything.

The first step is to add the Dag GPG key to RPM's list of keys. To do this, open a console, become root, and type the following:

```
# rpm --import http://dag.wieers.com/packages/RPM-GPG-KEY.dag.txt
```

Use Yum

The next step is to add the Dag repository. How you add the Dag repository depends on whether you use *yum* or *up2date* to install packages. Fedora and CentOS both have Yum installed by default for upgrades, while RHEL uses *up2date* by default. If you use Yum for upgrades, you edit */etc/yum.conf*. Below are lines to add to */etc/yum.conf* for Fedora, CentOS, and RHEL (if *yum* is installed):

Add this line if you use Fedora:

```
[dag]
name=Dag RPM Repository for Fedora Core
baseurl=http://apt.sw.be/fedora/$releasever/en/$basearch/dag
gpgcheck=1
enabled=1
```

Add this line if you use RHEL or CentOS:

```
[dag]
name=Dag RPM Repository for Red Hat Enterprise Linux and CentOS
baseurl=http://apt.sw.be/redhat/el$releasever/en/$basearch/dag
gpgcheck=1
enabled=1
```

Add this line for an older version of Red Hat Linux such as RH8.x and RH9.x:

```
[dag]
name=Dag RPM Repository for older Red Hat Linux
baseurl=http://apt.sw.be/redhat/$releasever/en/$basearch/dag
gpgcheck=1
enabled=1
```

After you have edited *yum.conf*, save your changes, update the list of *yum* packages, and then install the *xmms-mp3* package to get MP3 support:

```
# yum update
# yum install xmms-mp3
```

Use up2date

If you use *up2date* for upgrades, then you must edit */etc/sysconfig/rhn/sources* instead. For RHEL4 or CentOS4, add this line:

```
yum dag http://apt.sw.be/redhat/el4/en/$ARCH/dag
```

If you use RHEL3 or CentOS3, replace el4 in the above line with el3. If you use Fedora, add this line to */etc/sysconfig/rhn/sources*:

```
yum dag http://apt.sw.be/fedora/4/en/$ARCH/dag
```

Replace 4 with 3, 2, or 1, if you use Fedora Core 3, Fedora Core 2, or Fedora Core 1, respectively.

Now you can install the *xmms-mp3* package from *up2date*:

```
# up2date xmms-mp3
```

HACK #17 Configure Network Sound

Set up local sound to play across the network.

In "Mix Your Audio for Perfect Sound" [Hack #13] I discuss how to use EsounD as a sound server to mix sounds from multiple programs for a sound card that supports only one input. One extra feature of EsounD is the ability to send and receive sound over the network. This can be particularly useful if you use programs like VNC over a local network, because you can use audio applications remotely and hear them on your local machine. Plus, in general, it's just pretty cool to be able to send sound around over the network.

To do this *esd* must be installed on the server (the machine on which you hear the sound). You don't have to have *esd* installed on the client—your client doesn't even need a sound card—but make sure your programs are EsounD-compatible. Most distributions should have EsounD packaged, so install it from your package management tool. If you use GNOME, EsounD is probably already installed. Once *esd* is installed on the server, you need to start it with special options so that it knows to listen to the network. Kill any open *esd* processes, and then start *esd* from the command line:

```
greenfly@napoleon:~$ esd -promiscuous -tcp -public -port 16001
```

You should hear a series of beeps on your computer to tell you that *esd* has started. Now on your client machine open a terminal and type:

```
greenfly@moses:~$ esdplay --server="ip_of_server:16001" sample.wav
```

Replace ip_of_server with the IP address of the *esd* server. The audio file will play back on the remote server, so be sure to adjust the mixer on that machine so that you can hear it. This works fine on an application-by-application basis, but you can also set an environment variable so that any EsounD-compatible applications you start will output to the remote server. Type the following in a terminal:

```
greenfly@moses:~$ export ESPEAKER="ip_of_server:16001"
```

Now you can start *XMMS*, *mplayer*, *xine*, or any of the EsounD-capable audio players from this terminal and the sound will be sent over the network. Be sure to add this setting to your *.bashrc* so it's available each time you start a program.

You can also configure *esd* globally so that it automatically starts with these network options by default. This is particularly useful if you use GNOME on your *esd* server since GNOME is configured to start *esd* automatically. Edit your */etc/esound/esd.conf* file and edit the default_options line to say:

```
default_options=-promiscuous -tcp -public -port 16001
```

Save your changes, and the next time *esd* starts, it will automatically start with those options enabled.

HACK **Manage Your Audio with XMMS**

#18   XMMS is a classic Linux audio player you can use to easily play a number of different audio file types.

A number of audio players are available under Linux, but XMMS is a classic that you are likely to find available no matter which Linux distribution you use. XMMS has an interface similar to Winamp under Windows and can play most popular audio formats, including MP3, WAV, Ogg Vorbis, and audio CDs, along with many other formats, if you install the proper input plug-in.

The default XMMS interface has controls to play, pause, stop, and skip forward and backward in your playlist—believe me, they're all there, just very tiny. To open the playlist editor, click the button labeled PL on the interface, right-click on XMMS, and select Playlist Editor, or type Ctrl-E. Within the playlist editor, you can add, delete, arrange, and sort tracks. To add tracks, select the add button and browse to the directory, or simply drag and drop files from your file manager onto the playlist. You can also save playlists you have created so that you can refer to them later. All playlist options that are available via buttons on the bottom of the interface can also be accessed if you right-click on the playlist. The audio settings are adjusted with the equalizer. To display the equalizer, click the EQ button next to the PL button on the interface, right-click, and select Graphical EQ, or type the keyboard shortcut Ctrl-G.

> XMMS supports streaming audio. To add a streaming audio source to the playlist, click Add → URL and type in the URL.

Once the playlist has been set up, click the play button or type **x**. The buttons to control playback including previous track, play, pause, stop, and next track can be accessed with z, x, c, v, and b, respectively. Notice how all of the keys on the keyboard line up in the same order as on the interface. As a track is playing, you can control the volume and balance directly from the main window. To skip ahead in a track, just click and drag the long bar that slowly progresses along the window. The main window also has checkboxes so that you can toggle shuffle and repeat modes for the playlist.

Plug-ins

XMMS is a highly configurable application that supports a number of plug-ins for input, output, visualization, and other options. The most popular plug-ins can be downloaded directly from *http://www.xmms.org* and extracted into your *~/.xmms/Plugins* directory. Right-click XMMS and select Options → Preferences or type Ctrl-P to access additional XMMS options. The preferences window (see Figure 2-3) has tabs organizing different XMMS plug-ins and options:

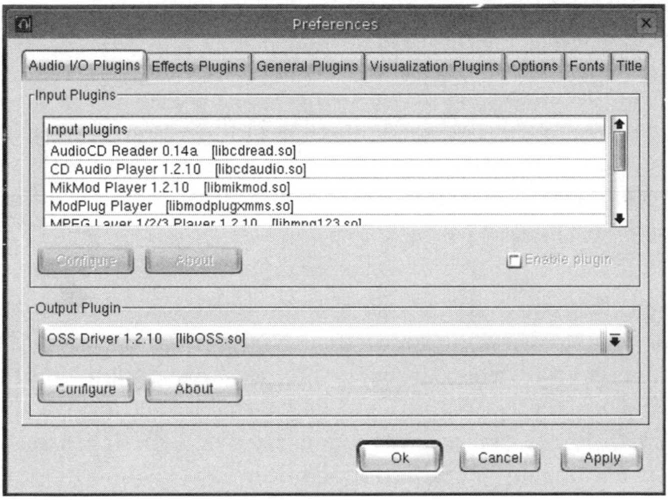

Figure 2-3. XMMS Preferences

Audio I/O Plugins

This tab lets you enable a number of input plug-ins that XMMS supports. You can enable support for different audio file formats including Ogg Vorbis and FLAC, plug-ins that let you play MPEG videos, and a number of other types of input. The Output Plugin section lets you configure how XMMS outputs sound. If your sound card supports OSS (whether natively or through the ALSA OSS compatibility layer), the default OSS driver output plug-in should work fine. Alternatively, if you want to directly use ALSA, choose that output plug-in. If you use EsounD to manage multiple audio streams, enable that output plug-in here.

Effects Plugins

This tab lets you enable and configure several effects plug-ins written for XMMS. For instance, you can install a Volume Normalizer plug-in that makes all the sound output stay around the same volume so you don't find yourself raising the volume for a particularly quiet song, just to have your eardrums blasted if the next song is extra loud. There are a number of other useful effects plug-ins, including ones that cross-fade between tracks, provide extra stereo, and create echoes in the music.

General Plugins

This tab is a catch-all location for plug-ins that don't fall into any of the other plug-in categories. Here you will find plug-ins that let you control XMMS with a joystick or remote control (if you have an IR receiver configured; see "Take (Remote) Control" [Hack #79]), along with a number of other miscellaneous features. To configure one of the plug-ins, select it and then click the Configure button.

Visualization Plugins

This tab shows all of the different visualization options XMMS has beyond the standard display in the main window. These plug-ins can be pretty fun to enable, as they provide a lot of colorful visuals to match the music you are listening to. Plug-ins in this category range from simple and three-dimensional spectrum analyzers, to plug-ins that have Tux the Linux mascot disco-dancing to your music (which is a fun thing to run in the background at a party).

Options

This tab lets you configure most of the common XMMS options you might want to change. One particularly interesting option is the Use real-time priority when available. To use this option, you must run XMMS with root privileges, and when enabled, XMMS will run with real-time priority, which gives it priority over other apps seeking CPU time, resulting in fewer skips during heavy CPU load.

> Some people find the default look of XMMS too "techno." You can download new skins directly from XMMS's official site at *http://www.xmms.org* and save them in *~/.xmms/Skins*. Right-click on XMMS and select Options → Skin Browser to choose one of the skins you downloaded.

XMMS Command-Line Control

One of the particularly useful features of XMMS is that you can control much of it directly from the command line. Table 2-2 lists some of the more useful XMMS command-line arguments.

Table 2-2. Common XMMS command-line arguments

Argument	Function
-r, --rew	Skip backward in the playlist.
-p, --play	Start playing the current playlist.
-u, --pause	Pause the current song.
-s, --stop	Stop the current song.
-t, --play-pause	Toggle between paused and play states.
-f, --fwd	Skip forward in the playlist.
-e, --enqueue	Add the following file(s) to the playlist without clearing the playlist first.

The playlist control options are especially handy if you have a multimedia keyboard, as you can use your desktop environment's keybinding editor to run the particular XMMS command for that function. Even if you don't have a multimedia keyboard, you might want to bind a key sequence to some of these keys. For example, to toggle between pause and play, tell your keybinding program to run **xmms --play-pause**.

The -e option is also useful to quickly add tracks to the playlist. To add, for instance, your entire Ramones collection to the playlist, you could type:

```
$ xmms -e ~/mp3/ramones
```

Of course, change the path to the path of the files you wish to add. If you ran that same command without the -e option, XMMS would still load those files into the playlist, but it would also clear out the playlist beforehand. When XMMS exits, it remembers the contents of the playlist, and next time you start it, it will reload that playlist unless you tell it otherwise.

> Since XMMS can be controlled from the command line, you can also control it remotely or from a script. Simply write a script containing the commands you want to run and schedule it via *cron* or *at*. I've used this feature along with *aumix* to control the volume and create a quick alarm clock. This also means you can control XMMS over *ssh*—a fun way to play a trick on a co-worker or roommate.

Shuffle Your Music the Smart Way

HACK
#19

Use IMMS to weight your music collection based on your listening habits.

Think of all the ways you interact with a computer each day. Any action you take, or even don't take, conveys some meaning. For example, when listening to your music collection, you might sometimes skip songs. What does that mean? There are a number of possibilities. Maybe you do not like the song that was playing, or it does not suit your current mood, or, possibly, you've listened to this song too much and would rather it be played less often.

Is it possible to build a system that uses this information to learn which music you prefer and play it more often? Yes! Intelligent Multimedia Management System (IMMS) is an attempt to create such a system—an adaptive playlist framework that tracks your listening patterns and dynamically adapts to suit your personal music tastes. Plug-ins are currently available for two popular Linux media players: XMMS (*http://www.xmms.org/*) and Beep Media Player (*http://beepmp.sourceforge.net/*).

The main feature of IMMS is its complete transparency to the user. It is incredibly unobtrusive—you never have to interact with IMMS directly. Just continue using your player as usual and, over time, IMMS will influence the song selection to cater to your preferences. When your music player chooses the next "random" track in shuffle mode, IMMS weights its choice, based on which songs you've played and which songs you've skipped previously.

IMMS also offers a number of features beyond basic rating. For example, it keeps track of when a song was played last and makes sure the same song does not repeat too often—a common complaint with traditional shuffle-based systems. Moreover, it is able to recognize different versions of the same songs (for example remixes) and treat them as the same song.

IMMS also learns which songs should be played together and which should not. It does so by both watching and learning from the user, and performing acoustic analysis on the actual songs to determine their tempo and spectral "color," and then attempts to group more similar songs together.

Get IMMS

Depending on the distribution you use, there may already be an IMMS package available to install. There is an up-to-date Debian package for IMMS, as well as a Gentoo ebuild. If you are unable to find a pre-packaged version of IMMS, you can easily build one from source. The tarball can be downloaded from the IMMS homepage at *http://www.luminal.org/wiki/index.php/IMMS*. A list of required dependencies and instructions on building IMMS are included with the source in an *INSTALL* file.

Once you have IMMS installed, you will need to enable it in XMMS. Open the Preferences dialog, go to the General plug-in category, select IMMS, and click the "Enable plugin" checkbox in the lower-right corner.

That's it. From now on your music player will be imbued with IMMS intelligence. You will notice that music selection will improve over time without your having to do anything at all. Of course, you should not expect this to happen overnight. It will take time for IMMS to learn your preferences. You may find IMMS to be a little slow at first, since it needs to read the tags and calculate checksums of all your files. Depending on the size of your collection, this process should not take very long. In the meantime, type:

```
$ tail -f ~/.imms/imms.log
```

and watch IMMS rate your music.

More IMMS Magic

Although IMMS is built from the ground up to require no direct user interaction, it is possible to do some useful things with the data it accumulates. For example, if you own a portable MP3 player, you may want to fill it with the songs IMMS has identified as your favorites. James C. Jones wrote an excellent program called IMMS Magical Favorites Collector, or IMFavorites for short (*http://imfavorites.sourceforge.net*), for just that purpose. Simply specify how much space your player has, and IMFavorites will create a directory of symbolic links to the gems of your collection (see Figure 2-4).

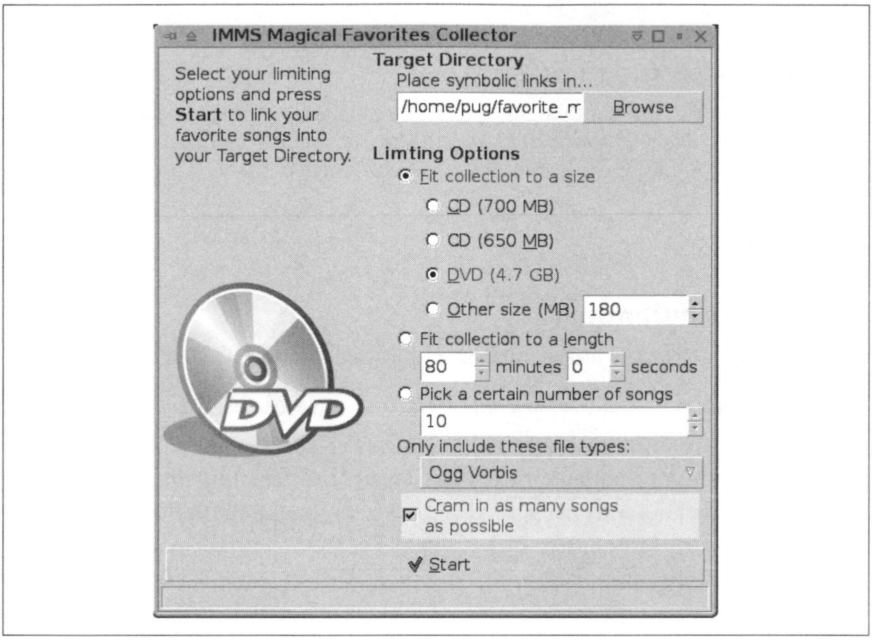

Figure 2-4. IMFavorites in action

A lot of the flexibility of IMMS comes from the fact that it is based around an embedded SQL database — SQLite (*http://www.sqlite.org*). SQLite allows users with even a very basic knowledge of Structured Query Language to generate neat statistics and reports about their music collection and preferences. To harvest its power, you will need to use the command-line client that comes with SQLite 3.0 and above—*sqlite3*. IMMS stores all of its data in *.imms* directory in your home directory, and the database is located in *~/.imms/imms2.db*. So to run an SQL query on it, you need to execute:

```
$ sqlite3 ~/.imms/imms2.db '<your query>'
```

Here are some queries you can use:

```
SELECT path FROM Identify NATURAL INNER JOIN Rating WHERE rating > 145 ;
```

This query will effectively generate a list of favorites, because ratings in IMMS range from 75 (really bad) to 150 (really good).

A more involved example that allows you to list the top ten artists for last month would look like this:

```
SELECT SUM( delta ) as sumdelta, readable FROM Journal
NATURAL INNER JOIN Library
NATURAL INNER JOIN Info
NATURAL INNER JOIN Artists
GROUP BY Artist ORDER BY sumdelta DESC LIMIT 10;
```

To familiarize yourself with IMMS schema run:

SELECT FROM sqlite master;

This lists the tables present in the database and their attributes. Also refer to the description of query language understood by SQLite at *http://www.hwaci.com/sw/sqlite/lang.html*.

—Michael "mag" Grigoriev

Try Rhythmbox

HACK #20

Use Rhythmbox to manage your audio collection much like the iTunes audio player.

There are many different approaches to audio players under Linux. Some players focus on minimalism, others focus on features, and some aim to provide similar functionality to a media player on another platform. Rhythmbox falls into the latter category, as it was created to provide an iTunes-like interface for audio under Linux.

Rhythmbox is a popular package, and most major distributions package it. If your distribution doesn't, you can download the source from the official project page at *http://www.rhythmbox.org* and compile and install it yourself.

To start Rhythmbox, launch it from your application menu or type **rhythmbox** in a console. The first time you run it, Rhythmbox will take you through an initial configuration wizard so it can find your music files. This step is optional, but I recommend you go through the full wizard so that Rhythmbox can find your files.

After you are finished with the wizard, Rhythmbox will begin scanning your entire MP3 collection (or other media files) for its internal database. Instead of organizing your collection by directory path, Rhythmbox organizes your collection based on the ID3 tags it finds in your MP3s or Oggs, so you can quickly build collections or find songs based on the artist or album. The initial scanning process can be a bit time consuming (ten to thirty minutes, depending on your machine and the size of your collection), and you can watch the collection grow in the main window as Rhythmbox finds new music.

Unlike music players such as XMMS, Rhythmbox has a large main window but displays only a basic set of controls. Most of the window is taken up with playlist and collection information (see Figure 2-5). The left panel displays music options, such as your complete library of music, playlists you created, streaming radio, and so forth. The right side of the main window is split into a browser and a track list. The browser provides filters that apply to the track list to make it easy to filter and find tracks based on attributes such as artist and album (or genre, in the case of streaming audio).

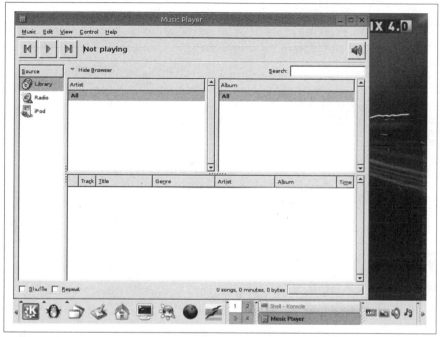

Figure 2-5. Main Rhythmbox window

A Hide Browser/Show Browser toggle above the track list lets you toggle whether the browser is visible. The track list shows the list of tracks for the current level of filtering. By default it displays all tracks for the current source, and if you execute a search or filter using the browser, the track list changes based on those criteria. When a source is changed, the track list changes based on that source, so music from your library displays various music tracks you have added while streaming audio sources display a list of streaming audio servers.

Click the Play button at the top of the interface or Control → Play to start the playback of a track. The navigation interface for Rhythmbox is very simple, with just the controls you need to play or change tracks displayed along with information about the current song. There are also toggles on the interface to change the shuffle and repeat modes for playback.

Rhythmbox can also display playlists in the source area. To create a new playlist, click Music → Playlist and select either New Playlist to create a new playlist location, or "Load from file" to load a playlist that you have saved to a file. You can also click Music → Playlist → New Automatic Playlist to add "Automatic Playlists." The dialog box that appears will let you create a new playlist based on criteria you specify, such as a particular title, artist, album, genre, or rating. You can choose songs that match or don't match a particular criteria and click Add to add them to the automatic playlist, then click New to create the playlist in the source area.

Rhythmbox can manage a number of audio streams, as well as local files. All the configured audio streams show up under the Radio source. To add a new stream, click Music → New Internet Radio Station and enter the information for your audio stream in the dialog that appears.

> Rhythmbox does take up quite a bit of desktop space by default, but you can click View → Small Display to display only the navigation controls. You can also minimize Rhythmbox completely and control it from the music note icon in your notification panel.

HACK #21   Let amaroK Rock Your Music Collection

Use amaroK to integrate great music features such as album art, Audioscrobbler, Musicbrainz, song lyrics, and great playlist management into one application.

As more people have started listening to their music collections on their computers, a number of Internet services have appeared to help manage collections and to utilize all this great metadata that exists on MP3s. The services have ranged from CDDB and FreeDB, which provide album and track information based on CD signatures, to services that provide album art and lyrics. A number of the music players under Linux have utilized one or two of these types of services either natively or through the use of plug-ins, but the amaroK music player seems to be one of the best at integrating them all by default into a useful and powerful interface. In this hack, I discuss many of the different features of the amaroK player and how to get the most out of them.

Get amaroK

amaroK is becoming a pretty popular music player, and many distributions already provide packages for it, so you can probably use your standard packaging tool to install it—but if your distribution doesn't provide it, go to the official page at *http://amarok.kde.org* and download a package for your distribution. If your distribution doesn't have a package, just grab the source and build it according to the installation instructions.

Once amaroK is installed, launch it from your desktop menu or type **amarok** into a console. The first time amaroK launches, it will run you through a configuration wizard so that it can find your music files. Point it to your collection and amaroK will scan through each of the files and collect all the metadata for its internal database. Depending on the size of your collection, this may take some time; however, I've found that amaroK is able to scan even a large collection pretty quickly.

> amaroK will update information about your collection automatically, but if you have made a large number of changes and want to force a complete rescan of your collection, click Tools → Rescan Collection. You can also click Tools → First Run Wizard to run through the initial configuration wizard again.

As part of the initial configuration wizard, amaroK will ask you to choose the default display style for the application. The *xmms* style splits amaroK into a small navigation window with controls to play, pause, and so on, and a large playlist window with the rest of the controls. The *juk* style combines everything into a single large window (it's named after another KDE music management program with a similar interface). Which style you choose is a matter of taste; however, I found that when I tried the *xmms* style, I was always opening the other window to glance at context-sensitive information such as album art, so I changed it to a single window interface. For simplicity, I will describe sections of the amaroK window as though it were in the single-window style for the rest of this hack.

amaroK Window Sections

Once you have finished the first run wizard and your music is loaded, you will see the main amaroK window (see Figure 2-6). This window is split into two main sections—a playlist on the right and a series of tabs along the left that open into a sidebar and display a number of different context-sensitive information panels. This sidebar is where the real power of amaroK lies, and I will talk more about it in a minute.

The playlist section is like most other playlist sections for media players and displays title, artist, album, and other metadata that amaroK has scanned from your music. To play a track, select it and click the play button along the bottom or click Actions → Play/Pause. This toolbar along the bottom has controls to play, stop, and skip forward or backward in the playlist, a visual-

Figure 2-6. Main amaroK window

ization section, and controls for the volume and to clear the playlist. You can also right-click on a track to access playback and playlist functions.

The right-click window also gives you the ability to edit metadata for the track. Select View/Edit Meta Information from the right-click menu, and you can change artist, title, and other information about the track manually or click Fill-In Tags Using MusicBrainz to take advantage of amaroK's MusicBrainz integration. MusicBrainz compares an audio signature from your track with its own database of signatures and provides you with a list of songs it thinks the track might be. In my experience, usually only one (or occasionally two) of the options it returns will be applicable, so it's easy to pick out the track. Select the track and MusicBrainz will fill in all the metadata for you. When you are finished editing the information, click Save & Close to save your changes. [Hack #30] provides more information about tagging your files using MusicBrainz.

Configure amaroK

amaroK has many different options, from basic features to advanced sound engine controls. Click Settings → Configure amaroK to display the configuration window. This window is split into a number of subcategories—General, Appearance, Playback, OSD, Engine, Collection, and Scrobbler. The General category lets you configure miscellaneous settings, including whether to remember the current playlist on exit and whether to show the splash screen at startup. The Appearance category allows you to tweak the font settings and color scheme for amaroK to give it a personal look. The playback category lets you control specific audio effects, including cross-fading and whether to resume playback upon start. The OSD category pops up a sample on-screen display that you can drag around your desktop to set its position. You can also configure the font and color settings for this display as well as what information to show.

The engine display is where configuration can get a bit complicated. amaroK itself doesn't know how to play MP3s, Oggs, and so on, and instead uses various audio engines that do. This makes amaroK very flexible in that it can adapt to a number of audio engines to suit its environment. Audio engines include the xine engine, GStreamer, aRts, and others. Which engine you choose depends on your specific environment, but for instance, if you use a KDE desktop you probably use aRts to manage your audio, so choose that engine. If you use GNOME you might want to try the GStreamer plug-in. If either of those engines don't work or seem buggy, try the xine engine, which I've personally found to be more stable than the others. Depending on which engine you choose, this display allows you to configure a number of advanced options for that engine, so tread carefully here.

The collection display lets you tell amaroK where to find your music on the system through a tree view of the filesystem. Click on a directory and check it to add it to amaroK's list. In this display you can also configure whether amaroK uses a local SQLite database or a MySQL database to store its collection database, including listening stats. By default, amaroK uses an embedded SQLite database, but [Hack #22] has information on how to configure and use amaroK with a centralized MySQL database.

Finally, the Scrobbler display will allow you to configure an Audioscrobbler account if you wish to submit your listening data to Audioscrobbler. Audioscrobbler is an Internet service through which subscribers upload their listening habits. Audioscrobbler uses this data to figure out listening preferences and displays suggestions in the sidebar or adds them to your current playlist. Set this option by clicking the small toggle box in the main window next to the volume slider. You'll know you have the right one when you see the tool tip "Append Suggestions on."

The Sidebar

The real usefulness of amaroK comes into play in the sidebar. This sidebar splits different types of context-sensitive information into a series of vertical tabs called Context, Collection, Playlists, Media Device, and Files. Each tab opens into a different sidebar full of information and controls for your music collection. Click on a tab to show that set of information and click a second time to hide the sidebar completely.

The Context Pane. The Context pane is the first tab in the sidebar and is the tab you will likely display most when you are just listening to your music. This pane has three tabs along the top: Home, Current, and Lyrics. Like the name indicates, the Context pane displays context-sensitive information based on the current playback state and the track that is playing. If no track is playing only the Home tab is enabled. This tab displays lots of different information about your listening habits and music collection, including a list of your favorite tracks from data that amaroK automatically collects based on your listening habits. In addition, the Home tab lists the newest tracks you have added to the collection and a list of least-played tracks.

When a track is playing, the Current and Lyrics tabs are enabled. The Current tab provides a lot of useful information about the current track split into a few sections. The first section displays information about the current track, such as the title and album, along with album art if it has been configured. If you haven't yet found album art for this track, click the question mark icon or right-click and select "Fetch from amazon.com" and amaroK will search Amazon.com for appropriate cover art. Cycle through the list of images until you find the correct cover and click Save to set that image as the cover art for this album. Once you set the cover art for one song, all the other songs for that album will display the cover art as well.

Click the Lyrics tab to attempt to retrieve lyrics for the current track and display them in that pane. If amaroK can't find a perfect match, it will list a number of possible matches or even allow you to enter your own search terms to find lyrics.

amaroK also keeps track of your listening habits and will display the first time and the last time that you listened to this particular track in addition to its current rating. amaroK calculates ratings based on your listening habits. The rating algorithm is a bit more complex than this description, but basically songs that you listen to all the way through are rated higher and songs that you skip or only partially play are rated lower, so to give a song a higher rating, listen to it more often and listen to it completely.

 If you want to perform general maintenance on album art for your collection, click Tools → Cover Manager. Amazon requests that all album art be deleted within 30 days of download and amaroK performs this chore for you automatically.

If you are connected to the Internet, the next section of this pane will display a list of suggested songs based on the current track using Audioscrobbler. With Audioscrobbler support enabled, amaroK will grab a list of suggested tracks from Audioscrobbler based on the track you are currently listening to, and display the tracks you happen to have in your collection, sorted by your ranking. Right-click a track and select Append to Playlist to add it to your current playlist. Click Settings → Append Suggestions to append these suggested songs to your current playlist—to quickly create a playlist that matches your current mood.

The next section in this pane displays a list of your favorite tracks by the same artist and underneath that a complete list of your albums by that artist, sorted by date, so that you can easily add them to the current playlist. You can also use this view to easily edit metadata for entire albums. Right-click on one of the album titles in the list and select View/Edit Meta Information, and you will be able to edit information about the album and apply it to all tracks for that album.

The Collections Pane

The Collections pane provides you with a complete list of tracks that amaroK has found in your collection sorted by artist and album. You can enter a keyword at the top of the pane to filter the list. Right-click on an artist, album, or specific track to add it to the playlist, queue it in the current playlist, create a new playlist, or edit meta information.

The Playlist Pane

The Playlist pane provides an interface for all of the playlists that you have created or that amaroK has found in your collection. You can add, delete, or edit existing playlists from the top part of the pane. The bottom section of the pane is titled "Smart Playlists" and provides a number of virtual playlists that amaroK has created based on your collection. These virtual playlists include all songs in the collection, your favorite tracks (based on amaroK's rating system), your most played tracks, and even a set of fifty random tracks.

Click Create Smart-Playlist to open a window where you can create your own rules-based playlist. For example, using this feature, you can tell amaroK to create a playlist of all Rock genre songs released between the years 1982 and 1988 that you have listened to less than five times in the past two months. The process is simple; just create one or more rules that specify your criteria and save. A rule is composed of three pieces: a database field to act upon which is chosen from the drop-down list; an operand that states how to match your criteria against the data; and finally a criteria string. The + button at the end of the default single rule line lets you add additional rules.

The Media Device Pane

If you use an iPod, the Media Device pane will let you drop files into a queue to transfer to your iPod. Click the Transfer button at the bottom and amaroK will initiate the transfer process.

The Files Pane

The Files pane is a general file system browser that lets you find tracks or playlists on your system and add them to amaroK. You can also use a keyword filter to display only files that match your keyword.

HACK #22   Store amaroK Data in MySQL

amaroK has the option to store its collection data in a remote MySQL database. Use this feature to create a centralized database of your listening habits so they follow you from computer to computer.

By default, amaroK stores information about your collection including listening habits and rankings into a SQLite database file on your filesystem. If you only use amaroK on a single computer this works fine, but if you run it on multiple computers you might want your information to be persistent across machines. amaroK supports the use of a MySQL database for this type of storage, but it does require a bit of setup beforehand to use. This hack will describe the steps necessary to migrate to a MySQL collection database.

First, you need root access to a MySQL database to create a new database for amaroK. If you plan on accessing this database from anywhere, you will want it to be on an Internet-facing machine that's always on. Log in to the database as root and create the initial database:

```
$ mysql -p -u root
mysql> CREATE DATABASE amarokdb;
mysql> USE mysql;
mysql> GRANT select, insert, update, delete, create, drop, create \
temporary tables, index ON amarokdb.* TO amarok@localhost IDENTIFIED \
BY 'password_here';
mysql> FLUSH PRIVILEGES;
```

Replace *password_here* with the password you want to use the for amarok user. Now that the database is created, click Settings → Configure amaroK and then click Collection from the amaroK configuration window. Change the Collection Database Engine to MySQL and then enter the hostname for your MySQL database along with the name of the database (amarokdb in this example) and the username and password (amarok and the password you chose in this example). Click OK. amaroK will now start using the MySQL database to store its settings.

Transfer SQLite Data to MySQL

To import SQLite data into MySQL, the amaroK team created this method, which is not officially supported. First, copy your *~/.kde/share/apps/amarok/ collection.db* file to your database server, and then type:

```
$ sqlite3 collection.db .dump | \
grep -v "BEGIN TRANSACTION;" | \
grep -v "COMMIT;" | \
perl -ne "s/INSERT INTO \"(.*)\"
VALUES/INSERT INTO \1 VALUES/; print" | \
mysql -u root -p amarok
```

HACK #23 Enable Your Multimedia Keyboard

LinEAK turbo charges the whole concept of customizing how your Internet/ multimedia keyboard works.

It's hard to find a keyboard these days that doesn't have special buttons to control your web browser, music player, or launch favorite applications. These keyboards include Windows software to activate these keys, but that obviously doesn't help a Linux user. Instead, this hack will show you how to use the Linux equivalent, LinEAK. LinEAK is a combination of packages, including the main daemon service and several plug-ins. It's a bit quirky and doesn't always launch successfully (at least in this author's experience), but it has support for many multimedia keyboards, so it's your best chance of getting the keyboard to work with Linux.

As of this writing, you can get Debian packages for some of the programs that make up LinEAK at *http://lineak.sourceforge.net/*, and you can get the source code for all the packages from the same site and compile the programs and plug-ins yourself. I compiled my own and it was a cinch. The RPM packages at this site are out-of-date but might be current by the time you read this. Until then, you can find a variety of RPM packages for LinEAK designed for Mandrake and other distributions at *http://rpm.pbone.net/ index.php3?stat=3&search=lineakd&srodzaj=3*. And you can also search *http://www.rpmfind.net*. Make sure you have XOSD and XOSD development libraries installed if you want to enjoy the on-screen display feature.

The following programs comprise LinEAK as it stands now:

lineakd
lineak_defaultplugin
lineak_xosdplugin
lineak_kdeplugins
Media Detect
lineakconfig
Klineakconfig

At minimum, install *lineakd*, *lineak_defaultplugin*, and *lineak_xosdplugin*. If you can't find packages for your distribution, download the source code and then compile and install the programs using these commands (assuming you place your source code in */usr/local/src*):

```
# cd /usr/local/src/lineakd-0.8.1
# ./configure
# make
# make install
# cd /usr/local/src/lineak_defaultplugin-0.8.1
# ./configure
# make
# make install
# cd /usr/local/src/lineak_xosdplugin-0.8.1
# ./configure
# make
# make install
```

Now log in as a regular user and type the following command to get a list of the supported keyboards:

```
$ lineakd -l
(The complete list is 3 pages long, this is just the first few lines)
LinEAK v0.8.1 -- supported keyboards:

 [TYPE]       [Full name]

 A4-KBS21       A4Tech Wireless Desktop KBS-21533RP & Office/Multimedia
Keyboard
 A4-KBS8        A4Tech KBS-8
 A4-RFKB23    A4Tech RFKB-23
 A4-RFKB25    A4Tech RFKB-25 (KBS-2548RP & KBS-2548RPC)
 ACE-6512UV     Acer 6512-UV
 ACE-TM290    Acer Laptop/notebook Travelmate 290LCi
 ACEAKV12       Acer AirKey V (12 keys)
 ADEL-9805    Adesso EL-9805
 APK7         Apple Pro Keyboard (7 keys)
 BEN-AM805    BenQ AM805
```

That kind of beats the tar out of Hotkeys support, doesn't it?

Find your keyboard in the list. For example, the code for the Logitech Elite keyboard is LTCElite. Now type this command to create a default configuration file for your keyboard (substitute LTCElite with the code for your keyboard):

```
$ lineakd -c LTCElite
```

The -c option creates a default configuration file, *lineakd.conf*, for the Logitech Elite keyboard and places the configuration file in the ~/.*lineak* directory. Fire up your favorite editor and customize this file's settings to your heart's content.

Here's a sample configuration I created for my Logitech Elite keyboard:

```
# LinEAK - Linux support for Easy Access and Internet Keyboards
# Copyright (c) 2001,2002, 2003  Sheldon Lee Wen <leewsb@hotmail.com>
#                and Mark Smulders <Mark@PIRnet.nl>
# http://lineak.sourceforge.net
#
# lineakd configuration file
# example key configuration:
#           play              = "xmms --play-pause"
#           eject             = EAK_EJECT
#
# Lineakd supports the following modifier keys:
#    control alt shift mod2 mod3 mod4 mod5

# Normally /dev/cdrom, but UDEV likes /dev/cdroms/cdrom0
CdromDevice = /dev/cdroms/cdrom0
Display_align = center
Display_color = 77FF00
Display_font = "-adobe-helvetica-bold-r-normal-*-*-240-*-*-p-*-*-*"
Display_hoffset = 0
Display_plugin = xosd
Display_pos = bottom
Display_soffset = 1
Display_timeout = 6
Display_voffset = 50
KeyboardType = LTCElite
MixerDevice = /dev/mixer
Screensaver =
conffilename = /home/nicholas/.lineak/lineakd.conf
keystate_capslock =
keystate_numlock =
keystate_scrolllock =

Arrow =
Email = "thunderbird"
Favorites = "firefox"
Go = "firefox -remote 'openURL( )'"
Media = "cdeject"
Messenger =
Mute = "EAK_MUTE"
MyHome =
Next = "cdplay +"
Play = "cdplay"
Pause = "cdpause"
Previous = "cdplay -"
Search = "firefox -remote 'openURL(http://www.google.com,new-tab)'"
Shopping =
Sleep =
Stop = "cdstop"
VolumeDown = "EAK_VOLDOWN"
VolumeUp = "EAK_VOLUP"
Webcam =
iTouch =
```

Note the use of some built-in commands, such as EAK_MUTE, EAK_VOLUP and EAK_VOLDOWN. These are preferable when figuring out how to configure a command-line mixer to do the same operations. Unfortunately, LinEAK doesn't automatically insert these as the default settings for the Mute, VolumeUp, and VolumeDown parameters (it leaves the definitions empty), so unless you know these generic settings exist, you might waste a lot of time figuring out how to create a command to mute your sound driver or change the volume. Well, now that you know they exist, by all means, use them!

Outside the internal EAK_ commands, the audio CD controls in this example are driven by a command-line package of programs called *cdtool*, created by a host of contributors but currently maintained by Max Vozeler. You can download cdtool from *http://hinterhof.net/cdtool*. You can choose any CD player that can be controlled via the command line, but it's nice not to have an actual graphical CD player clutter the screen when all the controls are already on the keyboard.

You can thank Mark Smulders (*msmulders@elsar.nl*), the original author, for this fine piece of software. Sheldon Lee Wen (*leewsb@hotmail.com*) is the current maintainer and developer of the latest versions, and wrote plug-ins from the ground up. Phil Woodland (*sir_taco@yahoo.ca*) is the contributions coordinator and maintainer. Finally, Chris Peterson (*rpm@forevermore.net*) does the RPM packaging for LinEAK.

—*Nicholas Petreley*

HACK #24 Rip CDs from the Command Line
Use command-line tools to rip CDs the old-school way.

There are a lot of CD-ripper and MP3- and Ogg Vorbis–encoder GUI programs out there nowadays that streamline and automate the process of turning a CD into a directory of digital music files. Most of these programs, however, still make use of the same old ripping and encoding tools that have been used on the command line for ages. If you want to hearken back to the era of command-line CD ripping—or maybe your machine isn't even running a graphical environment—this hack will walk you through the two-step process of ripping and encoding so you can quickly turn a CD into a directory full of MP3s or Ogg Vorbis goodness.

Rip the CD

The first step to convert a CD into MP3 or Ogg files is to rip the CDDA audio tracks from the CD to individual WAV files. My tool of choice for this is *cdparanoia*, which is a commonly used program for ripping CDs. Chances are that your distribution includes it, but if not, you can download the source directly from the official project page at *http://www.xiph.org/paranoia*. There are a number of other CD-ripping programs available including the original *cdda2wav* program, but I like *cdparanoia* because, well, it's more paranoid. CD drives and CDs themselves aren't perfect, and a jittery CD drive, or a scratched CD can often result in pops or other errors in your tracks when you are ripping. *cdparanoia* compensates for all these problems and reads the CD very carefully, bit by bit. It attempts to repair any scratches it finds and compensates for a jittery CD-ROM drive. The result is as accurate a WAV file as you are going to get from a CD, particularly if it is damaged. Of course, there's a downside to all this paranoia—speed. Even on a fast CD-ROM drive, don't be surprised if *cdparanoia* rips at 2x speed through the entire CD.

cdparanoia is pretty simple to use and has a few basic options. The simplest example is to rip an entire CD into WAV files:

```
$ cdparanoia -B
```

The -B option tells *cdparanoia* to go into batch mode, which causes it to split the output into multiple files at track boundaries and name each track "track[*number*]" where *number* is simply the number of the track. If you don't specify which tracks to rip, *cdparanoia* will default to ripping every track on the CD. As *cdparanoia* rips, you will notice live output, which tells you how far along it is in a particular track, and you will probably notice that there is an animated smiley face (hopefully) at the far right of the screen. This smiley isn't just for decoration; it alerts you to any problems *cdparanoia* is having at a particular point on the track. Table 2-3 lists the different smileys and what they stand for.

Table 2-3. cdparanoia status smileys

Smiley	Status
:-)	Normal operation, low/no jitter.
:-|	Normal operation, considerable jitter.
:-/	Read drift.
:-P	Unreported loss of streaming in atomic read operation.
8-|	Finding read problems at same point during reread; hard to correct.
:-0	SCSI/ATAPI transport error.
:-(	Scratch detected.
;-(	Gave up trying to perform a correction.
8-X	Aborted read due to known, uncorrectable error.
:^D	Finished extracting.

You don't have to rip the entire CD with *cdparanoia* either. If you only want to extract a certain range of tracks, specify the track number or track range on the command line. For instance, to extract tracks 2 through 5, type

```
$ cdparanoia -B 2-5
```

After *cdparanoia* is finished ripping the CD, you should have a directory full of *.wav* files. The next step is to encode them into MP3 or Ogg Vorbis.

Encode the WAVs to MP3s

Once you have a directory of WAV files and you want to convert them to MP3s, the next step is to choose an MP3 encoder. There are a number of different encoders out there, but probably the most common encoder under Linux is LAME. LAME stands for "Lame Ain't an MP3 Encoder," because originally it wasn't—it was a GPL'ed patch against the dist10 ISO distribution engine. Over time, that engine has been replaced and now LAME is a fully independent LGPL MP3 encoder hosted at *http://www.mp3dev.org*.

LAME is only distributed in source code form from the web site, so if you want to get it directly from the source (pun intended), download the tarball from the official page and follow the installation instructions to compile it. There are also a number of third parties that distribute LAME packages for various Linux distributions, but you will likely not find LAME prepackaged in a commercial distribution's official package repository. Why? Patents. The company Fraunhofer Gesellschaft owns a number of patents on specific parts of the technology that creates MP3s. While the legal ramifications of these patents are complicated, the short story is that, to avoid the risk of lawsuit, many Linux distributors have opted not to include MP3-encoding software in their distributions. For more information on this issue, check out the excellent FAQ at *http://web.media.mit.edu/%7Eeds/mpeg-patents-faq*.

Once LAME is installed, the basic encoding process is rather simple. To encode the file *track01.cdda.wav* to an MP3, type:

```
$ lame track01.cdda.wav track01.cdda.mp3
```

By default, LAME encodes in 128 kilobits per second at a Constant Bit Rate (CBR). This means that each second of audio will use 128 kilobits of disk space. For many people, the default is rather low, so you will likely want to use the -b option to specify your own bitrate. To double the bitrate to 256 kilobytes type:

```
$ lame -b 256 track01.cdda.wav track01.cdda.mp3
```

LAME also supports Variable Bit Rate (VBR) encoding. In VBR encoding, you specify a minimum and maximum bitrate, and LAME will vary the bitrate between those values depending upon the requirements of the audio it is encoding. Sections of the audio that don't need high quality will use a lower bitrate, ideally resulting in a file that sounds almost as good as a file encoding at the maximum bitrate, but with a reduced file size. LAME offers two different VBR algorithms, --vbr-old and --vbr-new. The new algorithm has undergone considerable tuning and is now considered to be on par with the original --vbr-old algorithm, but it is almost twice as fast. To encode an MP3 using VBR that ranges between 128 and 256 kb, type this:

```
$ lame -b 128 -B 256 --vbr-new track01.cdda.wav track01.cdda.mp3
```

With a little bit of shell scripting, you can use these commands to encode every WAV in your current directory to a 192 kbps CBR MP3:

```
$ for i in *.wav; do j=`echo $i | sed -e 's/\.wav/.mp3/'`; lame -b 192 $i
$j; done;
```

Or if you want to do the same thing, only with a VBR MP3 that varies between 128 and 256 kbps:

```
$ for i in *.wav; do j=`echo $i | sed -e 's/\.wav/.mp3/'`; \
lame -b 128 -B 256 --vbr-new $i $j; done;
```

LAME has an incredible number of advanced options you can use to get the most from your MP3 encoding. To see the complete list of options read the LAME documentation pages at *http://lame.sourceforge.net/using.html*.

Encode the WAVs to Ogg Vorbis

Because of the issues with the MP3 codec and patents, a group of developers got together to create a completely open source compressed audio codec to replace MP3. The result was called Ogg Vorbis, and it touts higher quality audio files at the same or even smaller sizes compared to MP3s. Most audio players under Linux now support Ogg Vorbis files, and because it is not encumbered with any patents, most distributions also ship with Ogg Vorbis plug-ins, encoders, and other software. *oggenc* is the command-line program used to convert files into the Ogg Vorbis format.

A recent study suggests that 12 percent of music shared online via P2P is in Ogg Vorbis format, so you're in good company should you decide to use it as your preferred audio format.

For basic options, *oggenc* is executed much like LAME and shares many of the common arguments. Ogg Vorbis files automatically use VBR encoding, so instead of specifying a hard bitrate to use, the -b option specifies an average bitrate to use. The simplest use of *oggenc* is this:

```
$ oggenc track01.cdda.wav
```

This will produce a file called *track01.cdda.ogg* with an average 128 kbps bitrate. To encode at a higher average bitrate such as 256 kbps, use the -b option:

```
$ oggenc -b 256 track01.cdda.wav
```

To automate this process for a complete directory of WAV files, we just modify the earlier *lame* shell script slightly:

```
$ for i in *.wav; do oggenc -b 192 $i; done;
```

 To find out more about Ogg Vorbis, visit the official site at *http://www.vorbis.com*.

H A C K   Rip CDs Straight from Konqueror
#25

The Konqueror file manager provides an incredibly easy-to-use CD-ripping program—just drag and drop files from the CD to convert them on the fly to MP3, Ogg, or FLAC.

Some people like to claim that almost everything under Linux (particularly when it comes to multimedia) is far too difficult. However, I think that after trying this next hack, even skeptics will agree that ripping a CD from KDE is about as easy as you can get.

First of all, even though this hack uses Konqueror and the KDE Control Center exclusively, you can use the hack in other desktop environments as well. To rip a CD from within Konqueror, put the CD in the drive and close any autorun CD-playing apps that might launch. Then open up Konqueror and if you are in file browsing mode, click Audio CD Browser from the sidebar; otherwise enter **audiocd:/** in the Location field. In the main window (see Figure 2-7) you will see a number of directories and files appear. These are all virtual files and directories, but become real files once you copy them. The main directory contains each of the tracks from the CD in WAV format. To rip one or more tracks from the CD, just select the tracks you want to rip and drag them onto your desktop or into a another Konqueror window opened to the directory of your choosing, or optionally right-click on the selected files and choose Copy To and then browse to where you want to copy the files. As Konqueror shows you its progress, it is actually ripping the files from the CD into WAV format.

Also in the main directory are a number of folders with names such as CDA, FLAC, MP3, and Ogg Vorbis. These folders contain the same tracks in the audio format the folder is named after. Each of the tracks is named based on CDDB data Konqueror automatically retrieves for you.

Location Edit View Go Bookmarks Tools Settings Window Help

Location: audiocd:/

Ars Technica Linux Today Register NYTimes Google Google Linux Debian Planet FARK Pr »

Name	Size	File Type
Audio CD Browser		
Devices		
Fonts		
Print System Browser		
CDA	13 B	Folder
FLAC	13 B	Folder
Full CD	5 B	Folder
Information	1 B	Folder
MP3	13 B	Folder
Ogg Vorbis	13 B	Folder
Elvis Costello - 01 - Welcome To ...	14.0 MB	WAV Audio
Elvis Costello - 02 - Miracle Man....	35.8 MB	WAV Audio
Elvis Costello - 03 - No Dancing....	27.4 MB	WAV Audio
Elvis Costello - 04 - Blame It On ...	29.1 MB	WAV Audio
Elvis Costello - 05 - Alison.wav	34.5 MB	WAV Audio
Elvis Costello - 06 - Sneaky Feeli...	22.2 MB	WAV Audio
Elvis Costello - 07 - (The Angels ...	28.4 MB	WAV Audio
Elvis Costello - 08 - Less Than Z...	33.3 MB	WAV Audio
Elvis Costello - 09 - Mystery Dan...	16.3 MB	WAV Audio
Elvis Costello - 10 - Pay It Back....	26.2 MB	WAV Audio
Elvis Costello - 11 - I'm Not Angr...	30.6 MB	WAV Audio
Elvis Costello - 12 - Waiting for t...	34.7 MB	WAV Audio
Elvis Costello - 13 - Watching th...	37.9 MB	WAV Audio

Services

19 Items - 13 Files (370.4 MB Total) - 6 Folders

Figure 2-7. Konqueror audiocd:/ location

To rip tracks from the CD into MP3s, enter the MP3 folder and then drag the tracks you want from that directory onto your desktop or any other location. Konqueror will perform the MP3 encoding on the fly as it copies.

While this all is certainly easy, you might wonder how you can change the bitrates and other settings Konqueror uses to rip the audio tracks. This is easy as well—just open the KDE Control Center from the K menu (or type **kcontrol** in a terminal) and then click Sound & Multimedia → Audio CDs. In this window are multiple tabs you can use to configure KDE audio CD settings. Click the File Names tab to change how KDE names the tracks it rips. Click the MP3 Encoder tab and you can adjust the bitrate KDE uses to rip, choose whether to use CBR or VBR, and find a number of other settings. The Ogg Vorbis tab configures similar settings for Ogg Vorbis ripping. Click the Apply button to save your changes.

HACK #26 Get a Grip on CD Ripping

Use the Grip program to automate all of your CD ripping tasks.

The command line is definitely a powerful tool, particularly for automation, but it can also make doing some tasks, like ripping a CD, more trouble than it's worth, especially if you plan on tagging the resulting audio with metadata such as ID3 tags. While there are several frontends to command-line tools, Grip, in my opinion, is an excellent example of a GUI frontend that balances the power and configurability of the command line, with the ease of use of a GUI interface. After you get to the end of this hack, your CD-ripping process will be so automated that once you start, you won't even have to pick up a mouse.

Grip is a pretty common program, so your Linux distribution will likely have it packaged for you already. Otherwise, you can download the latest version of Grip from the official web site at *http://nostatic.org/grip*. Grip is a frontend in that for the most part, it uses other command-line utilities behind the scenes to do all of the work and simply provides an easy-to-use interface to configure what commands it passes down to those tools. Because it is a frontend, Grip can make use of many different command-line CD ripping programs and WAV encoder programs and, as such, it supports ripping to a number of popular formats including MP3, Ogg Vorbis, FLAC, or even a custom encoder of your choosing. This also means that to use those tools, you will need to already have them installed.

Configure Grip

Before you rip your first CD, you will need to configure Grip. Grip's main interface is broken into a number of tabs:

Tracks
> This tab displays the current list of tracks for a CD that has been inserted into the CD player and allows you to check which of the tracks you want to rip. Grip also functions as a CD player, so you can select a particular track from this tab and click the play button at the bottom of the window to play the track.

Rip
> Here you can see the current progress of any ripping and encoding you have scheduled and start or abort the ripping process.

Config
> Under Config you will find a number of sub-tabs that configure how Grip rips and encodes a CD.

Status
> Look here for constantly updated text output for any jobs that have been done. You can look here to see any error messages or other output.

Help
> This tab provides buttons to launch help for different categories, including how to play CDs, rip CDs, and configure Grip.

About
> Here you'll find information about Grip itself, including the version and a link to the official web site.

To configure Grip, click the Config tab to reveal a number of sub-tabs that configure different Grip settings. The tabs we are interested in are CD, Rip, Encode, ID3, and DiscDB. The first tab, CD, lets you configure your CD device. For the most part the default settings will work, but for the purposes of automated ripping make sure that the "Auto-play on disc insert" option is off. To test whether Grip has the correct CD-ROM device, insert a CD and see whether Grip sees and can play it. If not, make sure */dev/cdrom* is pointing to your correct CD-ROM device, often */dev/hdc* or */dev/scd0*.

The Rip configuration tab is where things start to get interesting. Because so many people are used to automated programs that turn their CDs into MP3s, they often don't realize it is a two-stage process: first ripping the tracks from the CD into WAV files, and then encoding the tracks to MP3, Ogg, or whatever other format you wish. This tab controls the ripping stage of the process, and most of the options are pretty self-explanatory.

The first sub-tab, Ripper, lets you configure which CD-ripping program to use. Grip now includes its own version of *cdparanoia* by default, and I recommend that you use it unless you have a good reason not to. *cdparanoia* by default rips more slowly than most other ripping programs (on most of my CD-ROM drives it rips at 2x), but what it loses in speed, it more than makes up for in accuracy. *cdparanoia* is slow because it is particularly thorough about getting every bit it can from the CD. If you rip with faster but less thorough ripping programs, you might notice pops or gaps in your tracks. Even on many of my scratched-up CDs, *cdparanoia* has been able to recover the track. If you want more information about *cdparanoia,* see [Hack #24].

Once you choose your CD-ripping program, you can configure it further in the Ripper tab. In the case of *cdparanoia*, you can disable a number of its default options, including what it calls "paranoia" and "extra paranoia"— how thorough it is about reading the CD. I recommend you leave those and the scratch detection and repair options alone. The primary option in this sub-tab you should be interested in configuring is the "Rip file format" option. Here you can tell Grip where to put and how to name the WAV files it rips. Grip uses a number of variables that correspond to metadata from the CD. Table 2-4 lists a number of the common variables and what they represent.

Table 2-4. Grip naming variables

Variable	What it represents
%A	The artist name for the disc
%a	The artist name for the track (useful for multi-artist CDs)
%y	The year of the disc

Table 2-4. Grip naming variables (continued)

Variable	What it represents
%d	The name of the disc
%t	The track number, zero-filled so that 3 would be shown as 03
%n	The name of the track
%x	The encoded file extension (*mp3* for MP3 files, *ogg* for OGG files, and *wav* for WAV files)

For example, if you stored your MP3s in a directory called *mp3* in your home directory, you might put in this field:

```
~/mp3/%A/%y-%d/%t-%n.%x
```

Decoded, that line would turn Track 10 of the *London Calling* CD by The Clash, called "The Guns of Brixton" into the file *~/mp3/the_clash/1979-london_calling/10-the_guns_of_brixton.wav*

> You can use whatever naming scheme you wish for your audio files. I prefer this method because it organizes all my CDs by artist, then by each album sorted by date, then by each track. This way no matter what audio player I might use, by default the tracks are all in order.

With this sub-tab configured, click the Options sub-tab to get to other ripping options. There are a few options here that I like to enable, particularly Auto-rip on insert and Auto-eject after rip. With these options enabled, when Grip is running it will automatically start ripping a CD for you when you insert it, and then eject it when it's done. This means that once the rest of Grip is configured, you can set up a stack of CDs at your desk, start Grip, insert the first CD, and then minimize it and do something else. When you see that the CD has ejected, just replace it with another CD to rip and go on with what you where doing. Grip will handle the rest. It doesn't get much more automated than that!

The next main configuration tab is Encode. This tab lets you configure what audio files Grip will encode the WAV files into. The first option, Encoder, lets you choose what encoding program to use. What you choose here depends heavily on what encoding programs you have installed, and what kind of audio files you want. For instance, if you want to make MP3s, you will likely choose LAME, *mp3encode*, or your favorite MP3 encoder. I usually stick with LAME because it is fast and produces decent-quality MP3s. If you want to create Ogg Vorbis files, choose *oggenc*. If you want to create FLAC files (a lossless audio codec so there is no degradation in quality) choose *flac*. After you have chosen the encoder to use, make sure the encoder executable path points to where your encoder is (the default should be fine here). The defaults for the next two options, the encoder command line and file extension, should be fine unless you choose to use a special encoder not directly supported by Grip. The next field, "Encode file format," takes the same type of information as the similar field in the Rip tab. In fact, if you make sure to use %x as the file extension, you can likely just directly copy and paste from the same field under the Ripping tab.

In the Options tab for Encode, you can configure some specific options for your encoder. Probably the most important option in this tab is the "Encoding bitrate" option, which determines the bitrate at which to encode your audio file if you use a lossy encoding such as MP3 or Ogg. What you put here is largely a matter of taste, although the higher the number, the larger your resulting file will be. In the case of MP3s, some people can't tell the difference between 128 and 256 kilobits per second. For other people, the distinction is great. I usually use 192 or 256 kilobits per second here, but you might want to experiment with the output for your audio files and determine what bitrate is best for you—your choice may vary depending upon the type of music you are encoding. In this tab you also have the option to create an *.m3u* playlist file for each CD you rip and choose where to put the playlist file. Generally, the only other option I enable in this field is "Delete .wav after encoding."

The next major configuration tab, ID3, lets you control whether Grip inserts ID3 tags into your audio files. Generally this is a good thing, and you will want all these options enabled unless you want to go back later and manually set ID3 tags—an often tedious process.

The final configuration tab you might want to configure is the DiscDB tab. This tab lets you configure the primary and secondary CD database servers that Grip will query when you insert a CD. These servers contain information on many CDs, based on CD signatures. When you insert a CD, Grip will query this database and retrieve artist, disc, and track information for the CD so that it can automatically fill out the ID3 tags and name the files appropriately. I would recommend sticking with the default servers listed here unless you know what you are doing. Make sure that the "Perform disc lookups automatically" option is enabled here.

Rip a CD

Once you have configured Grip, the process to rip a CD is rather simple—just insert the CD into the CD-ROM drive. Grip will automatically scan the CD, retrieve the track information from your CD database servers, select all tracks for ripping, and start the ripping and encoding process. You can click on the Rip tab to watch the progress of both the ripping and encoding to monitor how far along in the process you are. If for some reason you want to stop the ripping process, click the "Abort Rip and Encode" button.

> If you notice that the track information that Grip retrieved is wrong, or Grip was unable to retrieve the track information at all, abort the ripping and encoding process, and then click the pencil icon at the bottom of the window. This will expand the window and provide a number of fields that you can use to fill out artist, title, genre, track name, and other CD information. Choose different tracks from the Tracks tab to change specific information for that track. Once you have finished your changes, you can click the envelope icon to submit your changes to your configured CD database so that the information is available to the next person who rips the CD. Once the changes have been made, select all of the tracks in the Tracks tab, and then go to the Rip tab and click Rip+Encode to start the ripping process.

As I mentioned before, the nice thing about configuring Grip in this way is that you can let it run virtually unattended and just feed it new CDs until all your CDs are ripped—which certainly beats typing long commands and editing ID3 tags by hand!

HACK #27   Edit ID3v2 Tags from the Command Line

Use the id3v2 tool to update your music tags either manually on the command line or through shell scripts.

If you ever need to hack the metadata in your MP3 files but wish to have more control over the metadata reading/writing process than you get with common GUI tools, the *id3v2* tool can help you. Using this tool, you can dump, change, or remove the ID3 tags from any MP3 file, which makes it perfect for calling from tools like *find* to dump, change, or remove all the tags in your entire MP3 collection.

The *id3v2* tool is a reasonably popular program and should be prepackaged by your Linux distribution of choice. Use your distributions software installation tool to install this program. If for some reason you don't have this tool prepackaged, download the tarball from *http://id3v2.sf.net*, compile, and install it according to the included installation instructions.

To list the ID3v2 tag contents of an MP3 file, invoke *id3v2* with the -l option:

```
$ id2v3 -l "Dr Greenthumb.mp3"
id3v1 tag info for Dr Greenthumb.mp3:
Title  : Dr Greenthumb              Artist: Cypress Hill
Album  : IV                         Year:     , Genre: Unknown (255)
```

```
Comment:                              Track: 13
id3v2 tag info for ../Cypress Hill/IV/13 Dr Greenthumb.mp3:
TIT2 (Title/songname/content description): Dr Greenthumb
TALB (Album/Movie/Show title): IV
TPE1 (Lead performer(s)/Soloist(s)): Cypress Hill
TRCK (Track number/Position in set): 13
```

This Cypress Hill track contains both ID3v1 and ID3v2 tags. ID3v1 tags appear at the end of the file and contain the name of the artist, album, and track names as well as a release year, a genre, a track number, and a comment field. ID3v1 limits the name fields to 30 characters, which all too often cuts off longer track names. The ID3v2 standard fixes this shortcoming by making many more fields of arbitrary length available to the user. Unlike ID3v1, v2 tags reside at the beginning of the file, which means that a file can contain both a v1 and a v2 tag, as does the example above. To see what you can store in ID3v2 tags, take a look at the ID3 specification pages at *http://id3.org*.

Each ID3v2 tag consists of a number of *frames*, where each frame has a four-letter identifying code and contains one piece of information (see Table 2-5). The artist name tag (Lead Performer/Soloist in ID3v2-speak) has the code TPE1, the album name TALB, and the track name TIT2.

Table 2-5. Frame identifying codes

Identifying code	Description
TPE1	Lead performer/soloist
TPE2	Band/orchestra/accompaniment
TEXT	Lyricist/text writer
TALB	Album name
TIT2	Track name
TOAL	Title of the original recording
TRCK	Track number
TENC	Encoded by
APIC	Attached picture

Using these codes and the ones listed on the ID3 specification pages, you can change any one piece of data in the ID3v2 tag. For instance, to change the album name using *id3v2*, type:

```
$ id3v2 –TALB "New album name" sample.mp3
```

This changes the album name to "New album name" in both the id3v1 and id3v2 tags. *id3v2* also has the -a, -A, -t, -c, -g, -y, -T shortcut options to set the artist, album and track names, the comment, genre, year, and track number, respectively. If you want to remove the ID3 tags from a file, use the –s, -d, and –D options to remove id3v1 tag, the id3v2 tag, or both tags, respectively.

Finally, if you wanted to dump all the ID3 tags in all your MP3 files, you could do this:

```
$ find /mnt/mp3 -name \*mp3 -exec id3v2 -l {} \;
```

This assumes that you stashed all your MP3 files under the */mnt/mp3* directory—change it according to your music collection organization. This find command executes id3v2 -l for each file it finds, which causes *id3v2* to dump all the tags it finds in the MP3 file.

> Pipe the output through *more* or *less*, because if you're like me, there will be *lots* of output.

—*Robert Kaye*

Add Album Art to ID3 Tags
Many MP3 players can display album art for a track if the art is embedded in the ID3 tag. Use the Album Cover Art Downloader tool to automate the process of adding cover art to your MP3s.

In this age of digital media and purchasing music from the Internet, there are still a few nice things about buying an actual CD. One of these things is the fact that a CD comes with album art. Album art not only can give you interesting photos of your favorite band and often song lyrics, but the cover of the album itself creates a distinctive look that you can use to identify the CD. Album art is popular even for MP3s, and a number of players can display album art that has been embedded in the ID3 tag. This hack will tell you how to use the aptly named Album Cover Art Downloader program to, well, download album cover art and add it to your ID3 tags.

The first step is to download and install Album Cover Art Downloader (called *albumart* for the rest of the hack). Go to the official web site at *http://louhi.kempele.fi/~skyostil/projects/albumart* and click on the link to the latest release. There you can download precompiled RPMs or DEB packages for your Linux distribution or, alternatively, you can download and build the source. To use *albumart*, you will need Python 2.3 or greater, QT 2.3 or greater (or QT 3.1 or greater), PyQT the QT Python bindings, and the Python Imaging Library.

> Debian users can get these dependencies quickly. Just type:
> ```
> # apt-get install python-qt3 python-imaging
> ```

Launch *albumart* from your applications menu or, alternatively, type
albumart-qt from a terminal. The initial interface is pretty basic and empty,
and the first step is to click File → Open and browse to a directory containing your music collection. *albumart* will then scan the directory and attempt
to guess appropriate album art for the MP3s based on image files in the
directories. Then it will display the MP3s, sorted by album, that do not yet
have album art in their ID3 tags, so you can easily see what you need to fix.
If you want to see your full collection instead, toggle View → Hide albums
with cover images.

To add album art to an album, click the album in the left-hand pane and
then click the Download Covers button. *albumart* will query Amazon.com
(and optionally Buy.com, WalMart, and Yahoo Images) for album art relating to your artist and album name and display any relevant images in the
right-hand pane (see Figure 2-8). Select the album art that matches in that
pane, and then click "Set as Cover" and *albumart* will add that cover art to
all MP3s for that album. If the correct cover isn't there, you can search the
Web on your own (or possibly scan it in), and then drag and drop the image
from your file manager into the right pane of *albumart*.

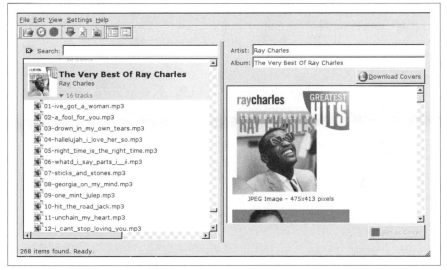

Figure 2-8. Albumart with downloaded cover art

> You can also have *albumart* automatically scan through
> every directory and install album art it finds automatically.
> Click Edit → Select All, and then click Edit → Download
> Missing Cover Images. This will take awhile, particularly if
> you have a lot of albums. You can also just select one or a
> few albums and run the same operation a few at a time.

Automate Music File Tagging

#29 Why tag your music files one by one? Use the EasyTag program to automate the naming and tagging of your music.

EasyTAG is a utility for viewing and editing tags for MP3, MP2, FLAC, Ogg Vorbis, MusePack, and Monkey's Audio files. Its simple and nice GTK+ interface makes tagging easy whether you're editing tags manually or taking advantage of EasyTAG's automatic tagging. This hack walks you through using EasyTAG to add tags to your audio files.

To get EasyTAG, go to the official EasyTAG download page at *http://easytag.sourceforge.net*. This page contains packages for most major distributions or, alternatively, you can download and compile it from source. The program depends on the following libraries:

- GTK 2.4
- id3lib to handle MP3 files,
- libogg and libvorbis for Ogg Vorbis files
- libFLAC (along with libogg and libvorbis) for FLAC files

After EasyTAG is installed, launch it from your desktop menu or type **easytag** in a terminal. The main window (see Figure 2-9) is split into a tree browser on the left side that is used to select audio file directories, and a tag editing section on the right. In the tree browser, select the directory that contains your media files and EasyTAG will search for supported files. All the files it finds are displayed in the middle pane with a variable background color to show, at one glance, the files in the same directory.

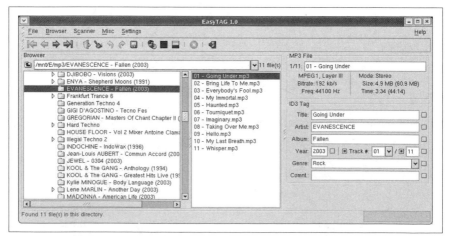

Figure 2-9. EasyTAG main window

Another useful viewing mode organizes the files by artist and by album to provide a quick look at all the artists of your collection and all albums for each artist. Click Browser → Tree View | Artist-Album View to toggle between the two.

The interface displays basic file information taken from the file header, such as bitrate or duration. You can manually edit common tag fields like title, artist, album, year, track number, genre, and comment (which were available in both ID3v1.1 and ID3v2.3 tags), but you can also edit special ID3v2.3 fields like disc album, composer, original artist/performer, copyright, URL, encoder name, and attached pictures.

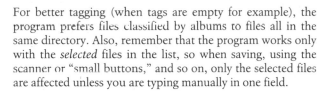

> For better tagging (when tags are empty for example), the program prefers files classified by albums to files all in the same directory. Also, remember that the program works only with the *selected* files in the list, so when saving, using the scanner or "small buttons," and so on, only the selected files are affected unless you are typing manually in one field.

Three Ways to Tag and Rename Files

EasyTAG offers three ways to tag or rename your files: manually, automatically with the scanner, or automatically with CDDB. The following sections describe each one.

Manually. This mode should be used when:

- Audio files from different albums are mixed in the same directory.
- There aren't many files to edit.
- There are few changes to make.
- You are adding only pictures to the tag.

If you have only a few albums to tag, this mode is very easy to use: you just type the information directly into each field.

When working by albums, some values, such as album name, year, and genre are the same for all files. To save time, selectthe small button on the right of each field to apply this value to all selected files. The genre field can be selected from the drop-down list or typed in manually. The year field also offers a little speed improvement; type the last numbers and the rest will be filled automatically, according to the current century and decade. For example, typing **4** will display 2004, and **94** will display 1994.

To number tracks quickly with the format track number/total tracks, use the first small button next to Track # to number each file according to its position in the list (so the order of files is important). The second small button is like a sticky button that applies the number of total tracks to each selected file.

To pass from one field to the next one efficiently, just press the Enter key. You can use Tab to move between fields but every other tap places focus on the buttons next to the fields so it isn't as efficient. The keys PageUp and PageDown jump to the previous and next files, respectively.

To rename the files one by one enter the new filename in the MP3 File field in the right top of the main window (its name changes to reflect the file format you are working with). The previous name remains in the file list until the changes are saved.

Any invalid characters you type (for Windows FAT partitions: '/', '+', etc) automatically will be replaced unless you disable the option "Replace illegal characters in filename (for Windows and CD-ROM)" in the Misc tab of the Preferences window.

To rename the directory directly in the browser, right-click the directory and choose "Rename Directory." The change takes effect immediately, and you can't undo it.

When renaming the directory manually, files aren't moved. As the directory is renamed, all files (even files not supported in EasyTAG, such as JPEG) stay in the current directory. This behavior differs from the scanner method, described next, which moves only files that match the pattern.

Automatically with the Fill Tag scanner. This mode is best when:

- The files are sorted by albums.
- The filenames or parent directory contain tag information (artist, album, title, etc.).
- There are empty or incorrect tags.

The Fill Tag scanner uses a pattern to associate words in the filename and directories with the tag entries. Once you press the green scanner button in the toolbar, the associated words are automatically entered into the appropriate tag fields. If the tag is partially completed, use the option "Overwrite fields when scanning tag" in the Scanner tab of the Preferences window to replace all fields with the new values. This pattern uses a series of codes that correspond to a particular field and follow rules listed in Table 2-6.

Table 2-6. EasyTag codes and values

Strings associated with code	Field value
%a	Artist
%b	Album
%c	Comment
%p	Composer
%r	Copyright
%e	Encoded by
%g	Genre
%i	None! Used to ignore a string
%l	Number of tracks
%o	Original artist
%n	Track name
%t	Title
%u	URL
%y	Year

> To avoid making mistakes, use a particular code only once in a fill tag.

Like when tagging manually, only the selected files are processed by the scanner. You can use the defined patterns in the list or write your own patterns to correspond to the format of your filenames and directories. To avoid mistakes when selecting the pattern, a preview area immediately shows the results before you apply the pattern.

If you need help with the different codes, press the Help button (the life buoy) to display the legend of each code. If you want to save your own patterns or edit or sort the full list of patterns, press the Mask button to display an editor on the Scanner window (see Figure 2-10). The following examples show how to use patterns.

Assume you have the following path and filename:

```
/mnt/MP3/EVANESCENCE - Fallen (2003) - Rock/01. Going Under.mp3
```

And you apply this pattern:

```
%a - %b (%y) - %g/%n. %t
```

You will fill the tag fields with the values shown in Table 2-7.

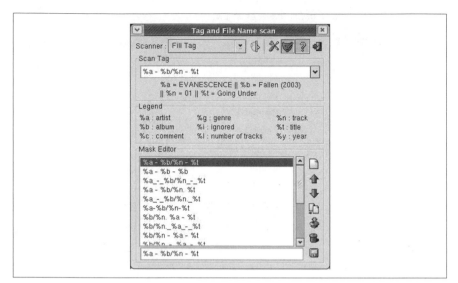

Figure 2-10. EasyTAG scanner window edit

Table 2-7. Example patterns

Field	Value
Artist (%a)	EVANESCENCE
Album (%b)	Fallen
Year (%y)	2003
Genre (%g)	Rock
Track (%n)	01
Title (%t)	Going Under

If you want to fix file and directory names along with ID3 information, choose the scanner mode "Rename File and Directory" from the drop-down menu, and you can easily fix names of lots of files and move them into new directories. The new filenames will be based on the tag values, so it is important to have correct tags. Like in the Fill Tag scanner, it uses the same codes to build the filename structure from the tag entries.

This scanner also offers the ability to move the files in new or existing directories using an absolute or relative path.

Relative path

Using a relative path causes the files to be placed in a subdirectory of the current directory. For example, */mp3/evanescence/01.Going Under.mp3* with the pattern %a - %b/%n - %t will be moved to */mp3/evanescence/EVANESCENCE-Fallen/01-Going Under.mp3* if the tag contains the values %a=EVANESCENCE, %b=Fallen, %n=01, and %t=Going Under.

Absolute path

Using an absolute path, the files can be moved to any directory. The current path of the file can be added to the pattern by pressing the icon to the left of the field (a directory with a green +). With this feature, it is easier to change the current path of the file.

For example, the file */mp3/evanescence/01.Going Under.mp3* with the pattern */mp3/%a - %b/%n - %t* will be moved to */mp3/EVANESCENCE – Fallen/ 01-Going Under.mp3"* if the tag contains the values %a=EVANESCENCE, %b=Fallen, %n=01, and %t=Going Under.

Unlike when renaming the directory manually, the scanner moves the files to the new destination—so it is important to know that the files not recognized by EasyTAG will *not* be moved to the new directory and will stay in the current location. However, the files are moved only once you save, so until you save, you can use Undo if needed.

Automatically with CDDB. Use this mode when:

- The files are sorted by album.
- The file audio data corresponds to the original CD (to use the Automatic Search).
- The album is found in CDDB.

To use tagging with the CD database, two modes are available. First try the automatic search, but if it fails to identify the album, try the manual search.

The automatic search mode generates the CDDBID from the audio files and queries the database. Select all files of an album (and only a single album's files) in the same order as the CD and press the Search button. All the corresponding albums found in the CD database are then listed (see Figure 2-11). Select an album to display the tracks for the album on the right. To fill files with the corresponding tags, select the tracks for the album you want to change and press the Apply button.

If no album was found with the automatic search, your last chance is to try a search using keywords such as artist name, album name, or track name. This search returns the same results as the search service on the freedb.org site and may return lots of lines. While browsing the albums list, the albums that already were displayed are shown in red. Press the red line button to keep these lines and remove the rest. When the right album is identified, follow the method for automatic search to select and apply the tags to your files.

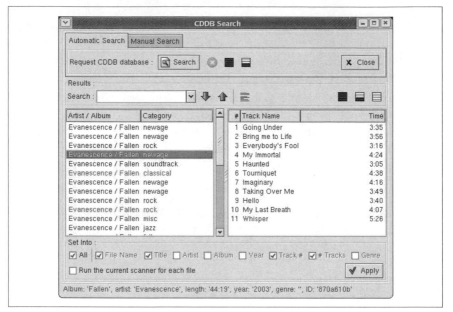

Figure 2-11. EasyTAG CDDB Scanner window

As for the tag fields, use the CDDB results to apply the new name to the file. With this method you can change only the filename and not the path. Activate the "Rename File" scanner, which will be run after applying the results.

Correct Tag Fields with the Process Fields Scanner

Here are the conditions where this mode is best:

- The filename or tag fields are already filled.
- You want to correct the case.
- You want to change some characters.

This feature is useful to normalize your filenames or tags. For example, you can fix the case or convert some characters in your filenames. To start this scanner, click Scanner → Process Field(s). At the top of the window, select the push-down buttons corresponding to each field that should be processed. Then press the green button to run the scanner on the selected fields.

If necessary, you can use one or both CDDB modes to fill your tags with FreeDB servers. You can also load the content of a simple text file containing filenames to set the name of each file.

—Jerome Couderc

Correct Music Metadata with MusicBrainz

#30 Learn about MusicBrainz and how to use and contribute to the project.

MusicBrainz aims to aggregate the "brainz" of thousands of music lovers to create an open, user-contributed, music encyclopedia. MusicBrainz collects information about the music artists have released and how musical works and musicians relate to one another. In turn, people can use the project along with tools that utilize MusicBrainz (see "Tools that Use MusicBrainz") to add metadata to their audio files and correct the data that is already there. The community of moderators (editors) collects information about all kinds of music, regardless of its genre, time period, ethnicity, or religion. Unlike some music information databases out there, MusicBrainz strives to eliminate duplicate data, fix incorrect data, and augment missing data. The end result is a project that can be used as a general music reference, a place to share your music trivia, and as a reference to use for cleaning up your music collection.

MusicBrainz got its start in 1998 as the CD Index, which intended to provide an open data/open source alternative to the formerly open CDDB project. After a short while, the CD Index reinvented itself as MusicBrainz and expanded its focus to include support for tagging digital music files and not just Audio CDs. Today MusicBrainz has more than 100,000 members and information for over 3,000,000 tracks.

MusicBrainz's Database

The MusicBrainz database contains a list of artists, the albums they have released, and a complete track listing for each album. MusicBrainz assigns each artist, album, and track a unique identifier (a UUID), so that client software can unambiguously talk about any of these musical entities. These identifiers should eliminate confusion about different versions of the same piece of music. For instance, the live version of Pink Floyd's *Great Gig in the Sky* has a different track identifier than the studio version.

Most albums in MusicBrainz have CD Index IDs (grandfathered in from the old CD Index project) derived from the Audio CD's table of contents, so MusicBrainz-enabled players can identify Audio CDs by reading the table of contents and retrieving the music metadata from the MusicBrainz server.

Recently MusicBrainz also added support for Advanced Relationships, which lets users create relationships between artists, albums, tracks, and URLs to web resources. For instance, the page for the rapper Snoop Dogg shows that Snoop Dogg:

- Has an official homepage at *http://www.snoopdogg.com*
- Is a performance name for the person Calvin Cordozar Broadus

The Advanced Relationships concept enables MusicBrainz to become a true music encyclopedia. Any contributor with any bit of information about an artist or a piece of music can now capture that detail in MusicBrainz.

MusicBrainz attempts to keep the numerous contributors all on one page by providing style guidelines (*http://musicbrainz.org/style.html*). Note the use of the term *guidelines* and not *rules*—MusicBrainz attempts to capture widely varying uses of metadata and few pieces of this data ever fit neatly into rules. MusicBrainz recognizes this and tries to keep the guidelines flexible, in hopes of capturing the world's unruly music metadata into one single database.

Open Source and Open Data

MusicBrainz embodies the principles of open source and applies the open source methods to data, coining the term "open data." Open data, much like open source, benefits from making data widely available under liberal licenses. Linus Torvalds famously said, "Given enough eyeballs, all bugs are shallow." This same concept applies to data as well: "Given enough users, all data problems and omissions are obvious."

With this idea in mind, MusicBrainz makes its data available for anyone to download at *http://musicbrainz.org/products/server/download.html*. MusicBrainz makes the core data (artists, albums, tracks, identifiers, relationships) available in the Public Domain. Ancillary data (search indexes, changes to the database, etc.) is available under the Creative Commons Non-Commercial Share-Alike 2.0 license. MusicBrainz makes its software available under the GPL and/or the LGPL.

Tools that Use MusicBrainz

The MusicBrainz project released two flagship tagging applications, Picard and *pimpmytunes*, that are covered in "Clean Music Metadata at the Command Line" [Hack #31] and "Clean Music Metadata with a GUI" [Hack #32] respectively.

The following applications also make use of MusicBrainz for metadata cleanup or audio CD lookup:

- amaroK (*http://amarok.kde.org*)
- Juk (*http://developer.kde.org/~wheeler/juk.html*)
- SoundJuicer (*http://www.burtonini.com/blog/computers/sound-juicer*)
- Zinf (*http://zinf.sf.net*)

More applications that support MusicBrainz can be found on their applications page at *http://musicbrainz.org/wd/MusicBrainzEnabledApplications*.

How to Participate

MusicBrainz needs all kinds of help. First and foremost, MusicBrainz needs the music knowledge that you have in your brain, so please go to MusicBrainz (*http://musicbrainz.org*) and create yourself an account. Once you've logged in, use the search page to find your favorite artist(s) and see if the artist pages are complete. Does MusicBrainz have all the albums for this artist and are they properly classified? Do they adhere to the official style guidelines? Check the release dates, album language, and CD Index IDs on albums and add missing ones or fix incorrect ones.

If the MusicBrainz database has all that data in order, consider grabbing your favorite album to see if anyone has captured the credits for the album using the Advanced Relationships feature. If not, use the Add Relationship link add relationships that capture contributions to this album.

Second, MusicBrainz needs developers—every open source project has more people coming up with ideas than it has people bringing those ideas to life, and MusicBrainz is no different. Once you've played with the MusicBrainz web site a bit, you may find shortcomings or think of features you'd like to see implemented. If you've hacked on Apache, Perl, or PostgreSQL, you'll likely make a great candidate for hacking on MusicBrainz. To find out more, visit the developer pages (*http://musicbrainz.org/development/index.html*) or the help wanted page listed next.

Finally, even if you don't hack on code, MusicBrainz can still use your help—the project always needs people to help test new applications, file bug reports, and write documentation for the site and the applications. For all the gory details on how you can participate, visits the MusicBrainz help wanted page (*http://musicbrainz.org/about/helpwanted.html*).

—Robert Kaye

Clean Music Metadata at the Command Line

Use Lucene-based tagging in MusicBrainz to automagically scan and tag all your MP3s from the command line.

Most people never understand the importance of clean metadata (e.g., ID3 tags) in their music until they shove their haphazard music collection into an iPod. If you have no tags or inconsistent tags in your music collection, it's nearly impossible to really enjoy your shiny new iPod. To help out with this dilemma, MusicBrainz has been working on creating intelligent tagging applications that take the pain out of fixing your music metadata (for an introduction to MusicBrainz, see **[Hack #30]**).

MusicBrainz offers a full-blown GUI application code-named Picard [Hack #32] that provides a visual approach to tagging your music. Musicbrainz also provides *pimpmytunes* for people who prefer to work on the command line. MusicBrainz tagging applications use the Lucene engine (*http://lucene.apache. org*) behind the scenes to identify tracks. This general-purpose text indexing engine, when applied to music metadata, allows tagging applications to perform metadata matching based solely on the incomplete metadata found in the source music track and a separate index file. MusicBrainz used to match a song to its online metadata by using acoustic fingerprints that attempt to identify music on the actual audio characteristics, but this was slow and inaccurate. These new tools are much better but do have one downside: they require very large index files to run, which delays the instant gratification of tagging your music collection *right now*, because you first have to download the index files.

Go to the pimpmytunes site at *http://musicbrainz.org/wd/PimpMyTunes*) to get started. Download the program and the index files pimpmytunes references. Follow the provided instructions for installing the program and its prerequisite software and for where to place the index files.

Configure pimpmytunes

Once you install the application and index files, run pimpmytunes (command line pmt) without command-line arguments to print out the usage for the program and write the default settings file to ~/.*pimpmytunes.conf*. Using your favorite text editor, edit this file and tweak the default settings to your taste. Pay close attention to the settings listed in Table 2-8.

Table 2-8. Important settings in pimpmytunes.conf

Setting	Purpose
IndexDirectory	The location of the MusicBrainz Lucene index.
FileMask	The file naming mask that specifies how to rename tracks (explained later).
VAFileMask	The file mask that specifies how to rename various artist (compilation) tracks.
DestDir	The directory where to save cleanly tagged tracks.
MoveFiles	Move files to the destination directory when saving.
RenameFiles	Rename files when saving.

pimpmytunes works best when you move cleaned tracks from your music directory to the destination directory. To organize files in place, either turn off the MoveFiles option or set the destination directory to be the same dir as your existing music directory. In the latter case, pimpmytunes will create subdirectories according to your selected FileMask.

Since no two people name their music tracks the same way, *pimpmytunes* supports *file masks*, which let you tell the program how to save your files (see Table 2-9). For example, the following file mask:

```
%abc/%sortname/%album/%0num - %track
```

will instruct *pimpmytunes* to save the track "Taxman from The Beatles" to the following file:

```
/mnt/mp3/clean/B/Beatles, The/Revolver/01 - Taxman.mp3
```

Table 2-9. pimpmytunes file masks

File mask	Description
%abc	The first letter of the artist name
%sortname	The name used to sort the artist
%album	Album name
%0num	Track number padded with zeroes
%track	Track name

Well, I'm assuming you have set DestDir to */mnt/mp3/clean*—which you don't have to do. Having a / in the file mask causes pimpmytunes to create a subdirectory, so that all your music gets cleanly organized on your hard drive. Please refer to the *pimpmytunes* documentation for a full listing of the supported substitution variables.

Run pimpmytunes

Now that you've configured *pimpmytunes*, you can invoke it with the command **pmt**, a mode (I'll explain modes shortly), and music files and/or directories containing music files on the command line. pimpmytunes will start up and examine the passed files and recursively search for MP3, FLAC, Ogg Vorbis, and WAV files in the directories.

pimpmytunes operates in two modes: automatic and manual. In the automatic mode (command line option –a), the program will check each file and directory passed on the command line to see if it can match the file against the index. If the application finds a match and its confidence rating exceeds the AutomaticThreshold setting, it automatically accepts the match, saves the new metadata to the file, and moves on to the next file. If pimpmytunes can't find a suitable match, it ignores the file and moves on to the next.

Matching files with the automatic mode allows the user to get the *mostly clean* files out of the way quickly and focus on the troublesome files that pimpmytunes can't readily identify. pimpmytunes in automatic mode can also act in the background to automatically tag files, without user interaction. Setting up a cron job to invoke pimpmytunes periodically allows you to automatically tag files in a download directory. If you download files with mostly clean metadata, pimpmytunes will identify, save, and rename your newly downloaded files automatically—all according to your preferences.

Operating pimpmytunes in manual mode (-m) presents the top matches found in the Lucene index for each of the files. You need to inspect the matches and enter the number of the match that fits best. Once the match is selected, pimpmytunes saves the file and moves on to the next file. If pimpmytunes didn't find a close enough match, enter **e** at the command prompt to edit the metadata for this track. pimpmytunes will show the metadata that this track has so far and allow you to edit the information so it can attempt another lookup.

In most cases where pimpmytunes cannot find a match, the metadata tags contained incomplete or incorrect information. For these cases, fixing the data in the tracks with the **e** command lets pimpmytunes find the right track.

Sometimes MusicBrainz does not have the album that matches your track— in that case enter **1** to open a web browser and look up the artist/track at MusicBrainz. Use the MusicBrainz web site to locate the right album or add a new album if the correct one isn't found. Once you locate the album, copy the album page URL that contains the album UUID (e.g., 8f468f36-8c7e-4fc1-9166-50664d267127), and then switch back to pimpmytunes. In pimpmytunes type **a** (for **a**lbum id) and then paste the UUID and hit Enter. This causes pimpmytunes to retrieve the album from MusicBrainz and match the current track to that album.

If pimpmytunes can't find the right match for a track, you can try one of the options from Table 2-10.

Table 2-10. pimpmytunes options

Key	Function
l	Look up this track at MusicBrainz.
a	Enter a specific album ID for this track.
s	Skip this track and try again after processing other tracks.
d	Delete this track from disk permanently.
r	Remove this track from pimpmytunes.

If you have trouble with pimpmytunes, go to the MusicBrainz Contact Us page at *http://musicbrainz.org/wd/ContactUs* and choose your favorite method of getting help.

—Robert Kaye

Clean Music Metadata with a GUI

HACK #32

Use the Picard GUI tool to access the MusicBrainz functionality for cleaning up your music files.

This hack focuses on the GUI version of pimpmytunes. If you prefer GUI tools over command-line tools, this hack presents the best way for you to clean up your music metadata. [Hack #31] explains pimpmytunes and why you should clean up your music metadata. For an introduction to MusicBrainz and its approach to metadata cleanup see [Hack #30].

To install Picard, go to the Picard Tagger homepage (*http://musicbrainz.org/wd/PicardTagger*) and follow the download and software prerequisite instructions listed there. Once you have Picard running, take a look at the Settings dialog box and tweak the settings to fit your tastes. In particular, notice and adjust the Directories and Naming tabs in the Settings dialog. The pimpmytunes hack talks a bit about file masks—please refer to it for a quick introduction to file masks.

Now that you've set up the basics of Picard, its time to take a closer look at the user interface (see Figure 2-12).

Picard has three main user interface areas:

Directory/file browser

This is on the left half of the screen. The top half of the panel allows you to browse your file system and find directories that contain your music collection. Click on a directory and the lower panel will show all the files Picard can work with. Note that Picard shows unsupported files in gray and does not let you drag those files.

Album browser

This panel on the right side of the window shows folders that organize your new files that are pending analysis by Picard, files that Picard hasn't matched, clustered albums, and albums loaded from MusicBrainz. I'll cover this panel in a lot more detail in just a bit.

Metadata information panels

This panel along the bottom of the window contains two tabs that show local metadata (for a selected file), MusicBrainz metadata (the metadata that MusicBrainz has for this file), match album information, and album cover art.

To tag your files with Picard, first use the directory browser to locate your music collection, and then use the file browser to select a handful of files to start. Next, drag the selected files from the file browser to the *New Tracks (drag files to identify here)* folder in the Album browser panel, which tells Picard to read the metadata from these files. If Picard identifies a file, it will

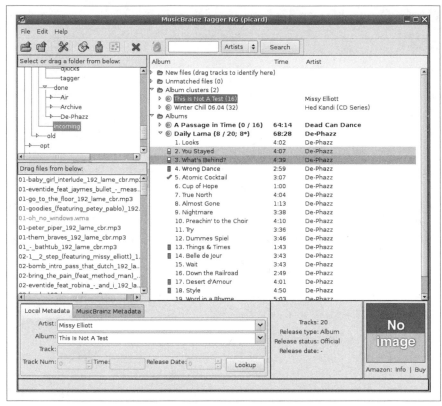

Figure 2-12. Picard user interface

open the matching album in the *Albums* folder and move the file to that album. Picard will add all other files to the *Unmatched Files* folder.

Once Picard completes reading the metadata from the files, click on the Cluster toolbar button to have Picard try to group the files into albums. If Picard finds tracks from the same artist and same album, it considers those files a *cluster* and adds a cluster entry under the *Album Clusters* folder. It is easy for Picard to create clusters when you have *almost clean* metadata that needs complete tagging or small corrections.

If Picard finds some clusters, the next step is to select a cluster and click the Lookup button to launch a web browser and find the right album using MusicBrainz. Once you've found the right album (be careful to select the album that has the same number of tracks that you have), click on the green tagger icon in the album web page to open this album in Picard. Switch back to Picard and drag the recognized album cluster onto the newly opened album (if Picard didn't already do it for you). This should match the files from the cluster to the newly opened album.

If Picard didn't find any album clusters, you can click on a track in the *Unmatched Files* folder and click the Lookup button to look up the album for this track. You could also enter the artist/album name and use the search function in the toolbar to look for the right album. Either way you do it, click on the tagger icon to open the selected album in Picard.

Once you have the correct album open in Picard, you can drag files from the *Unmatched Files* folder or an album cluster and drop it onto the appropriate track in an album. You can even drag a file onto the album to have Picard guess which track this file should be associated with. If Picard guesses incorrectly, simply drag the file from the wrong track onto the right track. If Picard doesn't find a good match, it will open the subfolder *Unmatched files for this album* and deposit unmatched files there. Table 2-11 shows a list of Picard's drag-and-drop operations.

Each file that has been associated with a track on an album has a small, colored icon in front of it. A green box indicates a good match between the file's metadata and the track with which it's associated. An orange box indicates a medium-level match, and a red box indicates a poor match. The background color of an associated track changes from the normal background color for good matches to a reddish background for bad matches. These visual cues make it easier for you to quickly grasp how well Picard matched your files to tracks and where you need to spend your time verifying Picard's work.

Once you're happy with a match, select the track or the whole album and click on the Save toolbar button to save the new metadata to the file(s). After Picard saves the file, the icon in front of the file changes to a green checkmark, showing that the file is done and checked off.

Table 2-11. Picard's drag-and-drop operations

Action	Function
Drag album cluster onto album	Match files from album cluster to this album.
Drag file onto album	Match file to this album.
Drag file onto track	Associate file to this track.
Drag album onto another album	Match the files from source album to target album.
Drag Unmatched files for this album onto Unmatched Files	Move all the files that Picard could not match to an album back to the *Unmatched Files* folder.
Drag a file from the file browser onto a track/album	Load the file into Picard and then associate the file with the track/album onto which it was dropped.
Drag a directory from the directory browser into the New Files folder	Load all the files (and files in all its subdirectories) from the directory into Picard.

—*Robert Kaye*

HACK
#33   Pass the Mic and Record Audio

You don't need a fancy GUI tool to record audio under Linux. Use SoX's rec utility to record audio from your microphone—and do it all from the command line.

Some people might wonder, with all the different graphical audio recording tools out there, why you would want to record sound from the command line. Audacity has everything you need to record, edit, and save audio in a nice interface, and I even cover how to use it to record audio in [Hack #34]. Even with these tools available, there are certain advantages to recording audio from the command line. For one, it's completely scriptable and can be easily scheduled with tools like *cron* and can be used to create a radio TiVo of sorts. For example, at one point there was a weekly radio show that I sometimes wasn't home to listen to. I wanted to record the broadcast and listen to it later, so I hooked up my computer microphone input with my radio's headphone output and left the radio tuned to that channel. Then I set a cron job to turn up my mic volume with *aumix* [Hack #13] and then run the recording program. This hack tells you how to use the SoX sound sample translator and its included *rec* frontend to start recording audio with just a few keystrokes.

The SoX sound sample translator is a very powerful audio editing tool. It not only can convert between a number of audio formats, but it can also modify audio input, adding echoes, fade in and out, and other effects. For this hack, I use a frontend included with SoX called *rec*, which uses SoX behind the scenes to record audio from your system's microphone.

The first step is to install SoX. Many other audio tools rely on SoX for their audio processing, so there's a really good chance that SoX is already installed on your distribution. If not, look for it with your distributions software installation tool. If for some reason SoX isn't available in a precompiled form, download the latest version from the official page at *http://sox.sourceforge.net* and compile it according to the included installation instructions.

The *rec* tool has only a few basic arguments, and for the simplest example you only need to pass it the output format and output file to use. Adjust your microphone volume in the mixer and type the following:

```
$ rec -t .wav output.wav
Send break (control-c) to end recording
```

Start talking into the microphone, and press Ctrl-C when you are finished. If you run the file command on the output file, you will be able to see the file format:

```
$ file output.wav
output.wav: RIFF (little-endian) data, WAVE audio, Microsoft PCM, 8 bit,
mono 8000 Hz
```

By default *rec* will save to a monoaural file at 8,000 Hz. This format might work just fine for you if you intend to play it back with tools like SoX's *play* tool or even tools like *mplayer*, but if you want to encode it into something like an MP3 later on, certain encoding tools might have trouble with the format. To solve this problem change the sample rate that *rec* uses to 44,100 Hz with the -r argument:

```
$ rec -r 44100 output.wav
Send break (control-c) to end recording
$ file output.wav
output.wav: RIFF (little-endian) data, WAVE audio, Microsoft PCM, 8 bit,
mono 44100 Hz
```

As you can see, the file is now encoded at 44,100 Hz. If you want to record in stereo sound, add the -c option to specify the number of channels to use, and set it to 2:

```
$ rec -r 44100 -c 2 output.wav
Send break (control-c) to end recording
$ file output.wav
output.wav: RIFF (little-endian) data, WAVE audio, Microsoft PCM, 8 bit,
stereo 44100 Hz
```

That's all there is to it. In addition to the radio TiVo I mentioned above, there are a number of other useful applications for this. The fact that it's a command-line tool means it would be simple to write a short shell script to adjust the microphone volume and start recording, and then bind the script to a key. Then you could start recording (say during a meeting) at the push of a button.

HACK #34 Edit Audio with Audacity

Record, crop, rearrange, and save audio with the cross-platform Audacity tool.

Often when you take a picture or write a paper, the first effort isn't perfect. Usually there are changes you need to make, whether cropping pictures or changing wording, before everything is perfect. Recorded audio is often the same. There are often periods of silence you need to remove from your recording, mistakes you need to edit, or other changes to make before the track is how you want it. Another more recent use of audio editing is *podcasting*, or the process of creating audio content that you then share and link to with RSS feeds so people can listen at their leisure. [Hacks #86 and #87] discuss podcast programs under Linux, or you could reference O'Reilly's *Podcasting Hacks* for more detailed information. Whatever your reason for editing audio, one particularly useful tool for performing these kinds of edits is Audacity.

Audacity is a cross-platform audio-editing program that runs on Linux, Windows, and Mac platforms. It is popular enough that you will likely be able to find a package for it for your distribution, but if not, you can download the latest release from the official web site at *http://audacity.sourceforge. net*. When you run Audacity for the first time, the interface that appears might seem a bit intimidating if you haven't worked with audio-editing software before. Audacity has a lot of powerful features that could take many pages to describe, but for the purposes of this hack I am going to cover only some of the basics: recording, editing, and cropping sound.

Record Sound

Audacity can accept input from a variety of sources, including previously created sound files, saved Audacity projects, and microphone input. There are a few initial steps to perform to set up audacity to record from your microphone. First, open your mixer program of choice and make sure that the microphone is not muted and that the microphone itself is at a reasonable volume. Next, locate the volume slider near the top of the Audacity window that has the picture of a microphone near it and make sure that it is at a reasonable volume as well. The exact volume levels for your microphone will depend on a variety of factors including what you are recording and what microphone source you use, so you might have to experiment to find the most suitable levels. To the left of the microphone slider is a drop-down menu that lets you choose from a number of audio sources including Vol, Line, CD, Mic, and other options. Make sure that this menu is set to Mic.

Once all of your volume levels are set, click the Record button (the button near the top that has a red circle as its icon) to start recording. When you are ready to stop recording, click the Stop button (a few buttons to the left of the record button represented by an orange square) or the Pause button to pause the recording. Audacity will show you the audio track live as it is being generated in the lower part of the window. To listen to your recording, click the Play button to the left of the Record button. To listen to a particular portion of the recording, just click on that section of the track and then click Play. Once you stop a recording, if you click the Record button again Audacity starts with a new track.

Edit and Crop Sound

Audacity makes the process of editing or cropping an audio track pretty simple. To edit a particular audio file you have previously created, click File → Open and choose the file to edit. Audacity can edit WAV, MP3s, and Ogg Vorbis files alike. To remove a section of audio from the track, click and highlight that particular section with your mouse. If you click Play at this point, Audacity will play only the portion you have selected, which can be useful to isolate exactly what you want to remove. Click Edit → Delete to remove the selected section. You can also move around sections of the audio with Cut and Paste operations. Just select the section of audio to move, and click Edit → Cut. Then click where you would like to paste and click Edit → Paste. If you would like to crop a particular section so only it remains, select it and click Edit → Trim. In between sections of a recording, you might notice that the microphone has picked up background noise that you would like to remove. Select the section you would like to silence, and then click Edit → Silence. Audacity will replace the section with complete silence.

If you need to undo any of your edits, click Edit → Undo. Click Edit → Redo to undo your undo.

Save Changes

When you are ready to save a project, close any unwanted tracks you may have been working from so that only the tracks you want are left behind. If you want to remember each of the tracks and resume the project at a later date, click File → Save Project As to save the entire project. To export to an audio file, click File → Export as WAV, File → Export as MP3, or File → Export as OGG to export to WAV, MP3, or Ogg Vorbis formats, respectively.

HACK #35 Convert from One Audio Format to Another
Use command-line tools to convert between audio formats.

While a desktop user may only encounter a few different types of sound formats on an average day, there are tens, if not hundreds, of different audio formats out there, each with its own specific use and set of features. In this hack, I tell you how to use standard command-line tools to convert between the major audio formats you might encounter.

There are different ways you could categorize audio formats, but one easy way is to split them into lossy and lossless categories. Lossy formats (like MP3s, WMA, and Ogg Vorbis files) not only compress audio, but also strip away parts of the sound that are inaudible or mostly inaudible to the listener. The degree of sound-quality loss varies based on the bitrate of the file and which format you use (certain formats are known for generating higher quality sound at the same or lower bitrates), but with any lossy format, there is a loss in sound quality—hence the name.

Lossless formats (like WAV, CDDA, and FLAC) provide maximum sound quality and do not strip away any sound from the file. This results in a (sometimes much) larger file because some lossless formats don't compress the file, while other lossless formats do.

 The distinction between lossy and lossless files is important, especially when you are going to convert between file formats. Generally speaking, converting from one lossy format to another will result in worse quality than a lossless to lossy conversion, since different lossy algorithms strip away different parts of the sound. Keep this in mind if you have a choice between a lossy and a lossless file as your source.

Some of the tools I will use in this hack can convert to a number of audio formats. For the purposes of simplicity, I'm going to use the WAV file format as the intermediary format because it is lossless and most audio encoders and decoders support it. This way, instead of describing how to convert Ogg Vorbis to FLAC, Ogg Vorbis to MP3, FLAC to MP3, and so forth, I will just describe how to convert to and from WAV files so you can piece the steps together to form whatever format you want.

MP3

MP3 is a very popular lossy audio format. Even though there are many competing formats that tout smaller file size and better quality, the large number of MP3 players and MP3-playing programs has kept this format one of the most popular. While there are many different tools to encode and decode MP3 files, for this hack I will use the LAME encoder. [Hack #24] covers installing LAME and encoding MP3s.

MP3 to WAV. To convert MP3s to WAV, pass the --decode argument to LAME. By default LAME will decode the MP3s to a WAV file, so you don't need to pass any extra arguments.

```
$ lame --decode example.mp3 example.wav
```

That code snippet is all it takes to convert *example.mp3* into *example.wav*.

WAV to MP3. LAME has a number of complicated and advanced options for MP3 generation, but for the purposes of this hack I will describe the basics—creating a CBR (Constant Bit Rate) and VBR (Variable Bit Rate) MP3. These terms describe whether the MP3 will use the same bitrate throughout the entire file (CBR) or whether it will vary the bitrate depending on the content of the audio at that moment (VBR).

The bitrate you choose is largely a matter of taste, so change these example values to a bitrate that suits you. To convert a WAV to a CBR MP3 with a 192 kilobits per second bitrate, type:

```
$ lame -b 192 example.wav example.mp3
```

To convert a WAV to a VBR MP3 that ranges between 128 and 256 kilobits per second, type:

```
$ lame -b 128 -B 256 --vbr-new example.wav example.mp3
```

Ogg Vorbis

Ogg Vorbis is another lossy format like MP3, but Ogg Vorbis is a completely Open Source format that touts higher quality audio files at the same or even smaller sizes. For these examples, I will be using the *oggenc* and *oggdec* programs from the Ogg Vorbis tool set. These tools should be packaged and easy to install for most major Linux distributions. To get more information about Ogg Vorbis, visit the official site at *http://www.vorbis.com.*

Ogg Vorbis to WAV. To convert Ogg Vorbis files to WAV, use the *oggdec* tool. This tool was created to decode *.ogg* files into WAV or PCM output, and the syntax is pretty straightforward. To convert *example.ogg* to *example.wav*, type:

```
$ oggdec example.ogg -o example.wav
```

WAV to Ogg Vorbis. Unlike MP3s, all Ogg Vorbis files use VBR encoding. *Oggenc* is the program of choice for creating Ogg Vorbis files out of WAVs, and when creating an Ogg Vorbis file, the bitrate you specify is the average bitrate Ogg Vorbis will attempt to use based on the content of the file. To convert *example.wav* to a 192 kilobit per second VBR Ogg Vorbis file, type:

```
$ oggenc -b 192 example.wav -o example.ogg
```

FLAC

FLAC stands for "Free Lossless Audio Codec," and the name says it all. FLAC offers a lossless audio format like WAV but at a high level of compression so you can store CD-quality sound at a fraction of the size. FLAC is an Open Source project. If the encoding tools and libraries aren't packaged for your distribution, you can download them directly from the official site at *http://flac.sourceforge.net.*

FLAC to WAV. The *flac* command-line tool is used for both converting to and from WAV files. To convert a FLAC file to a WAV file, add the --decode option:

```
$ flac --decode example.flac example.wav
```

WAV to FLAC. The default behavior of the *flac* tool is to encode files into the FLAC format, so simply specify the input and output filenames on the command line:

```
$ flac example.wav example.flac
```

Other Audio Formats

There are many other audio formats that you might want to convert. Linux doesn't necessarily support encoding into some of these proprietary formats, but if it can read them, it can at least convert them to WAVs for you so that you can convert them to your favorite open format. One of the best tools for this is actually the MPlayer program. Many people associate MPlayer with video files, but it supports so many video and audio formats that it is ideal as a universal converter for proprietary audio formats. [Hack #48] provides more information on installing and using MPlayer.

Anything to WAV. To convert a random audio format that Linux can play (in this example a WMA file, *example.wma*) into a WAV file (in this example a WAV file *example.wav*) type:

```
$ mplayer -vo null -vc dummy -ao pcm:waveheader:file=example.wavexample.wma
```

Since this is just an audio file, we pass null options to the *mplayer* video arguments (-vo null), and then tell the audio output argument (-ao) to output a WAV file (pcm:wavehandler) named *example.wav*. You can use this same method with any audio format MPlayer can play.

WAV

Sometimes you need to be able to convert a WAV file to a different WAV file. Usually this comes into play when you have WAV files you want to use on an audio CD that either aren't stereo or aren't at a 44.1 kHz sample rate, which is required for CDs. Use SoX for this kind of WAV conversion. SoX is short for Sound eXchange, and it acts like a universal sound sample translator. It is a very popular package and it might already be installed in your distribution. If not, it might already at least be packaged for you.

SoX offers a number of advanced options, but for the purpose of this hack I will discuss how to use it to change the sample rates on a WAV file. SoX is discussed in [Hack #33].

Change the Number of Audio Channels. If you have a mono WAV file that you want to convert to stereo, you need to use SoX to change the number of audio channels (in this case from 1 to 2). In SoX the argument to use is -c followed by the number of channels. To convert a mono *example1.wav* to a stereo *example2.wav*, type:

```
$ sox example1.wav -c 2 example2.wav
```

Change the Sample Rate. When you create an audio CD out of WAV files, the files need to conform to a 44.1 kHz sample rate. If you got your WAV files from ripping another CD or through conversion from another audio format, chances are the settings are fine, but if they aren't you need to use SoX to resample the audio to the appropriate sample rate. To resample a WAV file *example1.wav* to a 44.1 kHz sample rate in *example2.wav*, type:

```
$ sox example1.wav -r 44100 example2.wav resample
```

HACK #36 Normalize the Volume of Your Audio Files

Use the normalize tool to adjust the volume of audio files so they all have the same volume.

Many, if not most, people find TV commercials (or at least some of them) annoying. One particularly annoying trait of some TV commercials is their volume setting. The volume of the TV is set perfectly for the show you are watching, but the moment the commercial break starts, the advertising blares through the speakers, forcing you to adjust the volume again. Of course, this means that once the commercials are finished, you have to adjust the volume back to a level suitable for the program.

Music often suffers from the same volume issues that plague TV commercials—some CDs are recorded with particularly low volume, others with a particularly high volume. If you listen to your music on Random (or using a tool such as IMMS **[Hack #19]**), you end up fiddling with the volume control to account for these differences. Luckily, under Linux there is an excellent tool called *normalize* that can analyze a series of audio files and adjust them so they are all the same volume.

normalize has been around for years, and many other multimedia projects use it behind the scenes. As a result, your distribution probably already has it packaged (often called *normalize* or *normalize-audio*). If your distribution doesn't have *normalize*, download it from the official site at *http://www1.cs.columbia.edu/~cvaill/normalize* and compile and install it according to the provided documentation.

Normal Mode

Once *normalize* is installed, usage is fairly straightforward—type **normalize**
followed by a list of WAV files to normalize. The following command nor-
malizes all WAV files in the current directory to the default volume level:

```
$ normalize *.wav
Computing levels...
  file1.wav          100% done, ETA 00:00:00 (batch 100% done, ETA 00:00:00)
Applying adjustment of 20.10dB to file1.wav...
  file1.wav          100% done, ETA 00:00:00 (batch 100% done, ETA 00:00:00)
  . . .
```

By default, *normalize* will take any files it is passed and adjust the volume to
its default volume setting. In the above example, *file1.wav* was too quiet so
normalize increased the volume by 20.10 decibels. *Normalize* will output
progress information as it processes each file, but you can pass the -q argument to suppress this output.

> On newer *normalize* packages, the actual command-line pro-
> gram is called *normalize-audio* to differentiate the WAV nor-
> malizing program from the MP3 (*normalize-mp3*) and OGG
> (*normalize-ogg*) normalizing programs that the package now
> includes.

Mix Mode

One obvious application of the normalize tool is to help adjust the volume
on mixed CDs you might create. When you create a mixed CD, often you
don't necessarily care whether the tracks are the same volume as the rest of
your music collection as long as they are about the same volume as each
other. *Normalize's* mix mode computes the volume for each file and then
calculates the average volume and sets each file to that volume. Use the -m
option to turn on mix mode:

```
$ normalize -m *.wav
```

Once the WAV files have been normalized you can burn them to a CD. If
you've already created a mix CD that wasn't normalized you can rip the CD
[Hack #24], normalize it, and then burn it again with no loss of quality, because
the WAV files you ripped to are a lossless format.

Batch Mode

Some of you might be thinking that the fact that different tracks on an
album have different volumes is a feature, not a bug. Many albums feature
songs of many different relative volumes for effect, and you may not want to
just randomly assign them all the same volume if you plan to listen to the

album sequentially. All the same, if the album was recorded a bit too quiet, you might want to increase the volume of each track relative to each other, without setting the volume of each track to the same value. Batch mode accomplishes this.

In batch mode, *normalize* will scan through each file, compute its volume level, and compare it to the relative volume levels of each of the other files. Then it will compare the average volume of these files to *normalize's* default volume level and increase or decrease the volumes accordingly. In addition, *normalize* will throw out any tracks that are much louder or much softer when it computes the average, so as not to throw it off. Add the -b option to turn on batch mode:

```
$ normalize -b *.wav
```

Normalize MP3 and Ogg Files

It used to be that *normalize* only worked on WAV files, so if your files were in MP3 or Ogg Vorbis format, you would have to convert them to WAV, normalize them, and then convert them back. While you still need to do this in a manner of speaking, *normalize* has automated the process for you and created two tools, *normalize-mp3* and *normalize-ogg* to normalize MP3 and Ogg files, respectively. You can use these tools just like *normalize*, so to normalize all of the MP3 files in a directory, type:

```
$ normalize-mp3 -b *.mp3
```

HACK
#37

Make Your Computer Talk to You

Install Festival on a computer to convert text to speech.

Whenever I see a science fiction movie set in the future, computers almost always fit a certain profile. They are either a form of artificial intelligence (AI) that can talk to people, or they are bent on world domination (or sometimes both). While the AI part isn't exactly there yet, and hopefully the world domination bit is a ways off, computers talking to us is something we can have today. This hack shows you how to use Festival to convert text into speech.

Festival is a speech synthesis system hosted by the Center for Speech Technology Research at the University of Edinburgh (*http://www.cstr.ed.ac.uk/ projects/festival*). Actually, using Festival for basic text-to-speech is an underuse of the technology, because the system provides for all sorts of advanced speech synthesis in any number of languages.

To make Festival convert text to speech, you will need a few different components. First you need the core Festival program itself; next you need the

Edinburgh Speech Tools library; after that you need some sort of lexicon database Festival can use (popular ones are the *festlex* OALD (Oxford Advanced Learners' Dictionary) and *festlex* POSLEX (Parts of Speech Lexicons); and finally you need a speech database. Which speech database you choose basically depends on what sort of voices you want to hear. These *festvox* packages provide voices for American English males and females, British English voices, Castilian Spanish voices, and others. Most major desktop distributions have packages for all of these components either directly in the distribution or in third-party repositories, so check your packaging tool first. Alternatively you can download these source packages from the Center's official download site at *http://www.cstr.ed.ac.uk/projects/festival/download.html*:

- *festival-*.tar.gz* (choose the latest version)
- *speech_tools-*-beta.tar.gz* (choose the latest version)
- *festlex_OALD.tar.gz*
- *festlex_POSLEX.tar.gz*
- *festvox_rablpc16k.tar.gz* (or choose a different speaker)

If you go the compilation route, extract all the files from these packages, then build first the *speech_tools* directory, and then the *festival* directory:

```
greenfly@moses:~$ cd speech_tools
greenfly@moses:~/speech_tools$ ./configure
greenfly@moses:~/speech_tools$ make
greenfly@moses:~/speech_tools$ cd ../festival
greenfly@moses:~/festival$ ./configure
greenfly@moses:~/festival$ make
```

Once Festival is installed, send it some sample text to test it:

```
greenfly@moses:~$ echo "Hello World" | festival --tts
```

By default Festival runs in an interactive shell, but for general text-to-speech uses, you can just use the --tts argument and pipe text to it or, alternatively, pass it a text file to read as an argument:

```
greenfly@moses:~$ festival --tts filename
```

Festival works rather well when combined with Project Gutenberg's ebooks at *http://www.gutenberg.org*. I've found that I need to strip out the official Project Gutenberg text from the beginning of the ebook before Festival reads it, but otherwise it works reasonably well.

One issue I've had is that sometimes I'd like to be able to read the text that is being read to me. I've also found that ebooks and regular text files in different formats don't always have the proper pauses when being read. So I wrote a basic Perl script that runs through the text a paragraph at a time, converts some of the punctuation to make Festival pause where I want, and prints the paragraph to the terminal while simultaneously reading it. Since the script is only a few lines, it lends itself to outside modification to tweak Festival's reading habits even further. I named the following script *speak*, and it can accept either STDIN or a text file as an argument:

```perl
#!/usr/bin/perl

# usage: speak <filename>

$/ = "";
while(<>) {
    @paragraphs = split /((\n\W){1,})|(\n\r{2,})/;
    foreach $paragraph (@paragraphs) {
        next if($paragraph =~ /^\W*$/);
        $paragraph_unedited = $paragraph;
# strip away symbols
$paragraph =~ s/[^\w\s\d.,;:!?]//g;
# add appropriate pauses to newlines, periods, commas, etc
        $paragraph =~ s/\n\r/  /g;
        $paragraph =~ s/\s{2,}/ /g;
        $paragraph =~ s/\.(?=\w)/ /g;
        $paragraph =~ s/(\w)\./$1\. /g;
        $paragraph =~ s/(\w)\;/$1\. /g;
$paragraph =~ s/\.{2,}/ /g;
        $paragraph =~ s/(^\.)$/./g;

        print "$paragraph_unedited\n";
        system("echo '$paragraph' | festival --tts") == 0
    or die "festival exited$!";
    }
}
```

Save the file somewhere in your path (such as */usr/local/bin/speak*), and then to use it, either pass STDIN:

```
$ echo "Hello World" | speak
```

or pass a filename containing text you want to speak as an argument:

```
$ speak hello.txt
```

HACK #38 Search Audio for Hidden Messages

Use a simple effect from the SoX play tool to check audio for hidden messages.

Backward messages in music (or "backmasking") have provided quite a bit of controversy over the years. Music from the Beatles in particular has been popular to listen to backward in hopes of discovering hidden messages (one of the most famous being the phrase "Paul is Dead" at the end of "I'm So Tired" from the *White Album*). Since the Beatles, there have been numerous claims that music from a number of musicians contains hidden messages that are heard when played backward—messages that contain references to Satan, other evil things or, most commonly, drug use.

Of course, back in the days when most people listened to music on records, it was relatively easy to listen to a song backward—you just rotated the record on the turntable in reverse. This method won't exactly work (or at least not easily) for tapes or CDs, but for digital content, Linux has just the tool to aid you in your search for backmasking—the SoX tool and its frontend called *play*.

SoX is a universal sound sample translator and allows you to format audio with a number of interesting effects. SoX provides two frontend applications, *play* and *rec*, that make it easier to play and record audio, respectively (the *rec* frontend is discussed in [Hack #33]).

SoX is a popular program and should already be packaged, and possibly even installed, by your distribution. If not, you should be able to install it using your distribution's package manager. If for some reason you don't have a SoX package available, download the source from the official page at *http://sox.sourceforge.net* and compile it according to the included installation instructions.

With SoX installed, pick the track you want to play backward, and test it by playing it forward:

```
$ play file.mp3
```

The *play* tool will start playing the audio file back to your speakers. Make any mixer adjustments you need at this point. To play the file backward, just add the reverse argument to *play*:

```
$ play file.mp3 reverse
```

Keep in mind that the reverse sound filter will require some drive space to store the temporary sound file it uses, so it might take some time for *play* to finish processing large files, particularly on a slow system. Once *play* is finished processing the file, it will start to play it back backward. Listen to the file all the way through, jot down all the English-sounding words you hear, and then hit Ctrl-C to exit play.

Burn Audio CDs from the Command Line

HACK #39

Use cdrecord directly from the command line to create your own audio CDs.

There are a lot of advanced GUI programs for Linux that make it easy to burn your own audio CDs from files you have on your computer. Almost all of these programs, however, still function as a frontend for *cdrecord*—the command-line CD-burning Swiss Army knife. While GUIs are nice, for basic audio CDs, you'll find that it's almost as easy to burn the CD directly from the command line. This hack walks you through the process of preparing and burning your own audio CD from standard audio files you might have on your system.

The first step to burn an audio CD is to prepare the audio files. In the past audio files had to be converted to CDDA format for *cdrecord* to recognize them, but nowadays *cdrecord* works equally well with WAV files. Depending on the format of your audio files, you will use different tools to convert them to WAV files. Converting from autio format to another is discussed in **[Hack #35]**.

Once your audio files are ready, the next step is to discover which CD-ROM device *cdrecord* will use. Run *cdrecord* with the -scanbus argument and *cdrecord* will probe and detect any CD burners on your system and which device entry to use. The exact method to use will vary depending on whether you use the 2.4 or 2.6 kernel series. The 2.4 kernel series required that CD burners use SCSI emulation with the *ide-scsi* module, so your IDE CD burner on */dev/hdc* might be accessed through */dev/scd0* instead. Most modern distributions that still use 2.4 will turn on SCSI emulation for you so you shouldn't have to worry about setting it up. In the 2.6 kernel series you no longer have to use SCSI emulation and can write directly to the IDE device, but you have to tell *cdrecord* about this fact. To scan for IDE CD burners with 2.4 kernels (or if you use SCSI CD burners), run this:

```
$ cdrecord -scanbus
```

If you use the 2.6 kernel, add the dev=ATA: option:

```
$ cdrecord dev=ATA: -scanbus
```

In either case, you will see output much like the following:

```
scsibus1:
    1,0,0 100) 'MATSHITA' 'DVD-RAM UJ-822S ' '1.01' Removable CD-ROM
    1,1,0 101) *
    1,2,0 102) *
    1,3,0 103) *
    1,4,0 104) *
    1,5,0 105) *
    1,6,0 106) *
    1,7,0 107) *
```

In my case, my DVD writer is listed with the device number 1,0,0. If you had more than one CD-ROM drive installed, you would need to choose which one you wish to use by the extra device descriptions *cdrecord* outputs. Once your device number is identified, change to the directory containing the WAV or CDDA files you want to burn. If you use a 2.4 kernel, run:

```
$ cdrecord -v dev=1,0,0 -audio track01.wav track02.wav track03.wav
```

If you use a 2.6 kernel, modify the dev argument slightly:

```
$ cdrecord -v dev=ATA:1,0,0 -audio track01.wav track02.wav track03.wav
```

If you have converted files from some other audio format into WAV, add the -pad option to *cdrecord* so that it will ensure the WAV is padded to be a multiple of 2,352 bytes—a *cdrecord* requirement.

In both examples, replace the dev argument with the device number for your CD drive. This command tells *cdrecord* to burn *track01.wav*, *track02.wav*, and *track03.wav* to an audio CD. If your WAV or CDDA files are already in order in the directory, you can also use a shell glob (like **.wav*) instead of typing out each file manually. This example uses TAO (Track At Once) recording, which means that each audio track will be spaced by two seconds of silence. If you want more or less of a gap in between tracks you will need to resort to the more complicated DAO (Disk At Once) method if your drive supports it. Because of the many extra steps it involves, if you want to go the DAO route I recommend you use a graphical CD-burning tool as decribed in [Hack #40].

> Some *cdrecord* examples list a speed option, which you can use to set the recording speed. By default *cdrecord* will attempt to use the fastest speed it can detect for your CD writer, but if you want to purposely slow it down (perhaps because of a slow system) add the speed=2 option, but replace 2 with the speed at which you wish to write.

HACK #40 Automate Audio CD Burning with K3b

Use K3b to burn your own custom audio CD in just a few clicks.

Even with the advent of high-tech hard drive and flash memory–based media players and sophisticated peer-to-peer file-sharing software, sometimes the simplest way to take your music with you is on a good old-fashioned CD. After all, many home and car stereos still don't support playing MP3s or other audio formats so if you mix your favorite tracks and burn them to a CD you can play them just about anywhere. Plus, if your CD breaks, it's quick, easy, and cheap to replace with another burned copy.

Creating a CD used to be a bit of a dark science under Linux and required you to use a number of command-line tools to convert audio files into WAVs if they weren't already WAVs. Then you would execute another script to burn them onto a CD and, of course, hope that you calculated the song length correctly so your music would all fit on the CD. With K3b, those days are over. K3b (*http://www.k3b.org*) is a very powerful and very user-friendly graphical CD- and DVD-burning tool. It automates all of the steps that you would normally have to do on the command line and all within a nice simple interface. K3b is a popular package and most distributions have already packaged it for you, so you can install it using your standard software installation tool for your distribution, or alternatively, grab the source from *http://www.k3b.org* and compile it yourself.

Either launch K3b from your application menu or type **k3b** in a terminal. The screen that initially appears offers some quick links to start common CD-burning projects (see Figure 2-13), so click New Audio Project or click New → New Project → New Audio CD Project to select it from the application menu. The split screen interface shows you a view of your file system on the top of the screen and a view of your CD project at the bottom. To add tracks to your CD, browse through the top interface to the audio files you want to add in WAV, MP3, and Ogg Vorbis formats. You can also drag tracks from a CD you have inserted.

Figure 2-13. Main K3b window

As you add tracks, K3b automatically figures out how much space you have left on the CD and displays it in a progress bar at the bottom. K3b will also read any ID3 tags your music files may have and use the information to label the tracks on the CD so that the artist and title will show up on CD players that support CD-Text. Right-click on a track and choose Properties to edit any of the text fields, control what portion of the track to burn to CD, and change how long a gap to use in between tracks. If you want to save the project so you can burn another CD with the same settings at a future date, click File → Save As to store the project information to your disk.

Once you have arranged your new CD how you want it, click the Burn button at the bottom right-hand corner of the screen. The dialog that appears allows you to tweak any last-minute settings for your CD burner, including write speed, write mode, and which CD burner to use (see Figure 2-14). Unless you have specific needs, the default settings should work just fine. Once you have inserted the CD and are ready to burn, click the final Burn button in this dialog to start the burning process, or the Simulate button to simulate the process without actually writing to the CD. A new status window will appear and give you information on the progress of your burning session, including elapsed time, current track being burned, and other status information.

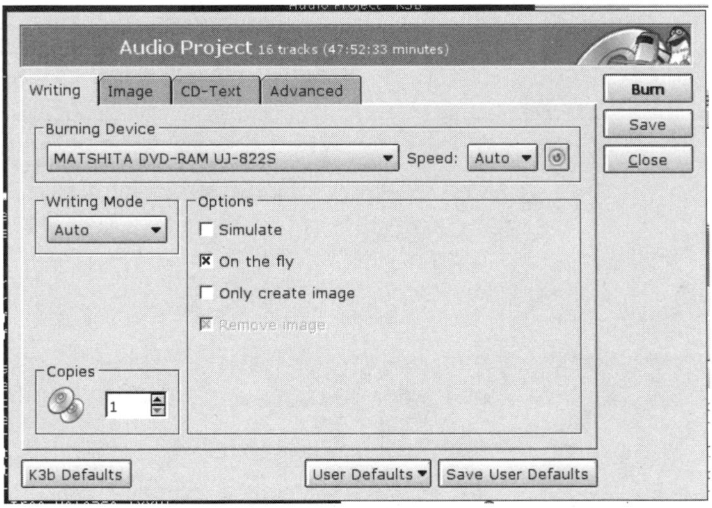

Figure 2-14. K3b Burn dialog box

While you can cancel the process at this point by clicking the Cancel button, doing so will almost certainly render your writeable CD useless, or if it's a rewriteable CD, you will need to blank the CD before writing to it again.

Turn Your Computer into a Turntable

HACK
#41

Use terminatorX to scratch on multiple MP3 tracks as if they were playing on a physical turntable.

terminatorX is a sample-based multiturntable deck. If you wonder why one would compare a software-sampler to a turntable, it's because of the feature that is largely responsible for the popularity of the software: *scratching*. TerminatorX provides the possibility to modify the playback speed with the motion of the computer's mouse and thus simulate the behavior of a turntable. This allows the user to create scratching tones that sound very similar to those produced by hip-hop DJs all over the world.

While this feature was the original intent for the project, terminatorX has evolved significantly from its initial scratching toy days. Today it supports multiple turntables and built-in as well as plug-in real-time effects. To manage more complex setups, terminatorX features its own sequencer—alternatively, it can be remotely controlled through the MIDI interface.

terminatorX is available at the project page at *http://www.terminatorx.org*. Download one of the precompiled packages available for a number of distributions or, alternatively, download and compile directly from source.

The Turntables

When you start up terminatorX, it will pop up with one empty turntable (called Turntable 1) with "empty" meaning there is no audio file loaded into that turntable. The terminatorX user interface is designed in a way to allow many turntables to be visible at the same time. To achieve this, each turntable is represented by two separate panels: the *control* panel on the left and the *audio* panel on the right side of the display.

The control panel is used to accumulate all the knobs, buttons, and sliders related to a turntable, while the audio panel's main purpose is to show a plot of the audio file loaded into the turntable and display the current playback position when the audio engine is turned on. To load a sample of your choice into a turntable, click on the button on the audio panel that reads "NONE." You are then offered a file dialog to select an audio file. Alternatively you can simply drag and drop files from your file manager onto the audio panel. When the file is read successfully, you will see a plot of the audio data in the audio panel. While terminatorX is focused on working with small loops, it is also possible to load complete audio tracks into a turntable. In such a case, you might find the zoom slider located right of the audio display useful, as it enables you to see more details.

 terminatorX supports a wide range of audio files through miscellaneous libraries and command-line tools; however, this depends on how terminatorX was configured at compile-time.

To actually produce some sound you have to get the audio engine running: hit the Power button located on the left of the upper toolbar, and you should hear your sample playing back at normal speed. You can now use the Pan, Pitch, or Volume controls of the turntable, or you can adjust the master controls on the right side of the window. Adjusting the master controls affects all playing turntables.

Typically one turntable is not enough. terminatorX allows you to use as many turntables as your machine can handle (see Figure 2-15). You can add new turntables by selecting Turntables → Add Turntable from the menu. This creates a new turntable with its own control panel and audio panel. To save space, click on the Minimize button in the upper-right corner to minimize the panels, just like the windows on your desktop.

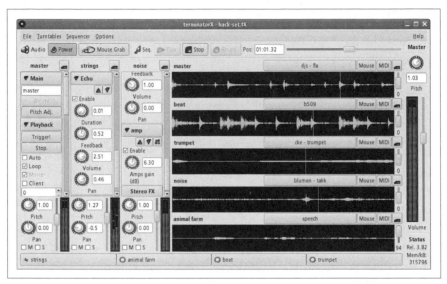

Figure 2-15. TerminatorX with multiple turntables

Scratching

When you use your mouse for scratching, you cannot use it for operating the user interface at the same time. So in order to perform some scratching you have to activate the audio engine and enter the *mouse grab* mode by hitting the Mouse Grab button next to the Power button. Your mouse pointer is now frozen—all mouse input will now be used for real-time turntable operation.

One of your turntables should now be highlighted in scratch mode. This is the one that currently has the input focus. You can select other turntables by pressing the Tab key. With no keys pressed, the turntable keeps on spinning by the speed of its motor. When you hold the Space key or the left mouse button, it's like you're putting your virtual hand on the virtual vinyl: the motor no longer spins the record, but you can spin it with your mouse. Move it from one side to the other and see how the cursor in the audio data plot moves the way you move the mouse. As soon as you release the Space key or the left mouse button you will find the turntable catches up with its motor again.

There are more keyboard shortcuts in scratch mode, most importantly:

- Both Alt and Ctrl allow you to mute the turntable—similar to using a crossfader.
- The F key enables scratching at warp speed, allowing you to quickly find a certain position in a large audio file.
- The Esc key exits mouse grab mode, allowing regular use of the mouse again.

The speed of the turntable is not the only thing you can control with your mouse—all sliders of a turntable can be mapped onto either the x axis (left to right) or the y axis (top to bottom) of your mouse. When you click on the Mouse button in a turntable's audio panel, you can configure the mappings.

The Control Panel

On the bottom of a turntable's control panel you find the most important controls that are always visible: the Volume slider, the Pan and Pitch knobs, the Mute and Solo buttons, and a level indicator displaying the turntable's current signal. The knobs in terminatorX are quite easy to use: click on the knob you want to adjust and move the mouse in either a horizontal or vertical direction while keeping the mouse button pressed. When you find the setting of your choice, release the button.

Above the fixed controls you find a scrollable area that holds all other controls of a turntable grouped into sub-panels. A sub-panel can be minimized when it is not required (click on the button that holds the name of the panel). The Main panel allows you to give a turntable a more useful name or delete it if it's no longer necessary. With the Playback panel, you can trigger or stop the playback of a turntable's sample or set up interturntable synchronization: when you work with loops you often want turntables to be triggered in relation to some other turntable. Activate the Master button of one turntable and the Client button of those you want to be triggered at the same time. You can choose whether you want the client turntable to be triggered with every master trigger or every 2nd, 3rd, and so on by adjusting the Spin button below the Client button.

The last two panels represent the effect queues of a turntable. At first the turntable signal is fed into the mono effect queue. The output signal of that first effect queue is then split into two channels and sent through the stereo effect queue.

Effects

terminatorX brings two built-in effects that are always available from the mono effect queue: Lowpass and Echo. To actually send the turntable's signal through an effect you have to activate the Enable checkbox. Now you can tweak the controls of the effect to achieve the sound that you prefer. The Lowpass filter is a pretty simple resonating lowpass filter—modify the cutoff frequency and the resonance intensity parameters to find out. The Echo effect is just as simple—the echo signal gets a special treatment, however (more on that later).

While they are fun to play with, the two built-in effects are not the limits of the interesting sounds you can produce. terminatorX supports the LADSPA interface (*http://www.ladspa.org*) and loads all the effect plug-ins installed in the default LADSPA lib directories (*/usr/lib/ladspa* or */usr/local/lib/ladspa*) that fit into the software automatically on startup. To add a mono effect, click on the FX button and select the effect of your choice from the menu. The effect will then appear in the queue just like the built-in effects.

The audio signal is fed top-down through the effect queue: the effect on top receives the original turntable output signal as input, and the effect below will use the upper effect's output signal as input, and so on. Obviously sequence matters here, which is why you can reorder the effects with the blue arrows below the effect's label. Click on the label itself to find out more about the plug-in. To remove an effect from the queue, just hit the small x button and it's gone (built-in effects cannot be removed—just disable them if you don't want them). Handling stereo effects works just the same way: create one by hitting the Stereo FX button and operate them just like mono effects.

I noted earlier that the echo signal is treated differently—it is not fed into the next effect, instead it is mixed separately. That way you can have the echo signal use a different pan position than the original signal to add some room to your mix. You can also do weird stuff with this. For example if you put the Lowpass below the Echo you will find that the actual echo signal has no lowpass filtering applied to it in contrast to the original signal.

Store Data and Audio

Once you have set up your turntables the way you want, you'll typically want to be able to save your setup so you can go back to it some other time. Select File → Save Set File to save and File → Open Set File to open a saved set. terminatorX set files hold all the structural information of your setup. The samples are not included within the set files; only their filenames are stored. So, to keep a terminatorX set file working you will also have to keep the referenced audio files on your hard disk and in the same location.

Often you want to record the audio output of a terminatorX session: select Turntables → Record Audio To Disk and choose the output file. TerminatorX will then record all audio generated from the next start (to stop) of the audio engine to a WAV audio file.

The Sequencer

With multiple turntables in your setup, you might find that you don't have enough hands or mice available to modify all the knobs you want. This is where the sequencer comes into play. Using the sequencer, you can record all kinds of events, play them back and record additional ones. To record events, click the Record button to arm the sequencer and then the Play button. Now move some knob up and down or perform some scratching in mouse grab mode if you want. After you hit Stop and then Play again you will see (and hear) how terminatorX performs the actions you previously recorded. For longer recordings you can use the Pos (position) slider at the top to choose the playback starting point.

terminatorX uses the popular touch-to-record approach: when you activate Record and then start sequencer playback all previously recorded events for each control will be played back until you "touch" a control by modifying it. As soon as a control is touched, old events are no longer played back. Instead, they will be overwritten by newly recorded ones. The "touching" is active as soon as you hit the Record button, even before starting playback. If you touch a control, the value will be recorded at the current sequencer starting point.

Sometimes you know you messed up before you hit the Stop button. In that case you might prefer to throw away the events recorded with such a take. When you activate Sequencer → Confirm Recorded Events in the menu, terminatorX will ask you to confirm applying the recorded events after each take. The Sequencer menu will also allow you to delete events for a specific control (you can also right-click on the control to do so).

All the events you record are stored along with your set file so you can restore all your actions easily.

Control terminatorX via MIDI

When you have access to some MIDI control hardware or want to use another application to control terminatorX, you can make use of the ALSA sequencer input port. First off, you have to "wire" the output port of your choice to terminatorX's Control Input port with a separate application like *aconnect*, *aconnectgui*, and so forth. The easiest way to map MIDI bindings to terminatorX's controls is by using the MIDI Learn menu item that appears when you right-click on the control you want to assign to a MIDI controller event. Then you send the MIDI controller event you want to use to modify this control (by rotating the button etc.) and the MIDI Learn dialog box will close automatically. From then on you can use your real knob (or application) to control this parameter. From my own experience, physical knobs really can make things a lot easier and allow you to find interesting settings much more easily.

> For some plug-ins, you might find that a parameter's range is too big, rendering the MIDI mapping ineffective. To work around such cases, you can set the upper and lower MIDI bound: set the value to use as a bound and then select "Set Upper MIDI bound" and repeat the same for the lower bound. Now the whole range of the MIDI controller will be mapped to the range of the plug-in control you selected.

Of course, all MIDI-related bindings, bounds and so forth are stored within the terminatorX set files as well.

Extend terminatorX

Instead of sending the audio output straight to your sound card you can also use the integrated JACK backend and route terminatorX's audio signal through the applications of your choice, apply additional effects, and so on. A lot of users enjoy creating their own turntables for use with terminatorX. To find out more about those (there's a gallery of turntables at the web site) and new terminatorX releases check out the terminatorX website at *http://terminatorX.org*.

—Alexander Koenig

Use an iPod with Linux
HACK #42
You don't need a Windows PC or a Mac to use an iPod.

Linux users' relationship with the iPod is a bit like a girl who can't get a date to the Sadie Hawkins dance—the users keep asking for a bit of attention, and Apple just pretends it doesn't hear. If this were a less hackish group of users, that would be the end of the story, but thanks to some clever programming, Linux users can use an iPod with Linux and this hack shows you how.

This is aimed at Linux purists—that is, people who don't want to have to use a Mac or Windows–based PC, nor Wine nor Windows software—to get going. (I fall into this category, not because of any religious convictions, but merely because Linux is all I have. For updates, visit *http://pag.csail.mit.edu/~adonovan/hacks/ipod.html*.)

Here's what you'll need if you want to use an iPod with your Linux box:

A Mac or Windows iPod (obviously)

The iPod is basically a FireWire hard disk with its own operating software stored in one partition. The two variants of the iPod are formatted with different filesystems: HFS+ in the case of the Mac and FAT32 in the case of Windows. Indeed, this is the only difference.

Ideally, you want to start with a Windows iPod. Linux has extremely limited support for the Apple HFS+ filesystem, and thus it is necessary to convert HFS+ iPods to FAT32, erasing the disk in the process. The iPod firmware is identical, though, so you must save this before you begin.

To do the conversion, don't mess around with Wine, or with Winnie-Pod Updater, the Apple-sanctioned tool for HFS-to-FAT32 conversion. The GNU instructions for how to convert are sufficient and require only `fdisk`, `dd`, and `mkfs.vfat`, which are standard Unix tools.

> The latest breed of iPod appears to come in a single flavor called "for Windows and Mac." They are actually HFS-formatted but come with software for Windows that invisibly does the conversion the first time they are used. So these are really just Mac iPods. If you have access to a PC with Microsoft Windows, you can use that to do the conversion to FAT32. (Thanks to Zach Hobbs for this information.)

A Linux system with a recent, FireWire-capable kernel (2.4.12 or later—now might be a good time to upgrade to RedHat 9.0 or similar)

Note that the version of RedHat Package Manager (RPM) that comes with RedHat 9.0 (Shrike) has an annoying bug: sometimes it will crash, and on subsequent executions, it will hang, waiting for a `mutex` (in the `futex` syscall, as can be observed using `strace`). If this happens, simply remove the */var/lib/rpm/__dbxxx* temporary files from the RPM database and try again.

A working FireWire interface

I use an Orange Micro PCMCIA card (*http://www.orangemicro.com/firewire.html*; $59.00) for a laptop. It still seems that the kernel support for FireWire is a little flaky, so try to avoid issuing and/or interrupting commands unnecessarily, or removing the interface while the drivers are doing something.

The GtkPod package

GtkPod (*http://gtkpod.sourceforge.net*; free) is a graphical tool for transferring files to and from the iPod. It is the Linux equivalent of the iTunes software used for the same purpose on the Mac.

I used the gtkpod 0.50 RPM, available free from *http://www.rpmfind.net*. This package requires the id3lib package.

You must use a tool such as GtkPod; you cannot simply copy files onto the iPod's hard disk, because the iPod's database must be updated for it to see the new tracks. Furthermore, the first time you use GtkPod, you must select File → Create Directories to set up the database on the iPod.

The grip package

Grip is a free graphical tool for ripping CDs and encoding them as MP3s.

Note that when ripping CDs to files, the actual filenames are not important to the iPod. However, because its music database is populated from the ID3 tags embedded within the MP3 files, it *is* important that these are accurate.

This means you should encode MP3 files from an album all together, or else you will lose the album track-numbering information. It also means you can use convenient filenames (such as *track07.mp3*) instead of using the actual track names (e.g., *07. Voodoo Chile [Slight Return].mp3*); the shell metacharacters present in the latter make them a pain to work with.

Setting Up Your Linux Desktop

Assuming you're using a PCMCIA FireWire card, once the card is inserted, the cardmgr daemon should take care of loading the ieee1394 and ohci1394 modules. If you have a PCI card, these should be loaded by system startup (*/etc/rc.local*).

When you attach the iPod to the FireWire interface, the sbp2 module is loaded automatically. (If it's not, load it with modprobe.) You should see messages appear in dmesg indicating that the device is recognized. Additionally, */proc/bus/ieee1394/devices* contains information on each device, including the string [Apple Computer, Inc.] for the iPod:

```
ieee1394: Host added: Node[00:1023]  GUID[00d0f5cd4008049d]  [Linux OHCI-
1394]
ieee1394: Device added: Node[00:1023]  GUID[000a2700020e545e]  [Apple
Computer, Inc.]
ieee1394: Node 00:1023 changed to 01:1023
SCSI subsystem driver Revision: 1.00
ieee1394: sbp2: Logged into SBP-2 device
ieee1394: sbp2: Node[00:1023]: Max speed [S400] - Max payload [2048]
scsi0 : IEEE-1394 SBP-2 protocol driver (host: ohci1394)
```

```
$Rev: 707 $ James Goodwin SBP-2 module load options:
- Max speed supported: S400
- Max sectors per I/O supported: 255
- Max outstanding commands supported: 64
- Max outstanding commands per lun supported: 1
- Serialized I/O (debug): no
- Exclusive login: yes
  Vendor: Apple      Model: iPod          Rev: 1.40
  Type:   Direct-Access                   ANSI SCSI revision: 02
Attached scsi removable disk sda at scsi0, channel 0, id 0, lun 0
SCSI device sda: 58595040 512-byte hdwr sectors (30001 MB)
sda: test WP failed, assume Write Enabled
 sda: sda1 sda2
```

The iPod appears as a fake SCSI device (typically */dev/sda* if you have no other SCSI devices) and can be accessed using the regular Unix tools for block devices. However, if you are using a Mac iPod, fdisk will not recognize the partition map, and you will get a message resembling "Device contains neither a valid DOS partition table, nor Sun, SGI or OSF disklabel." In this case, it is time to follow the GNU instructions (for conversion).

At this point, the Linux IEEE1394 drivers (ieee1394, ohci1394) should have recognized the hardware:

```
$ cat /proc/bus/ieee1394/devices
Node[00:1023]  GUID[0011060000000649a]:
  Vendor ID: `Linux OHCI-1394' [0x004063]
  Capabilities: 0x0083c0
  Bus Options:
    IRMC(1) CMC(1) ISC(1) BMC(0) PMC(0) GEN(0)
    LSPD(2) MAX_REC(2048) CYC_CLK_ACC(0)
  Host Node Status:
    Host Driver     : ohci1394
    Nodes connected : 2
    Nodes active    : 2
    SelfIDs received: 2
    Irm ID          : [00:1023]
    BusMgr ID       : [00:1023]
    In Bus Reset    : no
    Root            : no
    Cycle Master    : no
    IRM             : yes
    Bus Manager     : yes
Node[01:1023]  GUID[000a2700020ec65a]:
  Vendor ID: `Apple Computer, Inc.' [0x000a27]
  Capabilities: 0x0083c0
  Bus Options:
    IRMC(0) CMC(0) ISC(0) BMC(0) PMC(0) GEN(0)
    LSPD(2) MAX_REC(2048) CYC_CLK_ACC(255)
  Unit Directory 0:
    Vendor/Model ID: Apple Computer, Inc. [000a27] / iPod [000000]
    Software Specifier ID: 00609e
    Software Version: 010483
```

```
        Driver: SBP2 Driver
        Length (in quads): 8

$ cat /proc/scsi/scsi
Attached devices:
Host: scsi0 Channel: 00 Id: 00 Lun: 00
    Vendor: Apple    Model: iPod              Rev: 1.40
    Type:   Direct-Access                     ANSI SCSI revision: 02
```

Performing the HFS-to-FAT32 conversion involves the following steps:

1. Save the first 32 MB of the second partition, which contains the iPod firmware image. Keep this file safe somewhere on your PC:

   ```
   % dd if=/dev/sda2 of=backup_firmware
   ```

2. Splat zeros all over the partition map so that all disk data is effectively erased. Unload and reload the sbp2 driver to update its world-view:

   ```
   % dd if=/dev/zero of=/dev/sda bs=1M count=10
   % rmmod sbp2 && insmod sbp2
   ```

3. Create two partitions. The first should be large enough to hold the 32 MB file you saved earlier; the second will hold the remaining 30 GB of the disk. Tag the two partitions as Empty and FAT32, respectively:

   ```
   $ fdisk /dev/sda
   n    [make new partition]
   p    [primary]
   1    [first partition]
        [just press enter -- default first sector is 1]
   5S   [5 sectors -- big enough to hold 32MB]

   n    [make new partition]
   p    [primary]
   2    [second partition]
        [just press enter -- default first sector is 6]
        [just press enter -- default size uses all remaining space]

   t    [modify type]
   1    [first partition]
   0    [first partition has no filesystem; ignore warning]

   t    [modify type]
   2    [second partition]
   b    [second partition is FAT32]

   p    [show partition map]

       Device Boot     Start      End    Blocks   Id  System
       /dev/sda1         1          5     40131    0   Empty
       /dev/sda2         6       3647  29254365    b   Win95 FAT32

   w    [commit changes to disk]
   ```

4. Copy the firmware back to the first (small) partition:

```
$ dd if=backup_firmware of=/dev/sda1
```

5. Make a FAT32 filesystem on the second (large) partition:

```
$ mkfs.vfat -F 32 -n "My iPod" /dev/sda2
```

If all goes well, resetting the iPod (by holding down the Menu and Play buttons for 10 seconds) will cause it to reboot to the familiar menus. If not, go through the instructions again. Remember, the iPod is just a hard disk, so as long as you have the original firmware backed up correctly and safely on your PC, you can reformat it as many times as you like. (It worked for me the first time.) Be wary about installing different firmware from the one it came with, however.

At this point, you should be able to mount the disk in the usual way. Once this works, setup is complete and you can follow the normal usage instructions described in the next section.

Normal Usage

The Linux drivers for the iPod are still a little flaky; sometimes, the sbp2 driver gets stuck indefinitely in its initializing state and cannot be removed, and at other times the machine hangs.

To minimize the risk of such errors, I strongly advise you to follow a disciplined procedure for docking and undocking the iPod. Here's the order of events I usually employ:

1. Insert the IEEE1394 PCMCIA card into my laptop. Check that this succeeded by running lsmod and looking for ieee1394 and ohci1394.

2. Attach the iPod. This time the sbp2 driver should appear. If it does not, try detaching and reattaching it.

3. Mount the iPod as a disk, copy files across, and then unmount it again.

4. rmmod the sbp2 driver.

5. Detach the iPod.

6. Remove the IEEE1394 card.

Note that these steps are perfectly symmetrical. This seems to achieve greater reliability than performing them in an arbitrary order.

I use two scripts, *dock-ipod* and *undock-ipod*, whenever I attach or detach the iPod to or from the interface card. Here's *dock-ipod*:

```
#!/bin/sh

modprobe sbp2
mount /dev/sda2 /mnt/ipod/
```

And *undock-ipod*:

```
#!/bin/sh

umount /mnt/ipod
rmmod sbp2
```

They must both be run as root:

```
$ su - root -c ./dock-ipod
```

or:

```
$ sudo ./dock-ipod (if the user is a sudoer)
```

or:

```
$ su - root
Password:
root$ ./dock-ipod
```

Downloaded MP3 Files and ID3 Tags

The iPod does not care about the filenames of MP3 files; all its database information is supplied by ID3 tags within the MP3 files. Therefore, these must be present for transferred files even to appear on the iPod.

You might want to add MP3 files that did not come from a CD (e.g., those downloaded from Napster, Kazaa, etc.) to your iPod. The ID3 tags in such files are often inappropriate—for example, because they feature the original artist/album name from the CD they came from, instead of the logical group to which they will belong on your iPod (e.g., *Misc/80s Synth Pop*). If you do nothing about this, you will find each song appearing in its own artist/album category, with no useful grouping. You'll also need to tag manually when CDDB lookup fails (e.g., for *non-industry* CDs) or for MP3 files that were hand-encoded from WAV.

To change the tags, you need a tool such as ID3ed (*http://www.dakotacom. net/~donut/programs/id3ed.html*; free). This tool is pretty straightforward, and it comes with a helpful manpage. The synopsis says:

```
id3ed [-s songname] [-n artist] [-a album] [-y year]
[-c comment] [-k tracknum] [-g genre] [-q] [-SNAYCKG]
[-l] [-L] [-r] [-i] [-v] files...
```

Obviously, you don't need to include all those options. Here's an example:

```
$ id3ed -s "Red House" -n "Jimi Hendrix" \
-a "Are You Experienced?" -k 3 redhouse.mp3
```

Alternatively, use a graphical tool such as xid3 (*www.nebel.gmxhome.de/xid3/*; free), which has a Tcl/Tk-based frontend for ID3-tag editing that makes it a lot easier to use for this information. The main ID3 tags for the iPod are Artist, Album, Title, and Track Index (and Genre, if you bother to use that).

With minimal effort, your iPod will play nicely with Linux. No, you won't be able to buy songs from the iTunes Music Store, but you'll still have most of the functionality Mac and Windows users have.

—Alan Donovan

HACK #43 Sync Your iRiver with Linux

Use Linux to copy your songs and create the iRiver database.

Of the wide variety of "lifestyle" items that are competing for our disposable income, the personal music player is one of the most popular. Although many of us can remember the excitement of getting a personal cassette player when we were younger, the latest incarnation of music on the move is fully digital, and it can store your entire album collection.

A number of these personal music players are on the market, but one of the most intriguing is the iRiver series. Not only do these little boxes pack in upward of 40 GB of storage, but they also support a variety of different codecs beyond plain MP3. Some of you might be aware that encoding MP3 is actually a legally foggy area, as the codec was created and licensed by Fraunhoffer, and many free encoders are not properly licensed. A free MP3 alternative called Ogg Vorbis promises both higher quality and smaller file size. This format is gaining in popularity, and the iRiver, unlike the iPod, supports it out of the box.

To get songs on your iRiver, you need to rip your CDs to get the tracks onto the hard disk of your Linux machine, encode them as MP3 or Ogg Vorbis, and then upload them to the iRiver via USB. Optionally, you can then build the iRiver internal database for your MP3s (you cannot use the database for Ogg files). The iRiver IHP series of players uses a special internal database that stores all the details of your song titles, albums, genres, and other information. One issue to bear in mind is that the iRiver lacks support of Ogg Vorbis tags. This means Ogg metadata will not be included in the database. If you want to use ID tags (these tags store information about the artist, album, track number, and so on), you need to rip your songs as MP3s.

This hack does not cover how to rip songs, but a number of great ripping tools are available, such as Grip, RipperX, KAudioCreator, and Jack. Most of these tools are simple and intuitive to use.

Transfer the Songs to the iRiver

You can transfer songs to the iRiver by plugging it into one of the USB ports on your computer. To transfer files, you need to ensure that you have USB support compiled into your kernel, and then you need to mount the device.

These options are available in the kernel configuration tool in the USB Support section. You should ensure that you have UHCU, UHCI Alternate Driver, or OHCI selected, depending on the type of USB support on your motherboard. You can find out which USB support you have from your motherboard's manual. With the USB support compiled, you can mount the disk with the following command:

```
$ mount -t vfat /dev/sda1 /mnt/iriver
```

You will probably need to change the mount directory /mnt/iriver to something that is relevant to your system. Once it is mounted, if you look in /mnt/iriver, you will see either an empty directory (if you have not uploaded any songs) or a list of artist directories (if songs are already on the iRiver). Now you can copy over files by using a file manager such as Nautilus or Konqueror, or by using the following command if your Metallica songs are in /home/joeblogs/Metallica:

```
$ cp -r /home/joeblogs/Metallica* /mnt/iriver
```

Rebuild the Database

The iRiver database is essential in terms of making the iRiver as usable as possible. This database contains a detailed list of artists, genres, albums, song lengths, track numbers, and more; many of the features in the iRiver are available only if you have created the database. You still can use the iRiver without the database, but you can choose your songs and albums only via the clunky file manager on the iRiver as opposed to its special menus. Unfortunately, the installation CD does not come with a tool to build the database for Linux, but a simple utility available on the Internet, called iRipDB, can do the job. You can download *iRipDB* from *http://www.fataltourist.com/iripdb/*.

Once you have downloaded the latest version of *iRipDB*, unzip it onto your hard disk with this command:

```
$ tar xcvf iRipDB-x-x-x.tar.gz
```

Replace *x-x-x* with the actual version number of the *iRipDB* program. You need to ensure that you have the following libraries on your system before you compile the code:

libid3
    This library provides the use of ID3 tags in *songslibogg*.

libvorbis
    These libraries provide support for Ogg Vorbis files.

To compile the code, run the compilation script included with the code. Move into the directory where the code is stored and run this:

```
$ ./compile.sh
```

When the program is compiled, you will have an executable in the source directory called iripdb. Now you can run this to rebuild the database:

```
$ ./iripdb /mnt/iriver
```

The preceding command runs the iripdb command on the directory where you mounted your iRiver. You can also use the -e switch to include files that have not had tags added to them:

```
$ ./iripdb -e /mnt
```

To finish, you should unmount the device to ensure that all data has been copied over completely:

```
$ umount /mnt
```

Now full support for your iRiver is available on your system. Although you will mostly listen to music on your iRiver, try copying some text files onto the device. On the IHP series, you will find that you can read them on the screen. This can be handy if you need to carry around some notes or other text with you.

—Jono Bacon

HACK #44 Use Other Portable Audio Players

Access other USB storage device audio players under Linux and automatically sync them when you plug them in.

It's easy to feel left out if you have a portable audio player that isn't an iPod. It seems that most of the development efforts on all platforms are geared toward iPod compatibility before any other devices. Since most vendors only ship Windows and Mac integration software, that leaves us Linux users to fend for ourselves. Luckily most non-iPod portable audio players can be used not only as a USB storage device, they can also have music files added to them, just by copying the tracks to a particular directory on the drive. In this hack, I cover how to access these devices and how to leverage their USB storage device compatibility with *hotplug* and *rsync* to automatically synchronize your files the moment you plug your device in.

To access your media player, plug it into a USB port in your computer. Most modern Linux distributions have all of the USB drivers you need to access USB storage devices, and most are configured to automatically set up new devices you might plug in. After the device is plugged in, check */var/log/ messages* for information about your device. Here's a section from my file when I plugged in my media player:

```
Jul 23 15:29:17 moses kernel: usb 4-1: new high speed USB device using ehci_
hcd
and address 9
```

```
Jul 23 15:29:17 moses kernel: scsi1 : SCSI emulation for USB Mass Storage
device
s
Jul 23 15:29:18 moses usb.agent[2175]:     usb-storage: already loaded
Jul 23 15:29:22 moses kernel:   Vendor: HTC42603  Model: 0G7AT00
Rev:
 0 0
Jul 23 15:29:22 moses kernel:   Type:   Direct-Access
ANSI
SCSI revision: 00
Jul 23 15:29:22 moses kernel: SCSI device sda: 58605120 512-byte hdwr
sectors (3
0006 MB)
Jul 23 15:29:22 moses kernel: SCSI device sda: 58605120 512-byte hdwr
sectors (3
0006 MB)
Jul 23 15:29:22 moses kernel:  /dev/scsi/host1/bus0/target0/lun0: p1
Jul 23 15:29:22 moses kernel: Attached scsi disk sda at scsi1, channel 0, id
0,
lun 0
Jul 23 15:29:23 moses scsi.agent[2214]: sd_mod:loaded sucessfully (for disk)
```

As you can see, my computer detected the USB storage device and configured it as */dev/sda*:

```
Jul 23 15:29:22 moses kernel: SCSI device sda: 58605120 512-byte hdwr
sectors (3
006 MB)
```

It then detected a single partition on the drive:

```
Jul 23 15:29:22 moses kernel:  /dev/scsi/host1/bus0/target0/lun0: p1
```

With many desktop-oriented Linux distributions, this drive would now pop up on my desktop as an icon that I can just click to access the drive. Otherwise, to access it, all I would need to do is mount it as root somewhere on my system:

```
# mount /dev/sda1 /mnt/portable
```

Most media players have a preconfigured directory to store MP3 files, so you can now add new files to the device through your file manager or the terminal. You could also use the *rsync* command to synchronize between a directory on your local system and the device. The particular directory you would use varies for each device. On my media player the directory is called *Music*, so if I had it mounted at */mnt/portable* and wanted to synchronize between my local directory at *~/mp3* and it, I would type:

```
$ rsync -av --size-only --delete ~/mp3/ /mnt/portable/Music/
```

Use the --delete option with *rsync* carefully. It will delete all of the files inside the *Music* directory that aren't on the local system. If you only want to synchronize files between the two, but don't want to delete anything, remove the --*delete* argument from the command.

Notice that I used the --size-only argument. Because we are synchronizing between a Linux filesystem and a FAT32 filesystem, I've noticed that often the timestamps don't always match up. The --size-only argument tells *rsync* to base whether a file should be copied by the file size only, not the file's timestamp as well. This also saves on copying the same exact files over just because the timestamps are different.

Once you are finished copying files to and from your media player, you can unmount it from the system and then unplug it.

```
# umount /mnt/portable
```

 Be sure to remove the device only after it is unmounted to ensure you don't corrupt the filesystem on the device.

Automatically Synchronize Your Media Device

You can also leverage *hotplug* and *autofs* to automatically synchronize your computer and your media player just by plugging it in. The steps are almost identical to the steps outlined in "Automatically Synchronize Your Camera and Computer" [Hack #11], so follow those steps, replacing device settings with those corresponding to your media player. Stop once you get to the section called "Make a Synchronization Script," since we are going to create a different customization script here.

First, edit the *usb-storagehotplug* script mentioned in [Hack #11] so that it calls a new script, */usr/local/bin/portable_sync*. Here's a modified version of that *hotplug* script:

```
#!/bin/sh
sleep 3
DEVICE=`grep "kernel: Attached scsi .*disk" /var/log/syslog | tail -n 1 |
cut -f 10 -d " "`
set > /tmp/settings
case "$PRODUCT" in
# Archos PMA430
  e79/1106/0)
ln -s /var/autofs/usb/$DEVICE /mnt/portable
    echo -e '#!/bin/sh\nrm /mnt/portable' > $REMOVER
    chmod a+x $REMOVER
    /usr/local/bin/portable_sync &
;;
esac
```

Be sure to change the USB product ID from e79/1106/0 to match your device. Now create */usr/local/bin/portable_sync*:

```
#!/bin/sh

LOCAL_DIR="/mnt/audio/mp3/"
PORTABLE_DIR="/mnt/portable/Music/"
RSYNC_OPTIONS="-a -q --size-only --delete"

# only sync if the remote directory is available
if [ -x $PORTABLE_DIR ]; then
rsync $RSYNC_OPTIONS $LOCAL_DIR $PORTABLE_DIR
fi
```

Change the values of LOCAL_DIR and PORTABLE_DIR to match your system. Also keep in mind that this will remove any files on the portable device that aren't on the system. If that isn't how you want to synchronize, then remove the --delete argument from the RSYNC_OPTIONS variable. Now when you plug in your device, it will automatically run this script. The first time you set it up, monitor the processes on the system to make sure that the *rsync* has finished before you unplug the device. You can also just type *df* and check to see if the device is still mounted, since *autofs* will automatically unmount it for you once the *rsync* is finished.

> Since this script is set to run each time the device is plugged in, you might also want to do other things automatically. Just add the commands you want to run below the rsync command.

HACK #45 Use a Bluetooth Headset with Linux

Use a Bluetooth-enabled headset to make VoIP calls or listen to music while wirelessly roaming throughout your house.

One of the coolest wireless technologies to come along recently is Bluetooth. Unlike its more well-known cousin, Wi-Fi, Bluetooth is not intended to be a networking protocol, though it can be used as one. Bluetooth was designed to fill a more mundane purpose—cable replacement. When Bluetooth devices are talking to one another (defined as *pairing*), they form a *Personal Area Network* (PAN). There are many Bluetooth-enabled devices today, including PDAs, headsets, cellphones, and computers.

I own quite a few devices that are Bluetooth-capable, and I've used several of them under Linux. One of the more difficult things I've tried is getting a Bluetooth headset working in Linux, because the software isn't quite there yet. After a good deal of experimentation, I've finally gotten this working.

This has been tested under Ubuntu Linux (Hoary Hedgehog release), kernel 2.6.10. In theory, it would also work with Debian Linux with little or no modification. For users of other distributions, these steps might give you enough information to get a Bluetooth headset working.

Here's what you'll need:

- A Bluetooth headset (I'm using a Jabra BT250)

- A Bluetooth adapter for your computer (I'm using a D-Link DBT-120 USB adapter)

- The *Bluez* Bluetooth software stack and the associated development libraries installed:

  bluez-hcidump
  bluez-pin
  bluez-utils
  libbluetooth1 and *libbluetooth1-dev*

- The source code for *btsco*, available at *http://bluetooth-alsa.sourceforge. net* and its dependencies:

  automake-1.7
  libasound2-dev (otherwise known as *alsa-devel*)
  A kernel with *alsa* enabled
  The source code for the above kernel

The *btsco* code is the magic that makes the headset work. To get the *btsco* source code you'll need to use CVS, as the developers of the code haven't yet released a stable tarball. To check out the code from CVS, use the following commands (no password is needed for the anonymous access):

```
bill@excalibur:/usr/src$ cvs -d:pserver:anonymous@cvs.sf.net:/cvsroot/
bluetooth-alsa login
Logging in to :pserver:anonymous@cvs.sf.net:2401/cvsroot/bluetooth-alsa
CVS password:
bill@excalibur:/usr/src$ cvs -d:pserver:anonymous@cvs.sf.net:/cvsroot/
bluetooth-alsa co btsco
cvs checkout: Updating btsco
```

The source code will then be checked out (downloaded) from the development server. You will see a bunch of status messages as the files are downloaded to your system. Once the files are downloaded, you'll need to build the program from the source. Don't panic—it's a lot easier than it sounds. Let's get started on the build.

First, compile the code:

```
bill@excalibur:/usr/src/btsco$ ./bootstrap
bill@excalibur:/usr/src/btsco$ ./configure
bill@excalibur:/usr/src/btsco$ make
```

You'll need to be root (or have root permissions via *sudo*) for the next two steps:

```
root@excalibur:/usr/src/btsco# make install
root@excalibur:/usr/src/btsco# make maintainer-clean
```

Next, you have to build the *bluetooth-to-alsa* kernel module.

```
bill@excalibur:/usr/src/btsco$ cd kernel
bill@excalibur:/usr/src/btsco/kernel$make
```

You'll need to be root (or have root permissions via *sudo*) for the next three steps:

```
root@excalibur:/usr/src/btsco/kernel# make install
root@excalibur:/usr/src/btsco/kernel# depmod -e
root@excalibur:/usr/src/btsco/kernel# make clean
```

At this point everything should have built and installed properly. Now, we'll go through the configuration and basic playback steps.

To use the new code, first load the kernel module you built. Make sure that your Bluetooth hardware is online and ready to go. Load the module as root with *modprobe*:

```
bill@excalibur:~# modprobe snd_bt_sco
```

Verify that the module loaded:

```
bill@excalibur:~$ dmesg | tail
snd-bt-sco revision 1.6 $
snd-bt-sco: snd-bt-scod thread starting
```

Next, configure the Bluetooth adapter for voice using *hciconfig* as root:

```
bill@excalibur:~# hciconfig hci0 voice 0x0060
```

Turn on the headset and prepare it to be paired with the computer. On my Jabra BT250, this is done by holding the power button until the headset beeps and the power LED illuminates with a solid blue light.

Since you haven't paired the headset and the computer yet; you'll need to run *hcitool* as root to scan for available Bluetooth devices:

```
bill@excalibur:~# hcitool scan
Scanning ...
00:07:A4:03:26:5E JABRA 250
```

Now, run *btsco* with the Bluetooth address of the headset as an argument.

```
bill@excalibur:~$ btsco 00:07:A4:03:26:5E &
```

> *btsco* must run in the background as long as the headset is in use. This is the "helper" application that translates all the *alsa* calls across the Bluetooth protocol stack.

This should cause *bluez-pin* to pop up a Bluetooth PIN window where you can enter your PIN. I have populated the PIN with "0000"—that is the default PIN for pairing a Jabra BT250. Your headset's PIN and pairing instructions may differ slightly.

Now that this is done, you should be able to successfully play a sound file to your headset:

```
bill@excalibur:~$ aplay -B 1000000 -D plughw:Headset \
/usr/share/sounds/KDE_Logout.wav
```

Now if you look at your */dev* device tree, you'll see a new sound device:

```
bill@excalibur:~$ ls -l /dev/dsp*
crw-rw---- 1 root audio 14, 3 2005-07-07 14:11 /dev/dsp
crw-rw---- 1 root audio 14, 19 2005-07-10 20:34 /dev/dsp1
```

At this point, any ALSA-aware sound application will play through the headset if you configure it for */dev/dsp1*. This works with audio-recording applications as well.

Now that you've gotten your Bluetooth headset working under Linux, you can start using it as a free IP phone with Skype **[Hack #98]** or another VoIP application! Have fun!

—Bill Childers

HACK #46 Find All Your Media Files

Use standard command-line tools to track down all of the media files scattered around your computer.

Even with all the great ID3 tagging tools and other programs, we have to organize our media files; sometimes they just get put in strange places. When your collection becomes so scattered that you can't track down files you want, it's time for some spring cleaning. This hack tells you how to track down all the media files on your system, no matter where they are hiding.

The Fast Way

The quickest way to locate your media files is with, well, the *locate* command. *locate* uses a database that stores information about where all the files are on a system. On most Linux systems, this database is updated nightly. The up side of *locate* is that you get information quickly because it searches the database instead of the filesystem. The down side is that the data is up to a day old, so any media files added to the system since the last database update won't show up.

So, to locate all of the MP3 files on a system, type:

```
$ locate -i *.mp3
```

The -i option tells *locate* to ignore case, so this will find all files that end in *.MP3*, *.mp3*, or even *.Mp3*. Of course, you might want to locate not only all your MP3 files, but also all your OGG Vorbis and WAV files. While you could do this with individual commands, locate supports regular expressions, so you can combine it all into a single command:

```
$ locate -i -r '\.(mp3|ogg|wav)$'
```

> You can use this same idea to track down all of the video files on your system as well. Just replace the *mp3*, *ogg*, or other audio file extensions with video file extensions like *avi*, *mpg*, and so on.

Now that you have a complete list of files, you can store that to a file for use in a shell script or tar command later.

The Slow Way

locate is fast and works fine, as long as you don't need data that's up to date. If you just added some media files to your system and you want to make sure they are part of the list, you will need to use *find*. *find* doesn't use a pre-existing database for its information—it scans the filesystem directly. As a result it can take some time to find files, particularly if you run this against the entire root filesystem. So, to search the entire filesystem for all MP3 files using *find*, type:

```
$ find / -iname "*.mp3"
```

The -iname argument tells *find* to be case insensitive. Be prepared for this command to chug along and take some time, particularly on a large filesystem. To perform the same command, only on multiple extensions, you need to use the regular expressions pattern matching of *find*:

```
$ find / -iregex '.*\.\(mp3\|ogg\|wav\)$'
```

Holy leaning toothpicks, Batman! Yes, all those slashes are necessary to escape the regular expression. Notice I replaced -iname with -iregex to specify that the pattern was a case insensitive regular expression.

Now, one nice thing about *find* is that it makes it easy to search within a particular directory, so if you only wanted to know about all the MP3 files within your home directory, just change the path find searches in:

```
$ find ~ -iname "*.mp3"
```

Change ~ to the directory path you want to search. Of course, with all these examples, the output goes directly to the screen. That can be difficult to read through if you have a lot of files, so you probably want to redirect the output to a file you can read through later. To redirect the output of the last command into a file called *MP3files* in your home directory, type:

```
$ find ~ -iname "*.mp3" > ~/MP3files
```

Another powerful ability of *find* is to execute commands on each file it finds using the -exec argument. With the -exec argument you could, for instance, move or remove all the MP3 files on a system while leaving other files intact. To use the -exec argument, type -exec as the last argument to *find*, and then follow it with the command you want to run with "{}" instead of the file-name. When you are finished with the command, use \; to tell *find* where the command ends. *find* will run that command on every file it finds and fill in "{}" with the path to that file. So, to move every MP3 file in a directory (here ~/*mp3/*) to the /tmp directory, you would type:

```
$ find ~/mp3/ -iname '*.mp3' -exec mv "{}" /tmp/ \;
```

> Be very careful when using the -exec argument to *find*, especially when performing destructive operations. Test the command first with *echo* or a similar command to be sure you are acting on the files you intend to. I won't name any names, but a good friend of mine accidentally deleted all the files in his home directory *except* for MP3s due to mistyping a *find* command.

CHAPTER THREE

Video
Hacks 47–72

Using video under Linux is often regarded as voodoo. After all, many of the most popular video programs are complicated command-line utilities such as MPlayer and *transcode*, with upwards of one hundred options. What's worse, when you go online for help, many of the examples list long commands that look more like an incantation or line noise than a program.

Video formats don't make things easier either. Underneath that seemingly simple *.avi* file might be any number of video and audio codecs. With so many competing video codecs, different versions of those codecs, competing container formats, and the fact that many of these codecs require proprietary licensing, it's no wonder video under Linux mystifies people and leaves them running back to Windows.

It doesn't have to be this way. Out of the confusing and complicated command-line tools, a number of handy frontends have emerged that take a lot of the sting out of watching and editing video under Linux. When you find you need to stray from the basics, sometimes the command-line tools still provide you with the most power and flexibility, so it might comfort you to know that the command-line utilities themselves continue to improve as well. Nowadays they do a lot of the work of sorting out file formats on your behalf, so you don't have to worry nearly as much about endless strings of command-line arguments.

In this chapter, I cover a broad range of video hacks using mostly standard command-line tools. Many of these hacks build on each other, so I first introduce the basics of MPlayer, and then move into more advanced options in later hacks. While this isn't necessarily a guide to all things video, along the way I include useful information about video formats from VCDs and DVDs to the different ways MPlayer can output video. There are also a number of hacks that discuss video editing and conversion under Linux. Although this is a topic that can quickly get complicated, there are a few common tasks that most of us do over and over. I've tried to present you with the information you need for most of the general editing and conversion cases you will run into, with enough information that you can tweak it for those borderline cases.

When you know the tools, Linux can be a really powerful video platform. By the end of this chapter, you should be equipped with examples of how to make the most of these tools to do things under Linux that you might have been too intimidated to try or too busy to figure out before.

HACK #47 Master Video Output Options

Most video players support a number of output options. Understanding the difference between X11, xv, SVGA, and other output settings can help you make the most of your video playback.

Not all video cards are created equal. After all, you can't expect to play a game that just came out this year on a graphics card from 10 years ago. Similarly, when you watch video under Linux there are a number of different output options that are at your disposal depending on what your video card supports. Some of these options give you extra choices for video playback including hardware acceleration and the ability to scale the video. In this hack, I cover the major video output options and their advantages and disadvantages so you can better match your output selection to the abilities of your video card.

> Where you configure these video output options varies greatly, depending on which media player you choose. For the purpose of this hack, I will cover how to select these output options with MPlayer on the command line, but other players require you to go into advanced preferences, such as in the case of a graphical video player such as *xine-ui* **[Hack #55]**, or otherwise use a command-line switch to set the option. Check the documentation for your media player for information on where to change these settings. All these output options are supported in MPlayer and should also be supported in *xine-lib*–based players, provided the support is compiled in.

When choosing the appropriate video output setting, the ideal is to be able to push the work of displaying the video from the CPU to the video card. That way the CPU can be used purely for processing the video codec. In addition, many of the hardware-accelerated video output options allow you to scale the image to a larger size or even full screen. Video modes without hardware acceleration often can't scale the image, or if they can, you need a relatively fast processor to scale the image full screen. Experiment with the various output types and see which one suits your system best.

There are also a number of other hardware accelerated video modes that are designed for certain brands of video cards. For instance one particular mode provides hardware acceleration for 3dfx cards. For the purposes of this hack I've listed only modes that work for a wide range of cards. For more information about these modes and modes that are specific to certain types of cards, visit *http://www.mplayerhq.hu/DOCS/HTML/en/video.html*.

XV

The xv video output option is the primary hardware-accelerated type you will run into, and many media players are set to try xv video by default. xv uses the XVideo extension in X for hardware acceleration, so it requires XFree86 4.0.2 or newer as well as driver support for your video card. To test whether your card has support, use the xvinfo command. It should create a lot of output if your card is supported:

```
$ xvinfo
X-Video Extension version 2.2
screen #0
Adaptor #0: "Intel(R) 830M/845G/852GM/855GM/865G Video Overlay"
number of ports: 1
port base: 56
operations supported: PutImage
. . .
```

If you don't see a lot of output, the xv extension isn't supported by your current module. In the case of NVIDIA and some ATI cards, you can download and install the official driver from their site.

The XV mode not only offers hardware-accelerated video, but also allows hardware scaling, brightness, and contrast adjustment so you can resize the video without putting extra load on the CPU. To select this option in *mplayer*, type:

```
$ mplayer -vo xv filename
```

X11

This option outputs to X11 without any hardware acceleration. Any display or scaling of the video output is done in software. Ideally, you will only fall back on this mode when all other options fail, because it is the slowest and most CPU-intensive. One other time you might purposely use this option is in the case of a multi-head setup or TV output where hardware accelerated drivers display a bluish window instead of the video. In general avoid this mode unless you *must* use it. Also avoid scaling the output if possible and instead change to a lower resolution in X. To select this option in *mplayer*, type:

```
$ mplayer -vo x11 filename
```

Simple Directmedia Layer

Simple Directmedia Layer (SDL) is a unified video and audio interface that is often used by games because it provides an interface to video hardware underneath without the program needing to know how to access the video hardware. A program can output video to SDL, which can then output to a number of other video drivers it knows about. A downside to SDL is that it uses software rendering, so choose hardware-accelerated options before SDL. For media players, the SDL output option might possibly provide more stable, more correct, or more consistent video output than other video output options, so it is worth trying if other video output options seem buggy or slow. To select this option with *mplayer*, type:

```
$ mplayer -vo sdl filename
```

Direct Graphics Access

Direct Graphics Access (DGA) allows a program to skip the X server and write directly to the framebuffer memory. This method allows DGA to use less CPU and gives you a full screen display of the video, however it can only display full screen, which might be a downside for certain uses. Also, although this mode uses less CPU, it is not a hardware-accelerated mode, and the kernel gives access to this kind of mode only to the root user. Since this is a software renderer you might wonder when to use this instead of the standard X11 driver. Use this mode instead of X11 if you want full-screen output, because X11 won't scale the image or resize to fill your entire screen.

To use this mode, your X server needs to be configured to use the DGA extension. Test this by searching for the string DGA in your X log file (usually */var/log/XFree86.0.log* or */var/log/Xorg.0.log*):

```
$ grep DGA /var/log/XFree86.0.log
(II) Loading extension XFree86-DGA
```

If your computer supports this mode, type the following to use it with *mplayer*:

```
# mplayer -vo dga filename
```

SVGAlib

This output option allows media players to display video from a console without requiring the use of X. It requires that the *svgalib* libraries be installed on your system and renders in software, but again, SVGAlib provides an option to view video without X and possibly on older monitors and older video cards that don't support framebuffer display. Also, this mode requires root privileges to use. To use this option, become root. Then type:

```
# mplayer -vo svga filename
```

Framebuffer

Like the SVGAlib option, the framebuffer option allows you to display a video directly from a console without the use of X. Also like SVGAlib it supports a wide range of cards so you don't have to worry as much about hardware support. Your kernel does need to have framebuffer support (*fbdev*) compiled in (which newer prepackaged kernels should have), so kernels without *fbdev* support will not be able to use framebuffer mode. If you do have framebuffer support compiled in, type the following to use it with *mplayer*:

```
$ mplayer -vo fbdev filename
```

VESA

Like SVGAlib and framebuffer, this is another output option that allows you to display video from a console without X. One advantage to this option over framebuffer is that it doesn't require that any special graphics options be enabled in the Linux kernel—you just need a VESA-compatible BIOS. Another advantage to this option is that for some hardware (for instance, some ATI cards) this mode often works with TV-out even if you can't seem to get support otherwise in Linux. Like the other console options, however, it does all rendering in software, and has an additional downside in that it requires root privileges to use. To try this option, become root and then type:

```
# mplayer -vo vesa filename
```

> MPlayer supports a number of other output modes in addition to the ones listed. To see which of the above modes Mplayer supports (and more), type:
>
> ```
> $ mplayer -vo help
> ```
>
> You can find out more about each of these modes in the MPlayer manpage.

Use MPlayer

HACK #48

MPlayer is a great video player that can play just about any format. This introduction shows the basics you need to get up and running.

Every once in a while a tool comes along in Linux that impresses you in almost every respect with its flexibility. MPlayer is one of those tools. When it comes to video and audio playback, think of MPlayer as your universal translator. It can play basically any audio or video format you throw at it (provided it has the libraries available) in just about any container you throw at it. For instance, it can play DVDs from the disc, an image of the disc, or even just the VOBs from the DVD). Of course, depending on your taste, there is one downside—by default MPlayer is a command-line program. There is a graphical frontend for MPlayer for those interested, called *gmplayer*, or you might want to check out some of the other video players mentioned in this book such as xine **[Hack #55]** or VLC **[Hack #56]**. This hack discusses the basics of how to play multimedia files with MPlayer from the command line.

The first step to using MPlayer is to install it. Because of all of the different libraries *mplayer* supports and potential dependencies they cause, I recommend using a precompiled MPlayer package whenever possible. Most major distributions either ship with MPlayer packages available, or have third-party packagers that provide MPlayer (for instance, Debian users can add the following line to their */etc/apt/sources.list* file to create an excellent third-party repository:

```
deb ftp://ftp.nerim.net/debian-marillat/ sid main
```

The next step is to sync with your repository and install *mplayer*:

```
$ apt-get upgrade and apt-get install mplayer-686
```

Replace 686 with 386, 586, k6, or k7 depending on your processor.

If you can't find a precompiled binary for your distribution, or if your precompiled binary did not include some of the extra MPlayer options you need, download the source code from the official site at *http://mplayerhq.hu* and follow the directions in the documentation at *http://mplayerhq.hu/DOCS/HTML/en/install.html* closely.

With *mplayer* installed, basic file playback is as simple as:

```
$ mplayer file.avi
```

The console will immediately fill with a lot of different output. This can be useful because MPlayer is telling you what information it can figure out about the file you passed to it, along with information about how it will try to play it. MPlayer should also display the video in a new window and immediately start playback. Back in the console you will see output scroll by as MPlayer updates you on which frame is playing and how far along MPlayer is in the video.

MPlayer provides an extensive list of key bindings so that you can control playback. The manpage lists all of these options and Table 3-1 lists some of the more commonly used ones.

Table 3-1. Common MPlayer key bindings

Keys	Function
Left and right arrows	Seek backward/forward 10 seconds.
Up and down arrows	Seek backward/forward 1 minute.

Table 3-1. Common MPlayer key bindings (continued)

Keys	Function
Page Up and Page Down	Seek backward/forward 10 minutes.
< and >	Move backward/forward in playlist.
p, Space	Pause movie (pressing again unpauses).
q, Esc	Stop playing and quit.
+ and -	Adjust audio delay by +/- 0.1 seconds.
/,9 and *,0	Decrease/increase volume.
m	Mute sound.
f	Toggle fullscreen.
t	Toggle stay-on-top.

Most of these key bindings are pretty self-explanatory, but the + and - options to adjust the audio delay are worth mentioning further. Sometimes when you create your own videos or convert videos between formats, the audio and video fall out of sync. This can be very frustrating when you are watching a movie, but with MPlayer you can tweak the audio with the + and - keys. Just hit one of the keys a few times and see whether you have improved or worsened the sync problems, and then adjust until the video and audio is completely in sync.

> The f fullscreen key binding won't necessarily scale the video to fill up the entire screen. Whether the video scales depends on the video output option you select for MPlayer. More information on the available video output formats is in **[Hack #47]**.

MPlayer is truly a universal multimedia playback tool, and in the next sections, I'll list some examples for playing back specific video types. For most video files, it is sufficient to simply pass the filename as an argument to `mplayer`, but for special videos like DVDs, VCDs, and filestreams, things are done slightly differently.

DVD Playback

MPlayer has good support for DVD playback, however one thing it does not have support for is DVD menus. When you play a DVD with MPlayer, it skips the menu system and everything else upfront and goes right to the movie, which can actually be a feature if you don't want to sit through the numerous ads and FBI warnings some DVDs have. Most DVDs have a main feature—the movie you purchased plus several lesser features, such as behind-the-scenes footage or scenes that were cut. In the case of episodic disks like TV shows, each episode is a different feature. Each of these features is a *title*, and you can select which title to play when you run *mplayer*. To start playback of the first title on a DVD, type:

```
$ mplayer dvd://1
```

Replace *1* with the number of the title you want to play. If you want to play a range of titles, you can specify the range on the command line. For instance, to play titles three through six, type:

```
$ mplayer dvd://3-6
```

You can also specify individual chapters (scenes) or a range of chapters with the -chapter argument. To play chapter four through eight on title one, type

```
$ mplayer dvd://1 -chapter 4-8
```

MPlayer will attempt to play from */dev/dvd*, but if that device doesn't exist, or you want to point it to a different device, you may use the -dvd-device argument. The following command will play back from */dev/hdc*:

```
$ mplayer dvd://1 -dvd-device /dev/hdc
```

You can even use the -dvd-device argument to play back directly from a DVD image somewhere on your filesystem:

```
$ mplayer dvd://1 -dvd-device /path/to/dvd.iso
```

It is even possible to use a directory full of VOB files:

```
$ mplayer dvd://1 -dvd-device /path/to/directory/
```

You may also specify language and subtitle options directly from the command line. The -alang option controls the audio language option and can accept multiple languages separated by commas. In that case, MPlayer will try the first language and fall back on the next language if the first isn't available. For instance, to play a movie in Japanese and fall back to English if Japanese isn't available, type:

```
$ mplayer dvd://1 -alang ja,en
```

The -slang option controls which language's subtitles are shown. To show the English subtitles on the above example, type:

```
$ mplayer dvd://1 -alang ja,en -slang en
```

(S)VCD Playback

(S)VCD playback in MPlayer is much like DVD playback. Just use vcd:// instead of dvd:// in the command line with the track to play as an argument. So, to play track one of a VCD, type:

```
$ mplayer vcd://1
```

MPlayer can even play the *.bin* files from (S)VCDs. You don't even need to pass any special options—just point *mplayer* to the *.bin* file to start playback.

Streaming Playback

MPlayer supports playback from a number of different audio and video streams. Just pass the URL on the command line:

```
$ mplayer http://example.com/stream.avi
$ mplayer rtsp://example.com/stream
```

In fact, MPlayer's support for streams is such that a browser plug-in has been developed to leverage it [Hack #91].

Troubleshooting

There are a number of reasons MPlayer may not output your video correctly. If MPlayer has trouble identifying your video, all the video codecs *mplayer* requires may not be installed in your system. [Hack #53] explains how to find and install the various video and audio codecs you need under Linux.

If MPlayer plays the video but the video output either looks strange, you can't see it at all, or playback is very jerky, it's possible that MPlayer is configured to use the wrong video output option for your system. The different video output options MPlayer supports are numerous enough to a hack of their own, so check out "Master Video Output Options" [Hack #47] for more information.

Another reason for jerky video is simply that a system is too slow to play the video well. In this case, MPlayer will warn you in its output that your system is too slow to play the video and will recommend that you add the -framedrop option. This option tells MPlayer to drop video frames if the video can't keep up with the audio on the system.

More MPlayer Uses

MPlayer has a number of advanced and just plain fun uses. This hack only scratches the surface of options you can use with MPlayer, but other MPlayer uses can be found in [Hacks #49, #51, #52, and #53].

HACK #49   Advanced MPlayer Tweaks

There are a number of advanced tweaks you can use to get the most out of MPlayer. You can even store many of these tweaks to the MPlayer configuration file and save yourself from tons of command-line arguments.

[Hack #48] touched on the basics of multimedia playback using MPlayer, but one look at the MPlayer manpage tells you that MPlayer is much more than that. If you are new to MPlayer, wading through all of these options might leave you a bit cross-eyed, so in this hack I will point out some of the more commonly used advanced options and show you how to set up the MPlayer config file to save many of them.

MPlayer Config File

In this hack, I cover a number of different command-line arguments that you can use to tweak MPlayer. Basically, all of these options can also be set in the MPlayer config file. By default, MPlayer has a global config file in */etc/mplayer/mplayer.conf*, and a local config file for each user in *~/.mplayer/config* that overrides the global config. The format of this config file is pretty simple—take an *mplayer* command-line argument, remove the leading -, and set it equal to its setting with the = symbol.

For instance, if you read through the different display options you can set in MPlayer with the -vo option in [Hack #47], you might want to change the default video output option for MPlayer permanently. If you want to set the default -vo option to xv, edit *~/.mplayer/config* and add the line (or edit the line if it already exists):

```
vo = xv
```

From that point on, MPlayer will behave as if -vo xv were on the command line every time. You can override any of these config settings from the command line as well, so even if vo = xv is in the config file, if you type **-vo x11** on the command line, MPlayer will use the X11 video output option.

Go Full Screen and Set Monitor Aspect

Once video playback has started, you can hit the f key to toggle the full screen setting within MPlayer, but if you already know you want to immediately display in full screen mode, just pass the -fs option to *mplayer* (or fs=true in the MPlayer config file). In the case of video output arguments such as X11 that rely on software scaling, you will also have to add the -zoom option to turn on software scaling (or add zoom=true to the MPlayer config file). Note that software scaling can really bog down a CPU, so only use it if you have a fast processor.

By default, MPlayer will scale a video to full screen as if the screen had a 4:3 aspect ratio. Since most computer monitors have this aspect ratio, the default is fine, but if you have a widescreen flat panel, the full screen mode will look stretched, particularly on 16:9 or anamorphic videos. To fix this, pass the -monitoraspect option to mplayer along with the aspect ratio.

For instance, my laptop has a wide screen with max resolution of 1280×768, or 5:3 aspect ratio. To play a DVD full screen with the proper aspect ratio, I would run:

```
$ mplayer dvd://1 -fs -monitoraspect 5:3
```

Of course, since I want the -monitoraspect option on at all times on my laptop, I just add monitoraspect=5:3 to my *~/.mplayer/config* file.

Increase the Cache for Streaming Video

By default, MPlayer uses a 1 MB disk cache to store video it is displaying. For local files this works fine; however when playing streaming video, particularly over a slow link, you might find you run out of cache too quickly and then have to wait as the video chugs through a bit at a time. The -cache option allows you to configure how large a cache to use, so to increase the cache to 8 MB, type:

```
$ mplayer http://example.com/stream.avi -cache 8192
```

Rotate the Video Before Playback

This may seem like a strange option to have, unless perhaps you have a tablet-style laptop or other display device that neither Linux nor MPlayer will detect properly. With the -vf rotate option, MPlayer will rotate the image ninety degrees clockwise and flip it. You may also set the rotate option equal to zero through three to adjust how the image rotates. Table 3-2 lists the different values and their functions:

Table 3-2. MPlayer rotation values

Number	Function
0	Rotate 90 degrees clockwise and flip (default).
1	Rotate 90 degrees clockwise.
2	Rotate 90 degrees counterclockwise.
3	Rotate 90 degrees counterclockwise and flip.

You may also set rotate equal to four through seven; however that will only perform the above rotations provided the video geometry is portrait instead of landscape.

You can also use -vf flip and -vf mirror to flip the image upside-down and rotate it on the Y axis, respectively.

HACK #50 Create Family-Friendly Edits of Movies

Use the Edit Decision Lists option in MPlayer to create a special list of video edits to perform on a file to mute or skip entire sections of a video during playback.

When I was younger, some weekends we would have movie night at home where we would rent a movie and watch it together. I was the youngest in the group, and when a movie we rented contained some questionable content, my stepdad would sit, remote control at the ready, and mute offensive language or say "hide your eyes" while he fast-forwarded. I remember one movie in particular that contained a lot of profanity. It seemed that no matter how hard he tried, my stepdad would mute dialogue only to unmute right as a character screamed some profanity, and then he would quickly press mute again to silence the rest of the dialogue only to unmute at yet another profanity—a losing battle. If only he had MPlayer and its EDL (Edit Decision Lists) feature, he could have set up the mutes and edits ahead of time.

An EDL is basically a text file with start and stop editing points, and an action to perform (either mute or skip). If the action is set to mute, MPlayer simply mutes that section of the video; if set to skip, MPlayer skips the section entirely.

While the natural application for this might be editing out content in a movie that might not be suitable for children, you could also use it to edit content that is merely annoying. As an example, go back to the time when *Star Wars Episode I—The Phantom Menace* was released. The hype around *Star Wars Episode I* was immense (and if you ask some fans so was the disappointment). In particular a number of fans were turned off by the Jar Jar Binks character. One fan went so far as to take a VHS copy of the movie and edit out most of the Jar Jar scenes, as well as many of what were considered "cutesy" scenes with Anakin. The result was called "The Phantom Edit" and was covertly released in CD form and on the Internet.

If this person had had MPlayer, instead of performing the edits by hand and distributing an entire movie, he could have simply marked edit points in an EDL—a simple small text file—and had a much easier time distributing it. You can also use an EDL to skip commercials in a TV episode you've recorded.

The easiest way to start using EDLs is to play the video you want to edit with MPlayer, and add the -edlfile option with a filename as an argument:

```
$ mplayer -edlfile sample-edl.txt sample.avi
```

MPlayer will start the playback of the movie, and whenever you see a section you would like to edit, hit the i key to write an edit placeholder in the file. MPlayer will maintain all of these timings in the file you specify (in our example *sample-edl.txt*), and when you are finished with the movie, you can then go into the EDL file and use the timings you set as general markers you can tweak by adjusting the timing a bit, lengthening the time of the edit, or changing which editing action MPlayer performs.

An MPlayer EDL file has the following format:

```
[begin second] [end second] [action]
```

The begin and end seconds are in floating point format so you can specify fractions of a second, and the action is a number, either a zero or a one. If action is 0, MPlayer will skip the scene between the begin and end points entirely. If the action is 1, MPlayer will mute the scene. Here is a sample EDL file:

```
10.095428  12.095428  0
20.480814  22.480814  0
35.662663  37.662663  0
49.634968  51.634968  0
. . .
```

Notice that MPlayer set each of the scenes to be exactly two seconds long, and defaulted to skip the scene entirely. At this point you can modify the timings in the file and then use the -edl option to try them out:

```
$ mplayer -edl sample-edl.txt sample.avi
```

The nice thing about these EDL files is that they have such a simple format, and are text, so they don't take up a lot of space and can easily be emailed or hosted for other people to use and refine.

Crop Video During Playback

HACK #51

Get rid of those annoying black bars at the top and bottom of movies using special features from MPlayer.

For the longest time, I was living in a 4:3 aspect ratio world and I didn't even know it. When I watched a VHS movie on the television, I didn't know that parts of the image had been cropped or what "pan and scan" was. As I got older and DVDs came out, I noticed that they often had widescreen and fullscreen options, and I finally started to understand that movies generally have a widescreen aspect ratio (such as 5:3 or 16:9) that, when displayed correctly on a TV, results in black bars along the top and bottom.

Of course, when playing back a movie on the computer, most video players adjust their size so that all you see is the movie without any black bars (until you fullscreen the image at least). However, if you watch a VCD or SVCD (videos formatted so that they can be played off of a CD in many modern DVD players) on the computer, the black bars are part of the image and are there whether you watch at fullscreen or not. My laptop's display has a widescreen aspect ratio (5:3) so it's perfect for watching DVDs—especially on a plane trip—but when I play back VCD or SVCD files fullscreen, I get large black bars and an even smaller video (Figure 3-1). My widescreen display goes to waste. I found that with a few simple command-line tweaks to *mplayer*, however, I could crop those black bars from the top and the bottom so the video would completely fill my screen. I could even have MPlayer figure out the optimal crop settings for me. In this hack I discuss how to leverage MPlayer to automatically crop those annoying black bars from a movie.

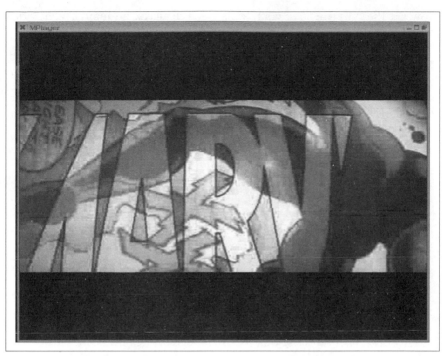

Figure 3-1. Video with black bands

The first step to automatically crop your video is to run *mplayer* with the -vf cropdetect argument. This tells MPlayer to scan the video as it is playing for those black bars and to output optimal crop dimensions for you to use to crop out the black bars:

```
$ mplayer -vf cropdetect movie.mpg
. . .
crop area: X: 0..479  Y: 80..496  (-vf crop=480:416:0:80) 2.5% 3 0 46%
crop area: X: 0..479  Y: 80..496  (-vf crop=480:416:0:80) 2.5% 3 0 46%
crop area: X: 0..479  Y: 80..496  (-vf crop=480:416:0:80) 2.5% 3 0 46%
crop area: X: 0..479  Y: 80..496  (-vf crop=480:416:0:80) 2.5% 3 0 45%
```

When you first start MPlayer with the option, you will notice a lot of output to your script as MPlayer tells you the width and height of the section to crop, as well as the dimensions of the image to keep. Let the video play back for a few seconds, particularly if the opening screen is black, so MPlayer can accurately find the sections to crop. Once the crop dimensions are consistently the same for a few seconds, close MPlayer.

The *mplayer* output tells you the exact argument you need to crop the black bars. In this example the argument is -vf crop=480:416:0:80. Now run *mplayer* again with this:

```
$ mplayer -vf crop=480:416:0:80 movie.mpg
```

Now get the full benefit of your widescreen displays, no matter what video format you happen to be watching (see Figure 3-2).

Figure 3-2. Video with black bands cropped

It takes extra CPU power for MPlayer to automatically crop each frame while it is playing, so be aware of this if you try it on a slower system. VCDs and SCVDs are in MPEG1 and MPEG2 formats respectively, which even a slower system can play without too much strain—but be aware of any skips or frame drops while using this method.

HACK #52 Add Custom Subtitles to Video

Use MPlayer's subtitle format to add your own commentary to your favorite movies.

When it comes to watching foreign films, I've found there are two types of people: those who prefer subtitles, and those who prefer dubbing. Even though dubbing has come a long way since the days of Godzilla and '70s Kung Fu movies, I still find that I fall into the subtitle camp. I prefer being able to hear the original actors say their lines in their own language. I read fast enough, so following along with the dialogue as it's printed hasn't been a problem for me.

Of course, not every foreign video is subtitled. In fact, there's a rather large movement of fans of certain programs who create subtitles (called *fansubs*) for them. Many of these subtitles not only contain translations of the dialogue on screen, but also extra explanation for any cultural references that were made, and so on. MPlayer supports its own rather simple subtitle format that you can use to add custom subtitles to your favorite videos. You might use this to add legitimate translated subtitles to a movie, or as you'll see in the section "A Sample .sub File," your own off-the-wall commentary on a movie. Think *Mystery Science Theater 3000*, but with text.

The MPlayer subtitle format was designed to be particularly easy to create and edit. There are only a few fields to worry about, as you can see from the beginning of this example:

```
TITLE=Pulp Fiction
TYPE=VIDEO
FORMAT=TIME

0 2
Welcome to Pulp Fsckion
```

The first field, TITLE, simply labels the name of the video that this subtitle goes with, in this case Pulp Fiction. You can choose whatever name you like, but it makes sense to name it something that associates it with the movie it is with. The second field labels what type of file the subtitle will be played with, and the FORMAT field specifies whether the following numbers refer to seconds (TIME) or frames (use a number, such as 25, for the argument).

Where the file gets interesting is in the next line, 0 2. This field always precedes some text to display as a subtitle. The first number specifies how long to wait after the previous subtitle disappears before appearing. In this case, since this is the first subtitle, I specified zero, but if you wanted to bypass some opening credits, you might increase this number. The second number specifies how long to display the following subtitle on the screen. In this example I chose to display for two seconds.

Probably the most difficult part of creating your own subtitles is timing. You might find that you must watch a scene multiple times so that the subtitles sync with the dialogue perfectly. Remember that each subtitle's numbers are based on the timing of any preceding subtitles, so if you adjust the amount of time a subtitle is displayed, you will need to adjust the amount of time before the next subtitle displays as well, so that everything remains synched.

After you have created your subtitle file, name it after the video it goes with so it's easy to find. Many people use *.sub* as the file extensions for these files. When you are ready to play back, add the -sub argument to *mplayer*, followed by the path to your subtitle file:

```
$ mplayer -sub video.sub video.avi
```

The subtitles you specify will advance along with the movie, even if you skip ahead while viewing. Note, however, that the *.sub* file contains no chapter information, so if you skip a chapter in a DVD, when MPlayer starts playing on the advanced chapter it will still display the subtitles with the same timing.

A Sample .sub File

So, to give an example of how these subtitles work, I have created a series of subtitles for the second chapter (which is the first scene with dialogue) for the movie *Pulp Fiction*. The following subtitle assumes the video will begin with the contents of chapter two, so if you have ripped your DVD to a file, you may have to adjust the timing for the initial subtitle a bit so things display properly. Save the following file as *pulp_fsckion.sub*:

```
TITLE=Pulp Fiction
TYPE=VIDEO
FORMAT=TIME

0 2
Welcome to Pulp Fsckion

0 4
Forget it, it's too risky, never dist-upgrading again.

0 2
You always say that...

0 3
"I'm through, never dist-upgrading again... too dangerous"

0 2.5
I know that's what I always say, and I'm always right.

0 2
But you trash your system after a day or two...

0 4
The days of my trashing my system are over,
The days of installing packages right has just begun

0 2
You know when you go on like this, what you sound like?

0 1.5
I sound like a sensible sysadmin

0 2
You sound like a penguin *quack*quack*quack*

1 3
Well, since I'm never going to dist-upgrade again

0 3
You're never going to have to fix my system for me again

0 2
After tonight's upgrade...
```

11 3
Way it is now, you take the same risks as a --force

2 2
Take more of a risk, apt-get is easier...

0 3
You know --force doesn't stop you in any way when you are upgrading...

2 3
Don't even need dependencies when ya --force...

With this file saved, pop the *Pulp Fiction* DVD into your computer and type:

```
$ mplayer dvd://1 -chapter 2 -sub pulp_fsckion.sub
```

The subtitles should start immediately and should be pretty well synched to the action. Feel free to add your own dialogue to the file.

HACK #53 Play Restricted Media Formats

For licensing reasons, not all distributions come preconfigured to play several popular media formats, but setting this up is not difficult.

Out of the box, many Linux distributions do not include support to play a few restricted media formats, such as DivX, Windows Media (WMV), Quicktime, and DVDs. The distros don't include the codecs to play these formats due to licensing restrictions. However, you can download the codecs yourself and use them with media player backends such as MPlayer and *xine*. Getting DVDs to play is a bit trickier.

Playing non-DVD Media Formats

MPlayer is a cross-platform multimedia player that is quite popular on Linux. The makers of MPlayer host the sites where you can obtain the codecs for media formats that aren't normally supported on Linux. These codecs are usually the *Win32.dll* files that are used on Windows systems, and MPlayer is programmed to let you use these codecs on Linux. You can obtain the most commonly used media codecs by downloading the essentials package from *http://www.mplayerhq.hu/homepage/dload.html*. These codecs can be used with the other popular media player on Linux, xine. Uncompress the download and put the contents in */usr/lib/win32*, which is where MPlayer and xine will look for codecs by default:

```
$ tar -jxvf essential-20050216.tar.bz2
$ sudo cp essential-20050216/* /usr/lib/win32/
```

Restart your media player, and you should now be able to play most restricted formats. For a full list of formats that are supported, visit: *http://www.mplayerhq.hu/homepage/design7/info.html*.

MPlayer and xine each have several frontend GUIs, such as
kMPlayer, Kaffeine, namp, Totem, and oxine. So, regardless
of the media player your distribution is configured to use,
you can probably drop the codecs into the */usr/lib/win32*
directory and have it just work.

Playing DVDs

Getting encrypted DVDs (most commercial DVDs) to play on your Linux
box is usually a bit trickier than adding codec support. To playback these
DVDs, you essentially need three things: a playback engine that supports
DVD playback, the *libdvdread* library, and the *libdvdcss* library for decrypt-
ing the content. A system that has a DVD playback-capable engine and *libdvdread* installed but doesn't have *libdvdcss* can play back only unencrypted
DVDs. A system that has *libdvdcss* installed but doesn't support DVDs in
the playback engine can't play any DVDs.

The media engines most often used for DVD playback are MPlayer and xine.
Depending on your distribution, these engines may or may not already have
support for DVD playing. Rather than working around this uncertainty, it is
often best just to grab a DVD-capable *mplayer* or *xine* package from a third-
party site. Since you'll nearly always need this site to add *libdvdcss*, it's no
more work to grab your playback engine from there as well. *libdvdread* is
usually installed as a dependency of your playback engine. If it isn't, you can
use either the one packaged by your distribution or one found on a third-
party repository.

To obtain the necessary software, Fedora users can choose from among several package sites, including *http://rpm.livna.org* and *http://freshrpms.net*. Both
sites contain easy-to-follow instructions for adding the repositories to your
Yum or *apt-rpm* configuration. Once enabled, installation is as simple as:

```
# yum install mplayer libdvdcss
```

Or for apt-rpm users:

```
# apt-rpm update
# apt-rpm install mplayer libdvdcss
```

Mandriva users need to add the Penguin Liberation Front (PLF) repository
in order to install *libdvdcss*. The versions of MPlayer and xine installed with
Mandriva already support DVD playback. An easy way to add the PLF
repository to your setup is to visit the website *http://easyurpmi.zarb.org* and
follow the insructions found there. This site is simply a web-based form that
asks a few questions about which version of Mandriva you are using, which
repositories you'd like to add to your configuration, and which mirrors

you'd like to sync with. After you answer the questions, the web page displays the commands you need to type in a terminal to enable the repositories. It takes only a minute or two to set this up. When you are done, the command to install *libdvdcss* is:

```
# urpmi install libdvdcss2
```

Note the 2 in this command. Depending on your distribution, this may be how your version of *libdvdcss* is packaged.

In addition, you can find RPMs of *libdvdcss* that should work on most RPM-based distributions at *http://cambuca.ldhs.cetuc.puc-rio.br/xine/*. You can also find a build of xine that supports DVD playback.

Once you have both software packages installed, DVD playback is as simple as inserting the disc, loading your media player application, and pressing Play. To view a movie with MPlayer, the command is:

```
$ mplayer -fs dvd://
```

This opens the movie in fullscreen mode and begins immediate playback of the movie. [Hack #48] provides more details about controlling video playback.

To do the same with xine, here is a recommended command:

```
$ xine -pfhq --no-splash dvd://
```

This command will autoplay the DVD (-p) in fullscreen (-f) with the xine GUI hidden (-h) and will quit the application when the movie finishes (-q).

> Running xine from the command line requires that the *xine-ui* package be installed. Depending on your distribution, this may have not been done for you when you installed the xine libraries.

[Hack #14] shows you how to configure Linux for surround sound and enable MPlayer and xine support for multi-speaker output.

DVD playback requires quite a bit of processing power. Depending upon your setup, you may be able to get by with a processor as slow as a Pentium II 500 MHz, but you probably can't go any slower than that. If playback is jerky but you have plenty of processor might, your problem may be that your DVD drive does not have DMA enabled. Enabling this with *hdparm* is covered in *Linux Desktop Hacks* and on numerous web sites.

—David Brickner

Watch Videos in ASCII Art

Use MPlayer's AAlib support to convert any movie into ASCII art.

If you have been on the Internet for any amount of time, chances are that you have come across ASCII art (drawings made with the ASCII text characters) either in an email signature, a web site, or some other place. Good ASCII art can take time and talent to look just right, but you can skip through that effort with AAlib (*http://aa-project.sourceforge.net/aalib*), a library devoted to converting any image into an ASCII art equivalent. Since a movie is basically a system of moving images, MPlayer has added support for AAlib as a video output option. This means that each frame in the movie is converted to an ASCII equivalent and displayed on the screen. This hack describes the basic options needed to convert a video into ASCII art.

To MPlayer, AAlib is yet another output format that it can support. Like with other output options, if you have compiled *mplayer* yourself, you will need to compile in support for AAlib. Many of the MPlayer packages out there already support AAlib, so if you use one of those, you should be fine. To turn on AAlib output, just add -vo aa to your mplayer command:

```
$ mplayer -vo aa video.avi
```

If you run this command from the console, MPlayer will display the movie with your console font and at your console's resolution. If you run this command from a terminal in X, by default a new X terminal will appear and display the movie with a rather large font for each pixel.

The default can be fine just to give a quick demonstration to your friends, but if you want to get higher resolutions out of AAlib, you will have to pass it some options. The first set of options to pass are width and height options. Note that these specify width and height in characters, not pixels, so don't simply pass along the resolution of your display. The width and height to use varies based on the size you want your screen and the size of the font you use. There isn't a hard and fast rule, so experiment with some options until you get the results you want. In this example, I will run *mplayer* with AAlib set to a width of 250 characters and a height of 80 characters:

```
$ mplayer -vo aa:width=250:height=80 video.avi
```

Even with the width and height settings, chances are that your video will still seem rather pixellated. The AAlib output option supports a font argument; however, all of the fonts to choose from are 8-point or larger. To pick a smaller font, run *mplayer* within a terminal in *ncurses* mode. A terminal has a lot more font choices including some below eight points. A small but common font to use is aliased as 5×7, so start a new *xterm* with that font size with an *mplayer* session executing inside:

```
$ xterm -fn 5x7 -geometry 250x80 -e "mplayer -vo aa:driver=curses video.avi"
```

The resulting video will run inside of the *xterm*; however, unlike with the X11 AAlib window, resizing this window will not result in a larger image—you will need to experiment with geometry settings to do that. Also, *ncurses* output is much more taxing on a CPU than the X11 output and even moreso as you increase the resolution, so keep that in mind on a slow CPU.

 I've found a very small 2-point font that may or may not be available on your system. If it is, it makes an excellent AAlib candidate because it is incredibly small, so you can get even more detail from your video. To use it, type

```
$ xterm -fn "-misc-nil-medium-r-normal--2-20-75-75-
c-10-misc-fontspecific" -geometry 450x150 -e \
"mplayer -vo aa:driver=curses video.avi"
```

In Living Color

So you may like AAlib, but sometimes those shades of grey just don't cut it. For that, I give you caca. Libcaca (*http://sam.zoy.org/libcaca*) is much like AAlib, except that it goes a step further and attempts to match colors, not just shapes or shades of grey in an image. As a result your videos look even more like the original.

MPlayer supports Libcaca as a video output option as well, although you pass extra arguments to it somewhat differently. A basic example of *mplayer* with Libcaca is:

```
$ mplayer -vo caca video.avi
```

If you run within X, it will default to an X11 output. To change to *ncurses*, you need to set the CACA_DRIVER environment variable, so to launch this within our *xterm*, type:

```
$ xterm -fn 5x7 -geometry 250x80 -e "CACA_DRIVER=ncurses mplayer -vo caca
video.avi"
```

Keep in mind that Libcaca uses even more resources than AAlib does, so you may need to turn down the resolution settings to get real-time playback.

Try xine-Based Video Players

#55   Use xine and xine-based players to view a number of video formats.

When it comes to multimedia programs under Linux, there are a number of alternatives to choose from and, in the case of xine, a back-end multimedia playback engine that is used by a number of frontends, such as Kaffeine and Totem. Although the selection of a media player is largely a matter of taste, a number of other factors apply as well. Even though in most cases the major media players under Linux all rely on the same codec libraries, I've noticed that some media players are able to play videos that cause other players to crash. Because of this, even in the cases where I choose other video players for files, I still have xine at the ready. This hack covers the major features of xine and discuss some of the frontends that are available.

Some people might associate xine with the video player, but xine actually refers to the portable multimedia engine that can play a number of audio and video files as well as support a number of different multimedia features. There are a number of different frontends that make use of the xine engine with the *xine-ui* frontend being the default frontend most likely associated with the project.

xine is a relatively popular library and most major distributions should package not only the *xine-lib* itself, but also the default *xine-ui* frontend. Otherwise you can download both *xine-lib* and *xine-ui* from the official xine page at *http://www.xinehq.de* and extract and build directly from the source.

After xine is installed, you can launch it either from your Media or Video menu in your desktop environment, or you can type **xine** in a console. The default interface (see Figure 3-3) is in two parts—the video window and the control window. The video window displays the current video being played and resizes to fit the current video. The control window provides a series of common controls such as play, pause, stop, and so on, as well as buttons to have xine open different media files, such as VCDs and DVDs. Other buttons on the control window allow you to change the playlist, change the current skin, and edit general xine preferences. All the buttons in the control window provide tool tips that explain their functions, in case the icons aren't descriptive enough. In addition, you can right-click on the video window to access all the different functions of the control window.

You can toggle the display of both the control and video windows. Hit g to toggle the control window, and h to toggle the video window.

Figure 3-3. Default xine windows

The steps to play a video under xine differ depending on the type of video. To play a VCD, DVD, CD, or DVB (digital TV input) press the corresponding button on the control window. xine will load the respective audio or video from its default location (typically */dev/cdrom* for CD-ROM-based video or audio, and */dev/dvd* for DVDs) and start immediate playback. In the case of video with menus, xine will load the main menu which you can navigate with the arrow keys or a mouse. To play a video file, right-click on the video window and select Open → File or press Ctrl-O to open the file selection dialog. Navigate to the file you wish to play, select it, and click the Select button. xine will start playback of the file immediately.

You can also choose files for playback within a playlist. Click the playlist button on the control window or type Ctrl-P to open the playlist editor. From this window you can add DVD, VCD, or other video sources as well as video files to the playlist. Once items are in the playlist, click the play button in either the playlist editor or in the control window to start playback. xine will play through the entire playlist. You can also save playlists for later or load previously saved playlists from this window.

Once a video has been chosen and is playing, you can control playback through either the control window or the right-click menu on the video window. The playback controls all have key bindings as well, so previous, play, pause, stop, and next can be accessed with Page Down, Enter, Spacebar, S, and Page Up, respectively. In addition you can skip forward or backward in the current video using the slider in the control window or by pressing the left or right arrows. You can also toggle full-screen mode either with the full-screen button on the control window, through the right-click menu, or with the f key.

The *xine-ui* frontend makes a large number of the *xine-lib* configuration options available. To access the *xine-ui* preferences, click the Setup window button on the control window, Settings → Setup on the right-click menu, or type Alt-S. The setup window (see Figure 3-4) has a number of tabs for General, Audio, Video, and other options. In the General window one of the first options lets you configure the configuration experience level. The level of experience you choose here, from Beginner to Master of the Known Universe, controls how many options will be revealed to you in the Setup Window. Some of the basic options you can configure in this window include the default skin to use for *xine-ui*, what video and audio output method to use, as well as various advanced options for those output methods, and which devices xine will default to for DVDs and CD-ROMs.

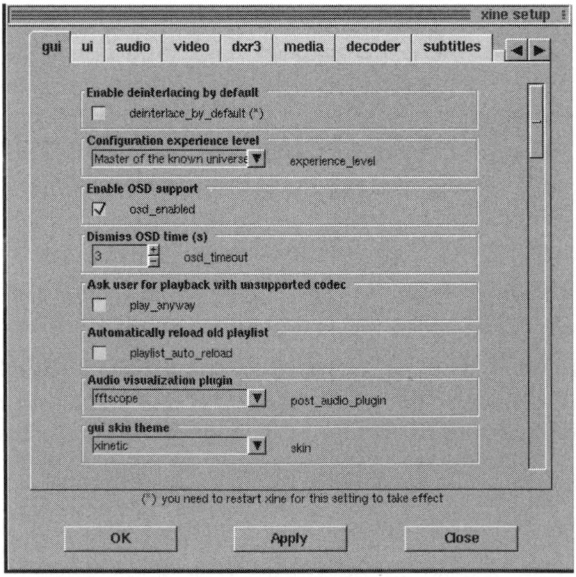

Figure 3-4. xine setup window

There are some very advanced options available in the setup window, so don't choose Master of the Known Universe unless you are prepared to face advanced and possibly confusing options.

Other xine Frontends

While the default *xine-ui* frontend can do the job, some people have found the interface difficult to use, and others prefer an interface that more closely matches their desktop environment. There are a number of other frontends to the xine engine, and two of the most popular are probably Totem and Kaffeine.

Totem is a GTK2-based frontend to xine and, as such, appeals to users of the GNOME desktop environment. Totem should already be packaged by most major distributions, but otherwise can be downloaded directly from the official site at *http://www.hadess.net/totem.php3*. Totem boasts a very simple interface, with both the video and control windows combined in a single window with a menu bar along the top of the window. The interface is pretty self-explanatory, and you can drag and drop videos to the window to play them, as well as open them from the Movie menu.

Kaffeine is another xine frontend based on the QT toolkit. You can install Kaffeine either through your distributions package manager or directly from the official site at *http://kaffeine.sourceforge.net*. Kaffeine and Totem both resemble each other somewhat, but Kaffeine is intended for use with KDE. Apart from look and feel, both UIs behave in similar ways and because both access the same xine engine underneath, both should be able to play the same range of video and audio files.

Visit *http://www.xinehq.de/index.php/releases* to see more xine frontends, along with links to other plug-ins or projects that use the xine engine.

View VLC, the Cross-Platform Video Player

Learn how to watch multimedia content with VLC, a video player you can use on Linux, Windows, and Mac.

There are a number of media players available for Linux, each with its respective pros and cons. Because all media players under Linux rely on basically the same codecs to play back video and audio, the media player you choose is largely a matter of taste—which media player fits best with how you watch video. VLC has gained popularity, on one hand, because of its simplified and easy-to-use interface and, on the other hand, because of its cross-platform nature. VLC has clients available for Windows, Mac OSX, various distributions of Linux, BSD, Solaris, and other platforms. If you use a number of platforms on a daily basis, it can be nice to have a single application that runs across all of them for your video needs.

VLC also touts a number of other features such as video streaming services, which I cover in "Stream Video with VLC" **[Hack #85]**. This hack, however, discusses the basics of installing and using VLC to watch video.

The first step to use VLC is to install the software. Visit *http://videolan.org/vlc* and scroll down to see the list of Linux distributions with precompiled binaries. Click the icon for your distribution and follow the installation instructions on that page. Some major distributions do prepackage VLC binaries, but the VLC installation page for those distributions will let you know whether or not you can use your distribution's packaging tool. In case your distribution isn't represented here, download and compile the VLC source according to the VLC installation instructions.

Once VLC is installed, launch it from your application menu or type **vlc** in a console. The default interface is small and rather simple with a standard navigation toolbar for play, pause, volume control, and so forth, and a menu bar. To open a video, click File → Open File to bring up the Open dialog. This dialog has a tabbed interface that lets you choose from local files, discs, network streams, Video4Linux devices, or a PVR (such as a Hauppage PVR card). To play a video file, click the File tab, and then click Browse to find the file to open. Click OK to start playback of the file.

Once a file is selected, you can choose from a number of menu options. The Video menu allows you to full screen or otherwise control the zoom level for the video. The Audio menu lets you tweak the Audio channels as well as enable various sound visualizations. Click Settings → Extended GUI to toggle the display of extra settings on the main interface including video controls for hue, contrasts, brightness, and so on, plus a full equalizer.

To edit general VLC preference, click Settings → Preferences. The Preferences page has an Advanced Options checkbox that will hide or show what VLC considers to be advanced options, so choose to leave this checked or unchecked based on your level of expertise. Beginners can configure a number of useful settings from this window including key bindings, device settings for CDs and DVDs, and video defaults. Advanced options allow you to tweak CPU optimizations, advanced video settings, and a number of other options for the experienced user.

Probe Video Settings

The tcprobe utility included with transcode provides an easy way to get specifications on a video using the command line.

As you begin to experiment with converting videos from one format to another you will find yourself searching for more detailed information about the video than simply whether it ends in *.mpg* or *.avi*. For instance, my portable media player is capable of playing a few different video formats up to a certain resolution, so before I copy videos to it, it helps to probe them beforehand to make sure they meet its specifications. Also to do video conversion you often need information such as resolution, video and audio bitrate, codec used, and so forth. There are a number of ways to retrieve this information on Linux. One way is to simply open up the video in your favorite GUI video player and check the file properties. Another is to play the video in *mplayer* and dig through the verbose output it creates for clues. Probably the fastest and easiest way however is to use the *tcprobe* utility included with the *transcode* suite of tools.

Information about the installation and use of transcode is covered in [Hack #63]. Once *transcode* is installed, it includes a number of useful tools that it uses when processing video, including *tcprobe*. *tcprobe* is pretty simple to use. The following command gives you general information about a video file named *sample.mpg*:

```
$ tcprobe -i sample.mpg
[tcprobe] MPEG program stream (PS)
[tcprobe] summary for sample.mpg, (*) = not default, 0 = not detected
import frame size: -g 480x576 [720x576] (*)
     aspect ratio: 4:3 (*)
       frame rate: -f 25.000 [25.000] frc=3
                   PTS=0.4494, frame_time=40 ms, bitrate=2450 kbps
 audio track: -a 0 [0] -e 44100,16,2 [48000,16,2] -n 0x50 [0x2000] (*)
PTS=0.4494, bitrate=224 kbps
                   -D 0 --av_fine_ms 0 (frames & ms) [0] [0]
```

The -i argument is used to specify the input file (otherwise it defaults to scanning STDIN). The input file can be an actual file, directory, device, or mount point. *tcprobe* provides you with a lot of information, but all of the labels make it easy to parse. To start it tells you that this is an MPEG stream. Next you see that the video itself is 480×576 pixels and has a 4:3 aspect ratio. Following that you get frame rate information telling you that this video is 25 frames per second and that the video has a bit rate of 2,450 kbps. *tcprobe* also provides you with information about the audio track such as the fact that it has a 44,100 Hz sample rate with 16 bits per sample and 2 channels (or stereo). You can also see that the video is encoded at 224 kbps.

Notice that a lot of the *tcprobe* output is in *transcode* argument form. If you look through the *transcode* man page, you will notice that each of the *tcprobe* arguments (such as -g 480x576) correspond to *transcode* arguments. This makes it easy to cut and paste these settings directly into a *transcode* command. Although for the most part this is unnecessary since *transcode* will probe for these settings itself, sometimes it can be handy as a basis to then override what transcode detects. These settings can also be handy when changing video formats for specific devices such as personal video players (see "Create Archos-Compatible Video" **[Hack #64]** for more information).

For most videos, *tcprobe* will work just fine with the -i argument. *tcprobe* provides some extra options though so you can work around problems with certain videos you might have. For instance, by default *tcprobe* will scan the first megabyte of video data to gather information. Certain videos, though, don't have all of the information (such as subtitle or audio tracks, for instance) in the first megabyte. For these files you can use the -H option followed by the number of megabytes to scan. So, to scan the first 10 megabytes of a VOB file, you would type:

```
$ tcprobe -i /mnt/dvd/VIDEO_TS/VTS__01_1.VOB -H 10
```

When you scan DVDs, you might want to scan a particular title for the DVD. *tcprobe* provides the -T argument, followed by the title number for this purpose. On certain files, you might need to skip ahead a certain number of bytes in the input stream before scanning (for instance to skip past file corruption). To do this, use the -s argument followed by the number of bytes.

HACK #58 Rip a VCD

Use vcdxrip from the VCDImager tool suite to extract MPEG video out of VCDs and SVCDs.

Video comes in all shapes, sizes, and formats. DVDs are great, but the video does take up a lot of space on a hard drive and until recently backing up a DVD to another DVD required expensive equipment. Alternate formats to DVDs, including VCD and SVCD, have been around for some time. These formats squeeze a video onto a CD instead of DVD using MPEG1 or MPEG2 video, respectively. The result is a much smaller file (albeit with lower quality) that you can burn onto inexpensive blank CDs and play back in many modern DVD players (most support VCDs if not both VCDs and SVCDs).

If you happen to have a video in VCD or SVCD format and would like to change the video or extract the MPEG from the CD, the VCDImager suite of tools (*http://www.gnu.org/software/vcdimager*) has a solution in the form of *vcdxrip*. *vcdxrip* is included in the VCDImager suite and allows you to extract the MPEG and XML files inside a VCD or SVCD, all from the command line.

By default *vcdxrip* attempts to rip from the default CD-ROM device. To extract the MPEG from a VCD or SVCD burned onto a CD, put the CD into the CD-ROM drive and type:

```
$ vcdxrip
```

vcdxrip will dump the resulting XML file and MPEG file (or multiple files if the CD has more than one track) to the current directory:

avseq01.mpg
> This is the first video track of the VCD in MPEG format. Each subsequent track is incremented accordingly.

videocd.xml
> A VCDImager-compatible XML file that describes the VCD's structure.

If you have VCD files that haven't yet been burned to a CD, you can point *vcdxrip* at the *.cue* or *.bin* files with the -c and -b options respectively:

```
$ vcdxrip -b videocd.bin
```

The -p option will provide progress output so you can see how much further you have to go in a rip. For multi-track VCDs, you can even specify a specific track to rip with the -t option. In the case that you simply want to extract the XML file and aren't interested in the MPEG, you can use the --norip option.

> If you want to convert VCD files into MPEG for a video player, note that many Linux-based video players can play both VCDs and the VCD *.bin* files without any extra extraction. Just point the video player to the *.bin* file.

HACK #59 Rip a DVD

Use dvdbackup to create a backup copy of your DVD to your hard drive for later encoding or burning to blank media.

Like with CD ripping and encoding, DVD ripping and encoding involves a number of steps. Like CD ripping, DVD ripping requires that you extract all of the tracks from a DVD onto your filesystem. Unlike CDs, DVDs have a much different file structure. Under Linux you can mount a DVD like a data CD and view the file structure. Unlike CDs, many DVDs have encrypted video tracks, so backing up a DVD to a hard drive, especially if you intend to perform any encoding later on, requires special tools to manage the CSS encryption. This hack describes how to use the *dvdbackup* tool to back up all or part of a DVD to disk so that you can later encode it to different video formats or burn it back to a new DVD.

dvdbackup is one tool in the DVD-Create suite of DVD tools. It may or may not already be packaged by your distribution. If not, download the *dvdbackup* source from *http://dvd-create.sourceforge.net* and build and install it.

Back Up an Entire DVD

dvdbackup can back up either an entire DVD, or just specific tracks you specify. To backup the entire DVD, use the *–M* option. Use the -i and -o arguments to specify the input file (path to the DVD device) and output directory to store the DVD files respectively. So, to back up a DVD at */dev/ dvd* to your *~/dvdrip* directory, type:

```
$ dvdbackup -M -i /dev/dvd -o ~/dvdrip/
```

This operation takes some time, as *dvdbackup* is copying over four gigabytes of data from the DVD. Once DVD is finished, a new directory under *~/dvdrip* is created and named after the title *dvdbackup* detected for your DVD. Inside that directory is the complete file structure for your DVD:

VIDEO_TS.IFO
> This is a configuration file that defines the general structure of the DVD along with region-coding information.

VIDEO_TS.BUP
> A backup of the *VIDEO_TS.IFO* file.

VIDEO_TS.VOB
> A placeholder that tells the DVD player it is at the beginning of the disk.

VTS_0X_0.IFO
> Contains information such as aspect ratios and other information for the corresponding *.VOB* file so that it will play correctly.

VTS_0X_0.VOB
> This is the first stream that is played on a DVD and is usually the menuing system for the DVD.

VTS_0X_0.BUP
> Backup file for the corresponding *VTS_0X_0.IFO*.

VTS_0X_1.VOB
> This file contains the video and audio streams for a title and is usually split into multiple files ordered in sequence. These are also usually the largest files on the DVD and what you are most interested in if you plan on encoding the DVD into other formats later.

Back Up Specific Titles

In some cases, such as when you plan on encoding the DVD files later, you may not want to copy every file from the DVD: you may want only the main feature. In this case substitute -M for -F:

```
$ dvdbackup -F -i /dev/dvd -o ~/dvdrip/
```

You can also back up specific titles on the DVD. If, for instance, you want to back up only the second title from the DVD, type

```
$ dvdbackup -T 2 -i /dev/dvd -o ~/dvdrip/
```

This will only copy the *VTS_02_** files from the *VIDEO_TS* directory.

You can even back up specific chapters within a title if you don't want the complete movie. The –s option specifies which chapter to start with, and the –e argument specifies which chapter to end with. So to rip chapters 10 through 13 on title one, type:

```
$ dvdbackup -t 1 -s 10 -e 13 -i /dev/dvd -o ~/dvdrip/
```

Encode a DVD to MPEG4 from the Command Line

Use mencoder 2-pass encoding to encode VOB files to MPEG4 .avi files (and other formats), all from the command line.

If you travel with a laptop over long distances, you might decide to take some DVDs along with you to pass the time. Of course, optical drives require a lot of power, and on some laptops you might not have enough power to get through an entire movie. However, if you rip and then encode the movie to a smaller format ahead of time, you can store a number of movies on your laptop and watch them directly from the hard drive, which saves a considerable amount of battery life, because you don't need to spin the DVD. This hack talks about how to encode a DVD to an MPEG4 (also known as "DivX") *.avi* file from the command line. This hack assumes that you have already ripped the DVD to your hard drive, as explained in [Hack #59].

There are a few DVD-encoding command-line tools available to Linux users, but one of the simpler methods involves 2-pass encoding with *mencoder*, part of the MPlayer project. If you don't have *mencoder* installed yet, follow the installation instructions in "Use MPlayer" [Hack #48] and be sure to grab *mencoder* packages along with your MPlayer packages. *mencoder's* 2-pass encoding actually processes the video twice using information gained in the first pass to create a final video with much better image quality in the second pass for about the same file size.

I provide several encoding scenarios in this hack, all of which assume that you have already ripped the DVD to a directory on the filesystem. For each example, you will need to choose a chapter from the DVD to rip. Often the main feature of a DVD is on chapter one, but there are exceptions. Each chapter will have the format *VTS_[Chapter]_[Section].VOB*, so chapter one, section one of a DVD would be named *VTS_01_1.VOB*. You can usually identify the main feature of a DVD just by looking at the file sizes of each chapter's files—the largest group is probably the main feature. If in doubt, open up the DVD in your favorite video player application and check the different chapters to see. In the following examples, I will encode all of chapter one from a DVD I have ripped into *~/example/VIDEO_TS*, so change the chapter and file paths to suit your DVD.

Full Quality Encoding with MP3 Audio

The simplest method for 2-pass encoding encodes the DVD at the full bitrate (or how many bits you can use to store a second of video). This method will create a larger resulting file, but it won't require a preliminary step of calculating a bitrate to create an output file of a specific size. This requires two different *mencoder* commands, one for each pass:

```
$ cat ~/example/VIDEO_TS/VTS_01*.VOB | mencoder -oac mp3lame -ovc lavc - \
lavcopts vcodec=mpeg4:vpass=1 -o example.avi -
$ cat ~/example/VIDEO_TS/VTS_01*.VOB | mencoder -oac mp3lame -ovc lavc - \
lavcopts vcodec=mpeg4:vpass=2 -o example.avi -
```

These commands concatenate all the VOB files for chapter one as input for *mencoder*. *mencoder* sets the output audio codec (-oac) to MP3, and sets the output video codec to MPEG4 (vcodec=mpeg4). At the end of the second pass *example.avi* will be finished and ready to play. On my 1.2 GHz Pentium-M processor, 2-pass encoding usually takes twice as long as the length of the movie, so a two-hour movie takes four hours to encode.

> You can encode into formats other than MPEG4 with this method; just view the *MPlayer* manpage for information on the different values you can pass the vcodec parameter.

Encode with Specified Bitrates

If space is a concern, you will likely want to specify a particular bitrate for *mencoder* to use so you can create a smaller output file. Although you could figure out which bitrate to use by picking different bitrates at random and seeing how big the resulting file is, or possibly through calculation, *mencoder* can calculate some acceptable bitrates for you. This calculation will add some extra time (on a 1.2 GHz Pentium-M, it adds 15 to 20 minutes for an average movie) to the process, but after you use it a few times you will probably notice a range of bitrates that fit with the file size you want. The first step is to remove any previous temporary files created by the calculation process and then launch the special *mencoder* calculation command:

```
$ rm frameno.avi
$ cat ~/example/VIDEO_TS/VTS_01*.VOB | mencoder -oac mp3lame -ovc frameno -o \
frameno.avi -
. . .
```

```
Recommended video bitrate for 650MB CD: 710
Recommended video bitrate for 700MB CD: 785
Recommended video bitrate for 800MB CD: 934
Recommended video bitrate for 2 x 650MB CD: 1679
Recommended video bitrate for 2 x 700MB CD: 1828
Recommended video bitrate for 2 x 800MB CD: 2126
```

Text will scroll by as *mencoder* processes through the video. The last lines of the output will give you rough estimates for bitrates to use for 600, 700, and 800 MB files (suitable for CDs). After you have chosen which bitrate to use, run the same 2-pass encoding commands as before, but with the addition of the vbitrate option (in this example 780):

```
$ cat ~/example/VIDEO_TS/VTS_01*.VOB | mencoder -oac mp3lame -ovc lavc -\
lavcopts vcodec=mpeg4:vpass=1:vbitrate=780 -o example.avi -
$ cat ~/example/VIDEO_TS/VTS_01*.VOB | mencoder -oac mp3lame -ovc lavc -\
-lavcopts vcodec=mpeg4:vpass=2:vbitrate=780 -o example.avi -
```

mencoder will process through the video as in the previous example, only this time with an output file that meets your space requirements.

> Reducing the bitrate for encoding will cause the output file to lose video quality. If you aren't pleased with the quality of a particular bitrate you might want to experiment with higher bitrates until you find one that has acceptable quality loss.

HACK #61   Rip and Encode DVDs with a mencoder Frontend

The *acidrip* utility gives you access to many of the common *mencoder* functions that rip and encode a DVD in a GUI.

In "Encode a DVD to MPEG4 from the Command Line" [Hack #60], I discuss how to use *mencoder's* 2-pass encoding to turn VOB files you have extracted from a DVD into an MPEG4 *.avi* file. This method works great; however, some people are turned off by the thought of doing encoding entirely from the command line. If you want to use *mencoder* to encode a DVD, but would rather have a GUI, the *acidrip* utility provides you with most of the major *mencoder* options you might want in a GUI interface.

First, install *acidrip*. If you search Google a bit, you can find third-party *acidrip* packages for most distributions. For example, Debian packages are available in Marillat's third-party repository that also houses packages such as *mplayer* and *mencoder*. If you can't find a pre-built package, then download the *acidrip* and accompanying *lsdvd* packages from the official site at *http://untrepid.com/acidrip* and follow the installation instructions.

With *acidrip* installed, type **acidrip** to start the program. The default screen that greets you (see Figure 3-5) can be a bit intimidating at first since it has so many options. For basic ripping there are only a few options you need to worry about, and the nice thing is that *acidrip* will remember your settings for next time. That means that after you have it set up, you can rip multiple DVDs with minimal effort.

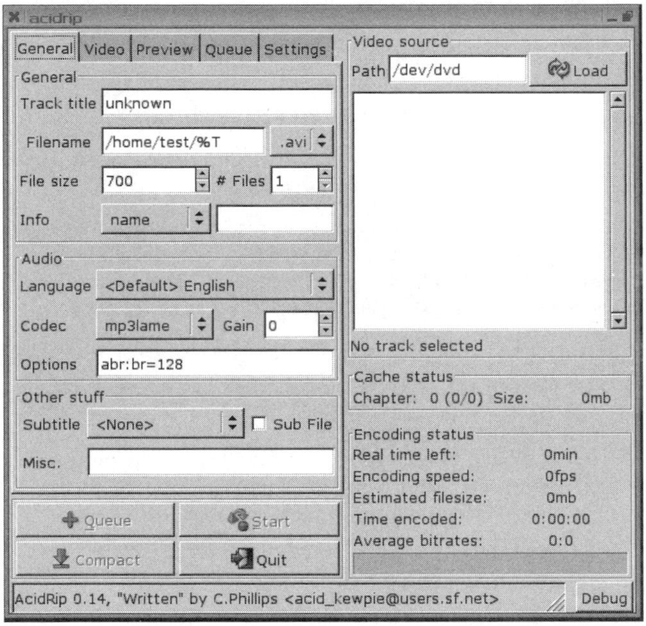

Figure 3-5. acidrip default window

To rip a DVD, first locate the section on the right side of the window labeled Video source and type the path to your DVD in the Path field. If you are ripping directly from a DVD, insert the DVD and type the path to your DVD device (such as */dev/dvd*). Otherwise if you have already ripped the DVD to the hard drive, type in the path to the directory that contains the *VIDEO_TS* directory. Click Load, and *acidrip* scans the DVD and displays each title with its playback time. Use the playback time to identify the main title you want to encode (generally the title with the longest playback time, and often the first title on the DVD) and select it.

If you are unsure of which title is the correct title, select the title and then click the Preview tab. Click the Preview button in that tab and *acidrip* uses *mplayer* to play that track inside the window. Uncheck the Embed window if you want to watch the video in its own window. If you enable any crop settings, you can also preview those here.

Now click on the General tab on the left side of the window and fill in the Track title if *acidrip* didn't automatically detect it for you. By default, *acidrip* uses this field for the final filename. In the Filename field, type in the path where you want *acidrip* to put the final encoded video. The %T in this field is a variable that gets replaced with the contents of the Track title field. In the dropdown menu next to the Filename, you can choose whether to give the final video an *.avi* or *.mpg* extension. Underneath that field you can configure the final file size for the video and whether to split it across multiple files. For instance, if you wanted to fit the video across two CDs, you would set File size to 700 and # Files to 2.

The above settings should be fine for the average case, but *acidrip* provides plenty of other options so that you can configure *mencoder* for your special case. The General tab also lets you configure what codec to use for the audio track along with whether to include a subtitle in the final video.

The Video tab gives the experienced *mencoder* user access to more advanced options. Here you can configure which codec to use for the output file and you can set the bitrate for the final file by hand. You can also crop the final video or scale it to a different width and height. If you want to add any special pre- or post-filters to *mencoder* you can also configure that here.

I noticed that my version of *acidrip* had the pp=de pre-filter enabled by default, which caused an error in *mencoder*. I simply disabled this filter and the *acidrip* worked fine.

After you have configured your settings the way you want them, click the Queue button at the bottom of the window to add the job to the queue. The Queue tab displays any queued jobs you have set. This tab can be handy if you want to learn more about the *mencoder* processes *acidrip* uses, because it displays the full commands it will run in this tab. This can also be good for debugging purposes if *acidrip* fails to start ripping. Copy and paste the *mencoder* lines from the queue to the command line and make note of any errors *mencoder* outputs. You can also queue more than one job, so you can line up a bunch of jobs and leave them running overnight.

The Settings tab lets you configure general *acidrip* options including what program to use for *mencoder*, *mplayer*, and *lsdvd* (useful if there is more than one instance of these programs in your path) and what directory to use to cache a DVD (if you have that enabled). From this tab you can also tell *acidrip* to automatically shutdown the computer after it is finished ripping.

Once you finish configuring your job and queue it, click the Start button to start the encoding process. *acidrip* shrinks down to a smaller window and displays its progress, including time left in the current process, encoding speed, and estimated file size. Click the Full View Button to go back to the full-sized window. When *acidrip* finishes, it goes back to full view, and you will be able to check out your new video files in the directory you specified.

As I said earlier, the nice thing about using *acidrip* over *mencoder* from the command line is that you can tweak *acidrip* with your favorite *mencoder* settings a single time and then just concentrate on adding encoding jobs. This will help eliminate the problem of trying to remember which options to use each time, plus it makes it easier to queue up multiple jobs one after another.

Rip and Encode DVDs with K3b

#62

Use K3b as an easy-to-use frontend to rip and encode DVDs without touching a command line.

The big success of a program such as K3b is how it gives you much of the power of the command-line tools it uses while still remaining easy to use. K3b is mostly used to burn CDs and DVDs, but you can also use it to easily rip and encode DVDs. This hack will take you through the process of ripping a DVD and encoding it using K3b.

> K3b's ripping and encoding features do work, however they are currently not maintained. This means that you might encounter bugs in the process. For instance, in the version I was using, I was able to crash K3b by checking certain options. The primary functions should work for you, so give it a try and see whether it can suit your needs.

Like with CD and DVD recording, K3b relies on command-line tools behind the scenes for much of what it does. K3b uses *transcode* for the encoding process, and K3b has a few dependencies for DVD ripping:

- Transcode version 0.6.0pre5
- An MPEG4 codec such as XviD or DivX4/5
- *libdvdread*
- *libdvdcss* (The developers prefer Version 0.0.3.ogle3 but Version 1.2.0 should work as well.)

With the requirements met, put your DVD in the drive and launch K3b. Click on your DVD drive from the filesystem tree on the left, and K3b reads and displays information about the DVD titles on the right side of the window. Choose the title you want to rip to your filesystem (generally the title with the longest runtime is the main feature, and it's often the first title on the DVD). Right-click on the title and select Copy. Now choose the location on the filesystem to store the DVD's *.vob* files. Keep in mind that you need over four gigabytes of space for the files, not to mention the final *.avi* file. Optionally, check "Open encoding dialog after ripping" and K3b will open the window for the next part of the process once the rip is complete. Click the Start Ripping button and K3b will start ripping the files to the filesystem.

> In my version of K3b, I noticed the progress bar had a bug that quickly filled up to 100% and then continued up to thousands of percents. It's just a bug in the progress calculation—the DVD itself ripped fine.

After the DVD has been ripped, if you checked "Open encoding dialog after ripping," you will see a new window filled out with information about your DVD. Otherwise click Tools → Encode Video and then click the button under "K3b DVD ripping file:" to browse to the directory where the DVD was ripped. Select the *.xml* file located there (it should be called *k3bDVDRip.xml* by default). Alternatively, you can just type in the full path to the file.

The Encoding Video window is split up into three tabs. The first tab is labeled Basic Audio/Video Settings and provides all of the basic options an average person would need when doing a standard encoding. The most important field to fill out here is the Final AVI filename as it won't encode otherwise. In addition, you might want to change the bitrate settings. By default it will encode the video so it will fit on a 700 MB CD. You can also configure which MPEG4 video codec to use.

The second tab, "Advanced Audio/Video Settings," lets you crop and resize the video. It also provides a preview of the video, with a slider that allows you to choose a representative frame from the movie for selecting your resizing and cropping settings. K3b provides you with red boxes that allow you to see the results of your crop settings on a frame of the video. At the bottom is a general resizing slider you can use to shrink the video to a smaller size.

The final tab is labeled "Expert Settings" and provides you with a few extra options, such as the ability to shut down the computer after you have finished encoding. You can also tell K3b not to use *normalize* to detect optimal audio settings. Enable this if you find audio settings are detected improperly.

After you have tweaked the settings to your liking, click the Encode button to start the process. K3b provides a progress window like it does with CD- and DVD-burning, so you can monitor how far along the process is. When it is finished, you will have a shiny new MPEG4 file in the directory you chose. You may want to experiment with different settings to get the optimal MPEG4 file for your tastes.

Convert from One Video Format to Another

#63

With transcode you can convert to and from many popular video formats and perform other video manipulation all from the command line.

They say that the problem with standards is that there are so many to choose from. This is definitely true when it comes to video formats. It would be nice to store all video just as it was recorded, but the fact is it would take up more space than many people have available on their computers. As a result, a number of different lossy compression formats have been developed to try to reduce the file size for video while still maintaining reasonable quality. There is also a battle raging between various companies such as Microsoft, Apple, and Real each with their own competing video formats. Plus, as the technology improves, new revisions of old formats appear. The end result is a jumble of MPEG1, MPEG2, DivX, ASF, XVID, and other video formats—all different from one another.

When wading through these choices, often you find you need to convert a video from one format to another. There are a number of special-purpose tools that excel at one particular formats or group of formats, but with *transcode* you have a single conversion tool you can apply to all of the various video files you might have. *Transcode* not only supports converting to and from a variety of formats, it also can perform cropping and resizing [Hack #68].

The first step is installing *transcode*. Because of the number of formats *transcode* supports, in general it's simpler to use a precompiled binary for your distribution. Most major distributions offer *transcode* either as part of the distribution or from third-party packagers. These are preferred since you can grab all of the library dependencies from the same place. To install from source, download the latest version from *http://www.transcoding.org* and follow the instructions at *http://www.transcoding.org/cgi-bin/transcode?Building_Transcode*.

The most important aspect of installation from source is the options you pass to the *configure* script. A majority of the useful import and export plug-ins, including *ogg*, *mjpegtools*, *libquickime*, *libdv*, and others, aren't enabled by default in the source (while usually they are enabled in prepackaged binaries). The number of arguments to pass *configure* are too numerous to list here, but check the install page linked above for the list of options that aren't enabled by default.

With *transcode* installed, the next thing to consider is which video format you wish to convert to. The *transcode* manpage lists all of the different video and audio export modules in the manpage under the -y option. Some export modules are only for video or for audio. In those cases, the manpage will list null next to the video or audio section of the description.

To see what modules your *transcode* install has, type:

```
$ ls -1 `tcmodinfo -p`/export*.so
/usr/lib/transcode/export_ac3.so
/usr/lib/transcode/export_af6.so
/usr/lib/transcode/export_debugppm.so
/usr/lib/transcode/export_divx5raw.so
. . .
/usr/lib/transcode/export_xvid2.so
/usr/lib/transcode/export_xvid3.so
/usr/lib/transcode/export_xvid4.so
/usr/lib/transcode/export_xvid.so
/usr/lib/transcode/export_yuv4mpeg.so
$
```

Table 3-3 lists some of the more popular video and audio export modules.

Table 3-3. Popular transcode video and audio export modules

Module name	Video codecs supported	Audio codecs supported	Description
ac3	N/A	AC3	Uses *ffmpeg* to encode audio to AC3.
divx4	DivX 4.xx	MPEG/AC3/PCM	Encodes MPEG4 video using the closed-source binaries from divx.com.
divx5	DivX 5.xx	MPEG/AC3/PCM	Encodes MPEG4 video using the closed-source binaries from divx.com.
dv	Digital Video	MPEG/AC3/PCM	Encodes DV into an AVI container. DV is a codec used in digital camcorders.
lame	N/A	MPEG1/2	Encodes audio to MPEG layer III (MP3) using LAME.
mjpeg	Motion JPEG	MPEG/AC3/PCM	Encodes MJPEG-based AVI files.
mp1e	MPEG1 video	MPEG1-Layer	Encodes into MPEG1 video and can encode VCD-compliant streams.
mp2	N/A	MPEG1/2	Writes an MP2 (MPEG1-Layer2) audio file.
mpeg2enc	MPEG1/2	N/A	Uses *mpeg2enc* to encode MPEG1, VCD, SVCD, MPEG2, and DVD videos.
ogg	N/A	Ogg	Encodes audio to Ogg Vorbis.
pcm	N/A	PCM	Encodes audio to PCM format.
raw	N/A	MPEG/AC3/PCM	Does no encoding and instead processes raw streams. Used also for pass-through mode.
xvid4	XviD 1.0.x	MPEG/AC3/PCM	Encodes MPEG4 video using xvid.org encoding libraries. The "xvid" option often is a symlink to this library.

Simple Example: Encode a Video to XviD

One of the easier examples for *transcode* is to turn a video (such as an *.mpg* file) into XviD format. XviD is a particular set of MPEG4 encoding libraries that provide high quality encodes with small file sizes. *transcode* has many different options you can use to tweak its output—so many it's easy to get lost in them all. For the purposes of this hack I'm going to try to limit it down to some essential arguments that you need to convert video between formats.

Many examples you see on the Web show people passing *transcode* import format options, but this isn't necessary, and if you omit the import format option, *transcode* will scan the video and figure it out for itself. I've found that for my videos, *transcode* is good at figuring it out, and one less option on the command line makes things easier to read and understand. So, to convert a sample MPEG file to an XviD AVI, type:

```
$ transcode -i sample.mpg -o output.avi -y xvid
transcode v0.6.14 (C) 2001-2003 Thomas Oestreich, 2003-2004 T. Bitterberg
[transcode] (probe) suggested AV correction -D 0 (0 ms) | AV 0 ms | 0 ms
[transcode] auto-probing source sample.mpg (ok)
[transcode] V: import format    | MPEG    (V=mpeg2|A=mp3)
[transcode] V: AV demux/sync    | (0) sync AV at PTS start - demuxer
disabled
[transcode] V: import frame     | 352x240  1.47:1  encoded @ 4:3
[transcode] V: bits/pixel       | 0.711
[transcode] V: decoding fps,frc | 29.970,4
[transcode] V: Y'CbCr           | YV12/I420
[transcode] A: import format    | 0x50   MPEG layer-2 [44100,16,2]  224 kbps
[transcode] A: export format    | 0x55   MPEG layer-3 [44100,16,2]  128 kbps
[transcode] V: encoding fps,frc | 29.970,4
[transcode] A: bytes per frame  | 5884 (5885.880000)
[transcode] A: adjustment       | 1880@1000
[transcode] V: IA32 accel mode  | sse2 (sse2 sse mmxext mmx asm C)
tc_memcpy: using mmxext for memcpy
[transcode] V: video buffer     | 10 @ 352x240
[import_mp3.so] v0.1.4 (2003-08-04) (audio) MPEG
[import_mpeg2.so] v0.4.0 (2003-10-02) (video) MPEG2
[export_xvid4.so] v0.0.5 (2003-12-05) (video) XviD 1.0.x series (aka API 4.
0) | (audio) MPEG/AC3/PCM
. . .
```

As *transcode* processes the file, it will indicate how many frames per second it is processing and how far along in the video it is, so you can track its progress.

By default *transcode* will encode XviD files at 1,800 bps. If you want to change that to a larger or smaller value, use the -w option followed by the bps, so to encode to an XviD like in the previous example, only at 1,500 bps, type:

```
$ transcode -i sample.mpg -o output.avi -y xvid -w
1500
```

Notice that, by default, *transcode* used MPEG layer-3 for the audio, since I didn't specify an audio format to use. If you want, you can change that. For instance, to create an XviD with Ogg Vorbis audio, you pass *transcode* an audio export module as well as a video export module. In this case you also need to provide *transcode* with a filename to save the audio track to with the -m argument, so that you can combine it and the video later on:

```
$ transcode -i sample.mpg -o output.avi -m output.ogg -y xvid,ogg
transcode v0.6.14 (C) 2001-2003 Thomas Oestreich, 2003-2004 T. Bitterberg
[transcode] (probe) suggested AV correction -D 0 (0 ms) | AV 0 ms | 0 ms
[transcode] auto-probing source sample.mpg (ok)
[transcode] V: import format    | MPEG    (V=mpeg2|A=mp3)
[transcode] V: AV demux/sync    | (0) sync AV at PTS start - demuxer
disabled
[transcode] V: import frame     | 320x240  1.33:1  encoded @ 1:1
[transcode] V: bits/pixel       | 0.782
[transcode] V: decoding fps,frc | 29.970,4
[transcode] V: Y'CbCr           | YV12/I420
[transcode] A: import format    | 0x50    MPEG layer-2 [44100,16,2]   224 kbps
[transcode] A: export format    | 0x55    MPEG layer-3 [44100,16,2]   128 kbps
[transcode] V: encoding fps,frc | 29.970,4
[transcode] A: bytes per frame  | 5884 (5885.880000)
[transcode] A: adjustment       | 1880@1000
[transcode] V: IA32 accel mode  | sse2 (sse2 sse mmxext mmx asm C)
tc_memcpy: using mmxext for memcpy
[transcode] V: video buffer     | 10 @ 320x240
[import_mp3.so] v0.1.4 (2003-08-04) (audio) MPEG
[import_mpeg2.so] v0.4.0 (2003-10-02) (video) MPEG2
[export_ogg.so] v0.0.5 (2003-08-31) (video) null | (audio) ogg
[export_xvid4.so] v0.0.5 (2003-12-05) (video) XviD 1.0.x series (aka API 4.
0) | (audio) MPEG/AC3/PCM
[import_mp3.so] MP3->PCM
[import_mp3.so] tcextract -a 0 -i "sample.mpg" -x mp2 -d 0 | tcdecode -x mp2
-d 0 -z 0
[import_mpeg2.so] tcextract -x mpeg2 -i "sample.mpg" -d 0 | tcdecode -x
mpeg2 -d 0 -y yv12
. . .
[export_ogg.so] Hint: Now merge the files with
[export_ogg.so] Hint: ogmmerge -o complete.ogg output.avi output.ogg

clean up | frame threads | unload modules | cancel signal | internal threads
| done
[transcode] encoded 15491 frames (0 dropped, 0 cloned), clip length 516.88 s
$
```

The transcode command even provides you with a hint on how to merge the audio and video streams once it is finished. In the case of Ogg files, use *ogmmerge* (part of the Ogg Vorbis toolset) to merge the video and audio streams:

```
$ ogmmerge -o final.avi output.avi output.ogg
```

```
Using AVI demultiplexer for output.avi. Opening file. This may take some
time depending on the file's size.
+-> Using video output module for video stream.
Using OGG/OGM demultiplexer for output.ogg.
+-> Using Vorbis audio output module for stream 1.
progress: 15490/15490 frames (100%)
$
```

In this example, *final.avi* would be the final combined video.

Other Multipart Video Formats

When creating other video files, particularly (S)VCDs, DVD, or other MPEG files, often *transcode* will output into multiple files that you then need to combine into a single file. The complete process of creating (S)VCDs and DVDs is covered in **[Hacks #69 and #70]** respectively, but if you want, you can also create these file types with *transcode*.

For this example, I have an MPEG1 file, *sample.mpg*, that I want to convert to an MPEG2 file. I use *transcode* with both video and audio export modules selected—in this case mpeg2enc and mp2enc for video and audio, respectively. In addition, since the mpeg2enc supports both MPEG1 and MPEG2, I need to pass an extra option, -F, to specify what type of video to create. The options for the -F argument vary depending on the type of video module you have selected, and all the various options are described in the *transcode* manpage. For mpeg2enc, the primary option for the -F argument is a number between 0 and 8. Read the manpage for more information on these options, but as an example, 0 specifies a MPEG1 (and is the default), 1 specifies VCD, 3 specifies MPEG2, 4 specifies SVCD, and 8 specifies DVD. Since I want MPEG2, I type the following:

```
$ transcode -i sample.mpg -o output -y mpeg2enc,mp2enc -F 3
```

Notice that I didn't add an extension to the output filename. That's because *transcode* is going to create two files for me, *output.m2v* (my MPEG2 video) and *output.mpa* (my MPEG2 audio). Since these files are MPEG format, the next step is to combine these two files into a single file with the *tcmplex* utility. *tcmplex* is part of the *transcode* toolkit up through 0.6.14, although it was removed due to lack of maintenance. If you have a newer version of transcode you can use the *mplex* tool that is part of the *mjpegtools* suite (*http://mjpeg.sourceforge.net*). To combine these two files, I type the following command for *tcmplex*:

```
$ tcmplex -m 2 -i output.m2v -p output.mpa -o output.mpg
```

The -m option sets the output to one of a few predefined modes. In this case I set it to 2, which is the predefined mode for MPEG2, but I could have set it to 1 (MPEG1 VBR), d (DVD), s (SVCD), or v (VCD). The -i option specifies the input video stream, and -p specifies the input audio stream. You can even specify multiple audio streams, just use -s to specify the second audio track. Finally, the -o argument specifies the output file to use.

In the case of *mplex*, type:

```
$ mplex -f 3 -o output.mpg -i output.m2voutput.mpa
```

The -f option is like the -m option in *tcmplex* and specifies a predefined mode for the output file. In this case, I chose 3 for standard MPEG2, but I could have set it to 0 (generic MPEG1), 1 (VCD), 2 (SVCD), or 9 (DVD). The manpage for *mplex* lists a number of other format options. Finally the -o argument specifies the output file to use.

Once the command completes, I have an MPEG2 file named *output.mpg*.

Final Notes

Transcode is a very complicated program with a large number of options. While I can't easily cover all the processes of conversion to every format you might want, the previous examples should be enough to get you started with converting files to various MPEG1, MPEG2, and MPEG4 or XviD files. Generally speaking, to change to a different output format, just change the argument you pass -y, and optionally add -F arguments if they exist for that output module.

For more information on tweaks to specific formats, be sure to read through the examples given in the *transcode* manpage (type **man transcode**) as well as the numerous examples on the official *transcode* page at *http://www. transcoding.org*.

Create Archos-Compatible Video

Use *transcode* to convert video files so that they work with the Archos line of video players.

The company Archos (*http://www.archos.com*) has released a number of portable media players over the past few years that play not only audio but also video files. The main problem with the video playback is that these video players can be rather choosy when it comes to which video formats they accept. The video must be within a certain resolution, have CBR MP3 audio, and use the MPEG4 video codec. Archos includes a Windows utility with the player that you can use to convert video files to a compatible format, but that isn't much help under Linux. In this hack I will describe how to use *transcode* to convert a video into a format compatible with the Archos line of video players.

I use *transcode* for this conversion because I've found that many of its default settings work well with Archos players. [Hack #63] provides an introduction to installing and using *transcode*.

While you can pass a number of options to *transcode* to specify input and output formats for videos, I've found in the case of the XviD video output format that *transcode* creates Archos-compatible videos without any tweaking. Even though the codec works, Archos video players can play back video only up to a certain resolution at a certain rate of frames per second, which varies for each player, but the AV400 series and the PMA400 series can play back up to 704×480 at 30 fps, and the AV300 series can play back up to 640×368 at 25 fps. So when converting a video, you first need to probe the video to see whether it fits within the specs, using the *tcprobe* utility [Hack #57]. Here's some sample output:

```
$ tcprobe -i sample.mpg
[tcprobe] MPEG program stream (PS)
[tcprobe] summary for sample.mpg, (*) = not default, 0 = not detected
import frame size: -g 480x576 [720x576] (*)
      aspect ratio: 4:3 (*)
        frame rate: -f 25.000 [25.000] frc=3
                    PTS=0.8233, frame_time=40 ms, bitrate=2530 kbps
audio track: -a 0 [0] -e 44100,16,2 [48000,16,2] -n 0x50 [0x2000] (*)
PTS=0.8233, bitrate=224 kbps
                    -D 0 --av_fine_ms 0 (frames & ms) [0] [0]
```

This video has a resolution of 480×576 and a frame rate of 25 fps, so it's well within the specs of both Archos series. To convert this, I just need to specify the input and output files, and which codec to encode to:

```
$ transcode -i sample.mpg -o sample-archos.avi -y xvid
```

Replace sample.mpg and sample-archos.avi with the input and output files you are going to use, respectively. *transcode* will convert the input file, and once it is finished, you can copy it directly to the Archos and play it back.

This works fine for videos that are within spec, but for videos that are outside of spec you need to add extra arguments so that *transcode* can change it for you. For instance, if the resolution of the file is within spec, but the frame rate is too high, use the --export_fps argument to bring it within spec:

```
$ transcode -i sample.mpg -o sample-archos.avi -y xvid \
--export_fps 25
```

If the input video's resolution is outside of spec, you will need to resize the video. Refer to [Hack #68] for more in-depth information on transcode's image resizing options. It's best in these cases to specify either the width or the height for the resize to ensure you keep the same aspect ratio on the video. Be sure to figure out beforehand what the final resolution will be, though, so you can make sure it is within spec. So, if I wanted to convert an MPEG video and resize it so that the width was 640 pixels with *transcode's* fast encoding, I would type:

```
$ transcode -i sample.mpg -o sample-archos.avi -y xvid -Z 640x,fast
```

HACK #65 Convert Dual-Layer DVD to Single-Layer DVD

Use command-line and graphical tools to shrink a dual-layer DVD to fit on a single-layer disk.

It used to be that most DVD movies were released on 4.7 GB DVDs. If you wanted to create an archival copy, you could just do a direct copy of the DVD. Nowadays, many DVDs are released on a dual-layer disc (sometimes referred to as DVD9) that can store twice the amount of data as a single-layer disc (or DVD4). While dual-layer DVD burners are available, if you only have a single-layer model, you can't directly copy the DVD to a new disc. First, you must shrink down (*requantize*) the MPEG2 video so that it can fit on a 4.7 GB disc and then create a DVD based on the new video. DVD Shrink under Windows is a popular tool to use for this task, and while there isn't a feature-for-feature direct equivalent under Linux (apart from running DVD Shrink in Linux using WINE, which is a route some people take), there are some tools available that can at least help you shrink down the main title of a DVD to fit on a 4.7 GB DVD.

Most DVD-shrinking tools under Linux act as frontends for *transcode* and a number of other command-line video tools. This hack covers *dvdshrink*, *batchrip.sh*, and their graphical frontend, *xDVDShrink*, but you may also want to check out a totally different graphical tool called *k9copy* at *http://k9copy.free.fr*.

The first step is to download and install the complete set of *dvdshrink* tools. Go to the official project at *http://dvdshrink.sourceforge.net*, click on Download XDVDShrink, and then download the latest *.tar.gz* file from the download page. Next, extract the *.tar.gz* file, cd to the newly created *dvdshrink* directory, and run the *install.sh* script inside that directory as root:

```
greenfly@moses:~# tar xzvf dvdshrink-2.6.0-2mdk.tar.gz
greenfly@moses:~# cd dvdshrink
greenfly@moses:~/dvdshrink# ./install.sh
DVDShrink installer v1.1

Checking for dependencies

Installing DVDShrink...
-------------------------------------------

Removing old version from /usr/local/bin if it exists
```

```
Creating application directories if needed

Installing files

Removing rc files if they exist

Checking for perl-gtk2    Found!

DVDShrink must be reconfigured the next time it's run
```

The *install.sh* script will check that you have all of the programs it depends on. These dependencies include *transcode*, *mjpegtools*, *subtitleripper*, *mkisofs*, *dvdauthor*, *growisofs*, *gocr*, and optionally Perl-GTK2 for the graphical frontend. The install script will tell you which programs you are missing so you can go grab the packages for your distribution.

The *dvdshrink* tools are split into three main programs, *dvdshrink*, *batchrip.sh*, and *xdvdshrink.pl*. *dvdshrink* is the command-line tool that shrinks a single DVD title, *batchrip.sh* can shrink multiple titles on a DVD into individual discs (useful for DVDs of TV series), and *xdvdshrink.pl* acts as a frontend for both. I generally recommend that you use *xdvdshrink.pl* if you can, since all the command-line options are accessible from there. That way you don't have to worry about remembering all the correct command-line arguments.

To start *xdvdshrink.pl*, type:

```
$ xdvdshrink.pl
```

The first time you run the utility a configuration window will pop up. Here, you can tell *dvdshrink* where your DVD input device is located (usually */dev/dvd*), where your DVD writer is located (for many people this might be the same device), where *dvdshrink* will store files (pick a directory that has 10 to 15 GB of space), the speed of the DVD writer, which X terminal to use, as well as specify a number of other options. Save your configuration a single time and it will be available both for the graphical frontend and the command-line tools.

> *dvdshrink* can also shrink a DVD that has been backed up to the filesystem already. Just type in the path to the directory containing *VIDEO_TS* (and optionally *AUDIO_TS*) in place of */dev/dvd*. [Hack #59] explains how to back up a DVD to the hard drive.

The main xDVDShrink window is split into two tabs. The Single Title tab acts as a frontend to the *dvdshrink* tool and will let you shrink a single title to a DVD. The Multiple Episodes tab is a frontend for the *batchrip.sh* tool and is intended for DVDs with multiple titles to rip, such as DVDs of a television series.

Shrink a Single Title

First, here's how to shrink a single title. In the main xDVDShrink window enter the name for your project. This is optional, but it helps keep things organized. Next enter which DVD title to rip. Often this is the first title on the DVD, but if you are unsure, click "Select from DVD" and choose the appropriate title (often the one with the longest run time in the case of movies) from the window that appears. Next choose which audio channel to rip. Usually the default is fine, but if you are unsure, click "Select from DVD" to be presented with the different audio channels the DVD has available. By default subtitles are not ripped, but you can change this from the main window.

With the main project configured, now you can configure the set of session options. The default behavior of *dvdshrink* is to shrink the title, create a new DVD filesystem, and then burn it to a blank DVD. However, you can change these session options (each of which correspond to a command-line argument) from the main window. Most of the options are self-explanatory, but some particularly useful options are "Save ISO with burn," which will not only burn the DVD but will also save a DVD image to your file system, so you can create more than one copy; "Create ISO file only"; and "Create MPEG files only". If you have different DVD-input and DVD-writing devices, you can enable the Force DVD burn option, and *dvdshrink* will automatically start writing to DVD when it is ready instead of prompting you. This way you can start the whole process and let it run unattended. You don't need to worry about conflicting options as the *xDVDShrink* program will disable any conflicting options for you.

 If drive space is an issue, be sure to enable the "Remove working files" and "Delete logs" options.

Shrink Multiple Titles

To shrink multiple titles, click the Multiple Titles tab instead. Most of the options are the same as the Single Title tab except that you can set either a range of titles to rip or a custom list of comma-separated titles. You can also configure how many titles to fit on a new DVD; generally you would set this to the number of episodes that are currently on the larger DVD (the default is 3). Also notice that the number of session options is the same as with a single title, except that there are fewer options to choose from.

Start Copy Process

When all of the options have been configured, click the "Start copy" button. A new X terminal will appear and prompt you to press Enter, after which the

Convert Dual-Layer DVD to Single-Layer DVD

shrinking process will begin. The terminal window will keep you up to date with what it is currently doing and how long each part of the process has taken. Here is some sample output from a test run against the *Spiderman 2* DVD, where I told it to create an ISO only:

```
DVDShrink 2.6.0 - May 21, 2005
Rick Saunders (ozzzy1@gmail.com)
_____


   INFORMATION

   Project:                          Spiderman2
   File cleanup?                     No
   Auto-burn?                        No, ISO only.
Save ISO with burn?             No
   DVD Title:                        1
Audio channel:                  0
   Subtitle channel:                 None


PROGRESS    Rip started at 12:32:55

   DVDSHrink Function                Status    Elapsed

   Checking for A/V desynchronization   Done!   [00:00:23]
   Reading the chapter list          Done!     [00:00:23]
   Ripping Title                     Done!     [00:16:00]
   Resizing MPEG2 video stream       Done!     [00:32:17]
   Remultiplexing                    Done!     [00:45:17]
   Building DVD on drive             Done!     [00:54:33]
   Building TOC                      Done!     [00:54:34]
   Creating ISO file                 Done!     [01:02:55]


   Your DVD ISO (/home/greenfly/dvd/Spiderman2.iso) is ready!

   Thank you for using OzWare!

Hit any key to close terminal and exit!
```

Notice that the entire process took about an hour on my 1.2 GHz machine with a DVD drive that can read at 8x. Each major step in the process took between 10 and 15 minutes. The total time will vary based on the speed of your DVD drive and the speed of your processor.

> If you didn't tell *dvdshrink* to remove working files, you will notice a number of interesting files in the output directory including *.m2v* and *.ac3* video and audio tracks, a final *.mpg* file for the movie, and a BUILD directory containing the final DVD filesystem. You can get extra use from these, for instance, to convert the video to a different format from the *.mpg* file.

Use a Digital Video Camcorder with Linux

With *dvdgrab* and Kino, you can pull video directly from your DV Camcorder and edit it.

One of the "killer applications" for the Apple Macintosh is iMovie. This application is designed to extract digital video from a camcorder or other source and easily edit it. I've been running a MacOS desktop for some time now, but really wanted to get this capability going on my Linux-equipped laptop so I could pull video out of my camcorder when my family and I are away on a trip. It so happens that Linux supports this use quite well, thanks to its excellent IEEE 1394 (Firewire) support and an application called Kino. Kino has all of the basic editing features of iMovie on the Mac, and is on par with iMovie for ease of use. Kino is missing some of the bells and whistles, but for standard editing tasks, Kino fits the bill nicely.

This was tested under Ubuntu Linux (Hoary Hedgehog release), kernel 2.6.10. It should also work with Debian Linux with little or no modification.

Here's what you'll need:

- A Digital Video (DV) camcorder with an IEEE 1394 (Firewire) port. Older Hi8 or Digital8 camcorders will not work with this hack.

- An IEEE 1394 cable to go from your computer to your camcorder. This could be a 4-pin or a 6-pin type connector on either end: be sure you've got the correct type connector for each end.

- The video-editing application Kino and its supporting command-line application *dvgrab*.

- The package *mjpegtools* if you wish to export your video to something other than DV format.

- A working 2.6 kernel with the following IEEE 1394 (Firewire) modules loaded:

    ieee1394
    ohci1394
    sbp2
    video1394
    dv1394
    raw1394
    cmp
    amdtp

Let's dig in a bit now and explain what each application does. *dvgrab* is a command-line program that does one thing and does it well—it pulls the DV stream out of your camcorder and saves it to your hard disk so you can edit it. Kino is the KDE-based GUI that provides all the editing features—it's like iMovie on the Mac. Kino also includes its own DV-capture routines; however, on CPU-challenged machines (like my 867 MHz Crusoe-powered laptop) it can occasionally drop a frame or mess up due to the added overhead. *dvgrab* has yet to drop a frame on me.

To start; verify that your kernel has all the required modules loaded:

```
$ lsmod | grep ieee1394
ieee1394 111416 7 amdtp,cmp,raw1394,dv1394,video1394,ohci1394,sbp2
```

If your line resembles the line above, your kernel and modules are ready to go. If not, use *modprobe* to load the above modules. If these modules don't exist, you may need to rebuild your kernel or grab a newer kernel from your distribution's package manager.

Next, we'll see if the device nodes exist: they should come into being when the module is loaded:

```
$ find /dev -name "*1394*" -exec ls -l {} \;
total 0
crw-rw---- 1 root video 171, 16 2005-07-24 13:08 0
crw------- 1 root video 171, 0 2005-07-24 13:08 /dev/raw1394
```

Note the permissions on */dev/raw1394*. This means I'll need to either **chmod** 660 */dev/raw1934* as root to give any user of the video group access to the node or run *dvgrab* under sudo.

Next; install *dvgrab*, Kino, and *mjpegtools* using your distribution's package manager. For instance, under Ubuntu, type:

```
$ sudo apt-get install dvgrab kino mjpegtools
```

Once these are installed, you're ready to begin processing video. We'll begin by using *dvgrab* to capture the video from your camcorder. Hook your camcorder to your PC using the Firewire cable, turn on the camcorder and cue up the tape to where you wish to begin capturing. Then run *dvgrab*:

```
$ sudo dvgrab --format raw testmovie
```

dvgrab will start your camcorder in play mode and begin capturing video to the filename *testmovie001.dv*. Since *dvgrab* is a command-line program, the only way to see where the capture is at is to monitor the camcorder's built-in screen. Once your capture has reached your desired endpoint, simply hit Ctrl-C to stop *dvgrab*.

Now that you've extracted your movie from the camcorder, it's time to fire up Kino. Once you start Kino (either via menu or command line), you'll see the window shown in Figure 3-6. If you're familiar with the Windows program VirtualDub, you'll feel right at home.

Once you load your *.dv* file by clicking on the Open icon, you can do basic editing on your video and can even add special effects! The key to using

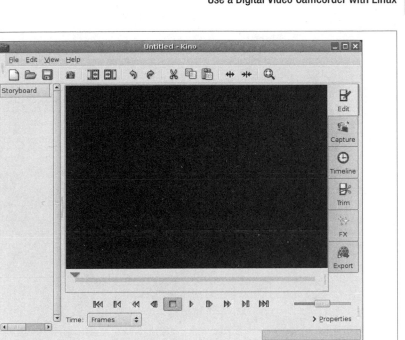

Figure 3-6. Kino default window

Kino is the six tabs along the right side—when clicked, the UI will change to fit whatever task you've selected. For example, Figure 3-7 shows Kino in Timeline mode with a movie loaded.

Kino's interface is very intuitive and easy to pickup. Spend some time playing with the edit functions, and you'll quickly see how easy it is to edit a video.

Kino'sreal strength is in the Export tab (see Figure 3-8). After you edit your movie and add any special effects, the Export tab allows you to export your video to any one of numerous formats. You'll probably use the MPEG tab under Export most often—this will let you export your movie to MPEG1, MPEG2, VCD, SVCD, or DVD formats. If you're exporting to DVD, Kino will automatically create an XML control file for use with *dvdauthor* and a DVD-compliant MPEG2 file.

With *dvgrab*, Kino, and some of the other tools described in this book, you should be able to create your own home movies on DVD **[Hack #70]**. If you have kids, home video DVDs make great Christmas gifts for nonlocal relatives—they'll get a chance to watch the kids grow up.

—Bill Childers

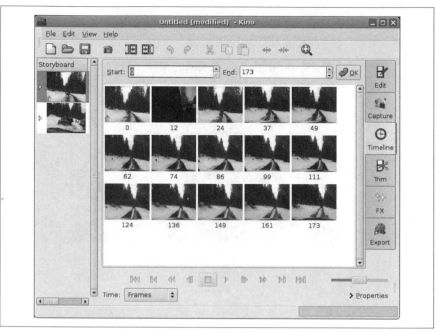

Figure 3-7. Kino in timeline mode

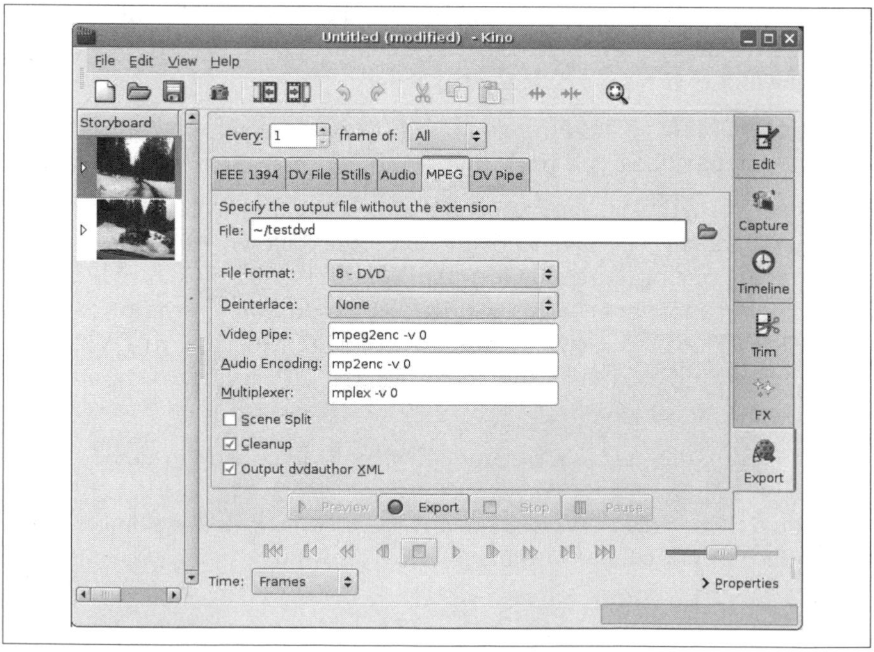

Figure 3-8. Kino's Export tab

Edit Video

#67

Cut and edit video from a number of formats with avidemux.

Like with other multimedia editing, video-editing tools usually fall into either the consumer or the professional user category. There are a number of video-editing tools under Linux, both command line or graphical, and consumer or professional. This hacks covers *avidemux*, a video-editing tool that is aimed at the consumer level and has plenty of features. I describe how to use this tool to perform basic video editing.

The first step is to download and install the *avidemux* software. This step varies based on your distribution, but visit the *avidemux* download page at *http://fixounet.free.fr/avidemux/download.html* and find the precompiled package for your distribution. If there is no precompiled version, then download the *.tar.gz* source from the site and follow the installation documentation at *http://fixounet.free.fr/avidemux/doc/en/install.xml.html* to install the software.

There are very few required libraries for *avidemux*: it requires GTK+ and glib2.x, *libmad*, *libxml2*, and *nasm*—all software that should be readily available on any major Linux distribution. Apart from that, other libraries are optional and only serve to increase *avidemux's* support for various video and audio formats. **[Hack #53]** explains how to find and install various extra codecs and libraries for your computer.

Once *avidemux* is installed, launch it from a menu or type **avidemux** from a console. The default interface has a lot of widgets, but for general video editing we only need a few of them. First, click File → Open and choose the video you wish to edit from the dialog box. *avidemux* will show you the first frame in the main section of the window. Along the bottom of the window are controls to navigate through the video. You can play through the video, skip through frames forwards or backwards, and set editing points. There's also a general slider bar you can drag to quickly move through the video.

> The first time you open an MPEG file, you might be prompted to index the file so that *avidemux* can keep track of where it is. Say yes to create an *.idx* file *avidemux* can use while editing.

With the file open, now is the time to start editing. Editing in *avidemux* involves finding a frame you want to cut, copy, or delete using the slider or frame skipping buttons, and then setting the beginning (Marker A) or ending (Marker B) editing point. Click Edit → Set Marker A to set the starting edit point, move to the end of the section you want to edit, and then click

Edit → Set Marker B. Once you've set the A and B markers, you need to tell *avidemux* what you want to do with that selection. All of the editing controls are under the Edit menu, so you can cut, copy, paste, and delete all from this menu. You also can set markers in reverse: just move to the end of a section of video to set marker B first, then move to the beginning and set marker A.

avidemux supports editing only a single track of video at a time, so if you want to add sections from another video, click File → Append Video and choose the video from the dialog box. That video will be appended to the current one, and you can then cut and paste from the combined video. You can, however, add a second audio track (so you could, for instance, add a sound track to a home movie). To add a second audio track, click Audio → Second Audio Track → MP3 File or choose AC3 file if you have audio in that format. Alternatively, you can use audio from a different file to replace the current audio track from the video. Click Audio → Source → External MPEG (MP2/MP3) to choose a different audio track. You can also choose the audio track from WAV or AC3 files.

To start playback of the current video, click Play → Play Video (or the Play button in the main window). You can't skip around in the video while in playback mode, so be sure to move where you want to play beforehand.

When you are ready to save the finished product, it is time to configure the final output. If you are fine with the *avidemux's* defaults, just click File → Save → Save Video and choose a filename for the output video. Otherwise, you can edit the output video and audio formats from the sidebar in the main window. *avidemux* supports a number of audio and video output formats provided you have the corresponding libraries installed. To change which video codec it uses, click the first drop-down menu under the Video header and pick the output format from the list. If you want to resize the video to VCD, SVCD, or DVD resolutions, click the V Filter button and select the resize option you want from the window that appears. Repeat this process for audio options under the Audio header. Finally, choose the container format you want to use under the Outp. fmt header. Then click File → Save → Save Video to start the video conversion process. *avidemux* will show a progress bar as it runs through the different encoding and other steps it must perform to save the file.

If you want to save your work as a project that you can open up later, click File → Project → Save Project and choose a filename for your project. To open that project later, start *avidemux* and then click File → Project → Open Project.

Resize a Video

#68 Use the powerful transcode utility to resize videos completely from the command line.

Normally, I don't find myself resizing videos. After all, you end up losing video quality if you lower the resolution, and usually I want to watch a video in the highest possible quality. However, there are certain instances where it can be useful to resize a video. One main reason people resize videos is simply to lower the file size. Each pixel in a video takes up space, so resizing a video is one good method for lowering the file size. Also, more and more portable devices are now supporting video playback. Since these devices often have screen resolutions of 640×480 or lower, they don't typically support playback of videos larger than their native resolution.

transcode is a versatile tool when it comes to video conversion, and [Hack #63] provides examples of conversions between video codecs using *transcode*. This hack takes that process a step further and uses *transcode's* video-resizing options. Because this hack uses *transcode* exclusively, you will definitely need to install it on your system. [Hack #63] explains *transcode* installation.

There are three primary arguments that *transcode* uses to resize video: -B, -X, and -Z. The -B and -X options are complementary—the -B option shrinks video resolution while -X increases video resolution. Both options perform a fast resize on the video, but have some rather particular requirements to use. The main requirement is that the resolution of the input and output files be a multiple of eight for *transcode's* fast-resizing algorithm. Although the algorithm is a bit less precise than the one used with -Z by default, it is substantially faster.

Both -B and -X arguments have the same three options; you can pass them separated by commas. The first option is the amount to resize the height of the image in rows, the second option is the amount to resize the width in columns, and the third option is 8, 16, or 32 (use whichever number works for your resolution). The rows and column values are calculated by multiplying the number you specify with the third option, so if you passed *transcode* the following command, it would increase the height by 96 (12 * 8) and the width by 128 (16 * 8):

```
-X 12,16,8
```

It seems a bit tricky at first, but once you calculate a few times, you get the hang of it. So, if I had a 512×384 video that I wanted resized to 640×480, I would type:

```
$ transcode -i input.avi -o output.avi -y xvid -X 12,16,8
```

Even with fast encoding, *transcode* will take some time to resize a file. *transcode* will output its progress so you can at least keep track of where it is in the encoding process. Note that both the input and output file resolutions are multiples of eight. Also note the -y argument. This option tells *transcode* what format to use for the output file (in this case XviD) and is required. Without this option *transcode* will use the null output format, which writes nothing. What argument you pass -y depends on the output format you want to use, and [Hack #63] covers the video format options at your disposal.

Now that I have a 640×480 *output.avi*, I can also resize it back to 512×384 with the -B option. Since the relative sizes haven't changed, all I have to do is switch -X with -B:

```
$ transcode -i output.avi -o output2.avi -y xvid -B 12,16,8
```

Of course, having to perform all those calculations whenever you want to resize isn't too much fun, but *transcode* has that covered as well. The -Z option allows you to simply specify the output resolution to use. *transcode* will then perform all the necessary calculations for you. You can even leave out one component of the resolution and *transcode* will calculate the appropriate value using the aspect ratio it imports from the video file. An added benefit is that you can choose resolutions that aren't divisible by eight, but the downside is that *transcode* no longer uses its fast-resizing algorithm, so the process will take longer.

To perform the same image resize as the previous example, only with -Z, I would type:

```
$ transcode -i input.avi -o output.avi -y xvid -Z 640x480
```

I could also say -Z 640x (x after the value for width) or -Z x480 (x before the value for height) and *transcode* will figure out the rest. The -Z argument also provides a fast option. This option actually will calculate the -B or -X arguments for you automatically and then perform the resizing operation with that algorithm. Since it uses the fast resizing algorithm, you still need to make sure that your input and output resolutions are divisible by eight. So to resize the video from 512×384 to 640×480 with fast resizing, I can just type:

```
$ transcode -i input.avi -o output.avi -y xvid \
-Z 640x480,fast
transcode v0.6.14 (C) 2001-2003 Thomas Oestreich, 2003-2004 T. Bitterberg
[transcode] (probe) suggested AV correction -D 0 (0 ms) | AV 0 ms | 0 ms
[transcode] auto-probing source input.avi (ok)
[transcode] V: import format    | XviD RIFF data, AVI (V=ffmpeg|A=mp3)
[transcode] V: import frame     | 512x384  1.33:1
[transcode] V: fast resize      | Using -B 0,0,8 -X 12,16,8
```

```
[transcode] V: new aspect ratio | 640x480   1.33:1 (-X)
[transcode] V: bits/pixel       | 0.244
[transcode] V: decoding fps,frc | 23.976,1
[transcode] V: Y'CbCr           | YV12/I420
[transcode] A: import format    | 0x55    MPEG layer-3 [48000,16,2]  132
kbps
[transcode] A: export format    | 0x55    MPEG layer-3 [48000,16,2]  128
kbps
[transcode] V: encoding fps,frc | 23.976,1
[transcode] A: bytes per frame  | 8008 (8008.000000)
[transcode] A: adjustment       | 0@1000
[transcode] V: IA32 accel mode  | sse2 (sse2 sse mmxext mmx asm C)
tc_memcpy: using mmxext for memcpy
[transcode] V: video buffer     | 10 @ 640x480
[import_mp3.so] v0.1.4 (2003-08-04) (audio) MPEG
[import_ffmpeg.so] v0.1.11 (2004-02-29) (video)  FFmpegcvsb4753: MS MPEG4v1-
3/MPEG4/MJPEG
[export_xvid4.so] v0.0.5 (2003-12-05) (video) XviD 1.0.x series (aka API 4.
0) | (audio) MPEG/AC3/PCM
[import_mp3.so] MP3->PCM
[import_mp3.so] tcextract -a 0 -i "input.avi" -x mp3 -d 0 | tcdecode -x mp3
-d 0 -z 48000
[export_xvid4.so] Neither './xvid4.cfg' nor '~/.transcode/xvid4.cfg'
[export_xvid4.so] found. Default settings will be used instead.
[mpeg4 @ 0xb5b20008]frame skip 8
[mpeg4 @ 0xb5b20008]frame skip 8
tc_memcpy: using mmxext for memcpy
Audio: using new version
Audio: using lame-3.96.1
[encoder.c] Delaying audio (0)
encoding frames [000000-030396],  16.37 fps, EMT: 0:21:07, ( 0| 0| 0)
clean up | frame threads | unload modules | cancel signal | internal threads
| done
[transcode] encoded 30397 frames (0 dropped, 0 cloned), clip length 1267.81 s
$
```

Notice, near the top of the output, the line that says:

```
[transcode] V: fast resize      | Using -B 0,0,8 -X 12,16,8
```

Here you see the actual -B or -X arguments *transcode* calculated for you—which is handy for helping you understand how the numbers are calculated.

> In general, you might as well use the -Z option and attempt fast resizing. *Transcode* will simply error out and tell you that fast resizing isn't available for your input and output resolutions. Then you can either change the offending resolution to a multiple of eight or let *transcode* resize it without the fast option.

Create a VCD

HACK #69 Use the tovid scripts to automate the conversion of many video formats to VCD and SVCD.

Before DVD burners and media were relatively inexpensive, creating your own video DVDs was a daunting prospect. Many people (both professionally and personally) used VCDs (or Video CDs) instead, as the media and hardware were much cheaper. VCDs allow you to put a video on one or more CDs and watch them either in your computer or in VCD-compatible DVD players (most modern DVD players support VCD playback, if not SVCD playback). Even with DVD burners and media coming down in price, VCDs are still a popular format in a number of countries. This hack tells you how to convert your own video files into a VCD or SVCD.

Choose VCD or SVCD

There are a number of standards for video on CD. These standards include VCD, XVCD, SVCD, XSVCD, and others. Some of these formats aren't even official standards (i.e., they may not even play in a commercial DVD player) but are instead variations on a standard. For the purposes of this hack, I will use the two more widely used formats—that will most likely work in your DVD player—VCD and SVCD.

The primary differences between VCD and SVCD, on a basic level, are video and audio quality and compression. The VCD standard was created based on MPEG1 video with CBR (constant bit rate) audio. The VCD 2.0 standard supports MPEG1 videos at a 352×240 resolution at 29.97 fps (NTSC) or 352×288 at 25 fps (PAL).

SVCD is based on MPEG2 video with VBR (variable bit rate) encoding for audio. The result is a higher resolution for the video stream in the same space requirements. SVCD supports MPEG2 videos at 480×480 at 29.97 fps (NTSC) or 480×576 at 25 fps (PAL).

It may seem like the decision between the two formats is simple—go for the higher resolution SVCD format. If you are creating the (S)VCD primarily for your own use, and your DVD player supports SVCD (or you plan to play it on your computer) then yes, go for the higher resolution. However, if you plan on distributing your video to a number of people, you might want to go with the VCD format simply because it has much wider support in hardware DVD players.

Whatever format you choose, you need the VCDImager suite of tools to create the (S)VCD file structures to burn to CD. Even if you use a GUI tool such as K3b to burn the CD, these libraries and tools are used underneath.

To get VCDImager, either download precompiled binary packages from the official site at *http://www.vcdimager.org* or, if you use Debian, run **apt-get install vcdimager**. If precompiled binary packages aren't available for your distribution, download the latest source tarball from the official site and compile it according to the installation instructions.

Create (S)VCD-Compatible Video

So you have a video (or a number of videos) that you want to convert into a VCD. The first step is to convert that video into a format compatible with the VCD standard. Although you could use *mencoder* or *transcode* directly to perform this conversion, the number of options involved can quickly get complicated and confusing. Luckily a great tool, *tovid*, has been created to solve this problem. The tovid suite is a series of scripts, which automate the process of converting a video into a VCD. The scripts involved have basic easy-to-understand arguments and, because the output shows you the commands that are being executed, you can also use the scripts to learn more about the underlying process.

To install *tovid*, download the latest release from the official project page at *http://tovid.sourceforge.net*. The main tool in the suite is called *tovid* and uses *mplayer*, *mjpegtools*, *ffmpeg*, and *normalize* to perform the video conversion so you will need to have these packages installed beforehand. Once these requirements are met, download the latest release and untar it:

```
$ tar -xzvf tovid_0.18b.tar.gz
```

Now become root, enter the *tovid* source directory that tar created, and then run the configure script inside. This script automates the process of installing *tovid* on your system and once it completes, you are ready to start.

```
# cd tovid_0.18b
# ./configure
```

With *tovid* installed, now it's time to convert the video. The *tovid* arguments are pretty basic. The only wrinkle is that you need to decide whether to use NTSC or PAL formats and which aspect ratio to use for the video so *tovid* knows how to properly resize the video. Whether to use NTSC or PAL formats depends on where you live (or more specifically, what your TV uses). If you live in the United States, use NTSC. If you live in Europe or Japan, use PAL.

tovid supports full-screen (4:3), wide-screen (16:9) and theatrical wide-screen (2.35:1) aspect ratios through the -full, -wide, and -panavision options, respectively. Generally speaking, if you are creating a VCD of a home video or TV show, you will probably use -full (and this is what *tovid* uses by default if you don't specify the option). If the video source is from a movie, you will use -wide or -panavision depending on how wide the video is. If you are unsure, run the *idvid* utility that comes with the *tovid* suite on the video file to output the width and height of the video, and then divide the width by the height:

```
$ idvid sample.avi
--------------------------------
idvid video identification script
Version 0.18b
Written in 2004 by Eric Pierce
http://tovid.sourceforge.net/
--------------------------------
Gathering video information. This may take several minutes,
so please be patient...
=======================================================
                File: sample.avi
               Width: 640 pixels
              Height: 288 pixels
. . .
$
```

In this example the video aspect ratio is 640/288 or, basically, 2.35:1.

With all this figured out, now run *tovid* on the input video. In this example, I will create a NTSC VCD out of *sample.avi* with a panavision aspect ratio:

```
$ tovid -vcd -ntsc -panavision sample.avi output
```

This example would create a new VCD-compatible video called *output.mpg* in the same directory. As *tovid* runs, it outputs the various commands it is running and gives you a general idea on how long it will take to complete the task. On my 1.2 GHz CPU it takes between an hour and two hours to convert a video. To create an SVCD instead, simply use the -svcd argument instead of -vcd. If you have a video that is too long to fit on a single CD, *tovid* will automatically split the video along CD-sized boundaries for you.

If you have more than one video you would like to convert, you can use the *tovid-batch* command instead. *tovid-batch* takes the same arguments as *tovid*, except that you don't specify an output filename—*tovid-batch* will determine the output filename based on the input filename. So if you had a directory of full-screen *.avi* files that you wanted to convert to SVCD, you would run:

```
$ tovid-batch -svcd -ntsc *.avi
```

Notice I didn't specify -full. That's because -full is set by default in both *tovid* and *tovid-batch*. When *tovid-batch* completes, your directory will be full of VCD-compatible *.mpg* files.

Create the (S)VCD XML File

With your video in the proper format, you can create the (S)VCD file structure to burn to CD. (You can skip this entire step if you use K3b to burn the
CD.) Just launch K3b, click File → New Project → New Video CD project.
Drag and drop your video file(s) onto the bottom pane and then click Burn
to start the process. At this moment K3b does not perform any video conversion or validation on its own—all it will do is create the proper file structure
for the video file and burn it to the CD along with the video you created.

If you don't want to use K3b and instead want to stick to the command line
or use another burning tool, the next step is to create the VCD XML file.
This file describes the structure of the VCD and is used by *vcdimager* to create the actual VCD image and includes any menus you might want to have
in the VCD as well. *tovid* includes the *makexml* script to help automate this
process. To create the XML file for the video in the previous example, type:

```
$ makexml -vcd output.mpg output
--------------------------------
makexml
A script to generate XML for authoring a VCD, SVCD, or DVD.
Part of the tovid suite, version 0.18b
Written in 2004 by Eric Pierce
http://tovid.sourceforge.net/
--------------------------------
Adding title: output.mpg as title number 1
============================================
Done. The resulting XML was written to output.xml.
You can create the (S)VCD .bin and .cue files by running the command:
  vcdxbuild output.xml
Thanks for using makexml!
$
```

To create an SVCD-compatible XML file, replace -vcd with -svcd. The
makexml script supports other options as well, and Table 3-4 goes over
some. These options come into play if you want to add a menu system to the
VCD, but if you just want to play back the video you don't need them.

Table 3-4. makexml command-line arguments

Argument	Function
-menu *VIDEO*	Use video file *VIDEO* as a menu from which you can jump to each of the listed video files. If you have multiple menus, include a top menu so they are reachable.
-topmenu *VIDEO* [-menu *VIDEO*] [-menu *VIDEO*]...	Use video file *VIDEO* for the top-level (VMGM) menu. The top menu will jump to each of the subsequent [-menu] videos listed. Use this only if you have multiple sub-menus to jump to. You can only have one top menu.
-slides	Create a slide show of still images.

Create the BIN and CUE Files

As you might have noticed in the *makexml* output, the next command to run is *vcdxbuild*. This script actually generates the *.cue* and *.bin* files that make up the VCD image you will burn to CD (the cue file contains the file structure for the VCD and the bin file contains the actual video). The syntax is pretty simple, just pass *vcdxbuild* the name of your *.xml* file. *makexml* is nice enough to tell you the command to use, and in the case of my example I would type:

```
$ vcdxbuild output.xml
```

> I noticed on my VCD *.xml* file that the *makexml* script added an SVCD-only option tag:
>
> ```
> <option name="update scan offsets" value="true"/>
> ```
>
> When I ran *vcdxbuild* the first time, it complained "parameter not applicable for vcd type." If you run into this problem, compare the XML file to the examples at *http://www.videohelp.com/~vitualis/general_xml_structure.html* and make sure the options are valid for VCDs or SVCDs, depending on what you are making. I deleted the offending line and was able to run *vcdxbuild* at that point.

When *vcdxbuild* finishes, it will create a *videocd.bin* and *videocd.cue* file by default (change these with the -b and -c options, respectively). Now you are ready to burn to a CD.

Burn to a CD

The *.cue* file is actually a special set of instructions as to the structure of your VCD. A CD recording utility like *cdrecord* doesn't automatically know how to handle such a structure, so you need to use *cdrdao*, which can perform DAO (disk at once) recording, instead of TAO (track at once) like you might use with *cdrecord*. *cdrdao* is used by many other applications, so it might already be installed on your system, otherwise it is likely already prepackaged, so use your distribution's package manager to install it.

The *cdrdao* syntax is much like *cdrecord*. Tell *cdrdao* the device to use like you would with *cdrecord* or, on Linux, you can even specify the actual device (such as */dev/sr0* for instance). My system has a CD burner on */dev/hdc*, so to burn the VCD in the example, I type:

```
$ cdrdao write --device /dev/hdc videocd.cue
Cdrdao version 1.1.9 - (C) Andreas Mueller
. . .
Burning entire 79 mins disc.
Starting write at speed 8...
```

```
Pausing 10 seconds - hit CTRL-C to abort.
Process can be aborted with QUIT signal (usually CTRL-\).
WARNING: No super user permission to setup real time scheduling.
Turning BURN-Proof on
. . .
Writing track 01 (mode MODE2_RAW/MODE2_RAW )...
Writing track 02 (mode MODE2_RAW/MODE2_RAW )...
Wrote 615 of 615 MB (Buffers 100%  98%).
Wrote 274259 blocks. Buffer fill min 87%/max 100%.
Flushing cache...
Writing finished successfully.
$
```

Now pop your new CD into your DVD player and enjoy.

HACK #70 Create a DVD

How to create your own DVD under Linux with the tovid suite and a host of other utilities.

"Create a VCD" [Hack #69] discussed how to use the *tovid* suite to take a video of almost any format and convert it into a video suitable for a VCD or SVCD. You can also use this tool to create DVD-compatible video. The nice thing about this method is that you use largely the same tools for the task with a few variations when it comes to creating the final DVD file structure.

This hack assumes that you already have the *tovid* suite of tools installed. If you don't, follow the steps in [Hack #69] to download and install *tovid*. Much of the syntax to create a DVD-compatible video file is the same. First identify the aspect ratio of your video file. *tovid* supports full-screen (4:3), wide-screen (16:9) and theatrical wide-screen (2.35:1) aspect ratios through the -full, -wide, and -panavision options, respectively. Generally speaking, if you are creating a DVD of a home video or TV show, you probably will use -full (which is what *tovid* uses by default if you don't specify the option). If the video source is from a movie, you will use -wide or -panavision, depending on how wide the video is. If you are unsure, run the *idvid* utility that comes with the *tovid* suite on the video file to output the width and height of the video, then divide the width by the height:

```
$ idvid sample.avi
-------------------------------
idvid video identification script
Version 0.18b
Written in 2004 by Eric Pierce
http://tovid.sourceforge.net/
-------------------------------
Gathering video information. This may take several minutes,
so please be patient...
=====================================================
```

```
                    File: sample.avi
                   Width: 512 pixels
                  Height: 384 pixels
  . . .
  $
```

In this example the video aspect ratio is 512/384, or 4:3.

With the aspect ratio chosen, run *tovid* with the -dvd option to create the new DVD-compatible MPEG2 file:

```
$ tovid -dvd -ntsc -full sample.avi output
Probing video for information. This may take several minutes...
Input file is 512 x 384 at 23.976 fps.
Reported running time is 1267 seconds.
Source is not 29.970 fps. Adjusting to 29.970 fps.
Scaling and/or padding with letterbox bars
Scaling 512 x 384 directly to 720 x 480
The encoding process is estimated to require 886 MB of disk space.
You currently have 21396 MB available in this directory.
===========================================================
Testing mplayer stability with -vc dummy option:
Test succeeded!
Creating WAV of audio stream with the following command:
mplayer -quiet -vo null -ao pcm "sample.avi" -vc dummy -ao pcm:file=stream.
wav
===========================================================
===========================================================
Encoding WAV to ac3 format with the following command:
ffmpeg -i stream.wav -ab 224 -ar 48000 -ac 2 -acodec ac3 -y "output.ac3"
Audio encoding finished successfully
===========================================================
Creating and encoding video stream using the following commands:
nice -n 0 mplayer -benchmark -nosound -noframedrop -noautosub -vo yuv4mpeg -
vf-add pp=hb/vb/dr/al:f -vf-add hqdn3d -vf-add scale=720:480 "sample.avi"
cat stream.yuv | yuvfps -r 30000:1001 -n -v 0 | nice -n 0 mpeg2enc -M 2 -a 2
-f 8 -b 8000 -g 4 -G 11 -D 10 -F 4 -v 0 -n n -4 2 -2 1 -q 5 --keep-hf -o
"output.m2v"
```

If you have more than one video you would like to convert, you can use the tovid-batch command instead. tovid-batch takes the same arguments as tovid, except that you don't specify an output filename—tovid-batch will determine the output filename based on the input filename. So if you had a directory of full-screen *.avi* files you wanted to convert to DVD, run this:

```
$ tovid-batch -dvd -full -ntsc *.avi
```

Unlike with VCDs, K3b doesn't yet support creating Video DVDs directly from the MPEG files—it expects a complete VOB file structure. This means you need to create a proper *.xml* file to describe the DVD structure. Like with VCDs you can use the *makexml* tool to create an XML file that is compatible with the *dvdauthor* tool. *makexml* supports more options when used for DVDs.

Table 3-5 lists the DVD-specific options.

Table 3-5. makexml DVD options

Argument	Function
-group -endgroup	List of video files to include as one single title. This is useful if you have split a movie into several video files.
-titlesets	Forces the creation of a separate titleset per title. This is useful if the titles of a DVD have different video formats—e.g., PAL + NTSC or 4:3 + 16:9. If used with menus, there must be a -topmenu option that specifies a menu file with an entry for each of the titlesets.
-chapters *n*	Creates a chapter every n minutes within the video. This option can be put at any position in a file list and is valid for all subsequent titles until a new -chapters option is encountered. Using this option may take some time, since the duration of the video is calculated.

These options are generally for special cases apart from the last option. By default *makexml* won't define chapters in your DVD, which means you won't be able to easily skip through. To add chapters, use the -chapters option and specify an interval such as five or ten minutes. That way you can more quickly skip through the DVD. To create an XML file for the example with a chapter every five minutes type:

```
$ makexml -dvd -chapters 5 output.mpg output
--------------------------------
makexml
A script to generate XML for authoring a VCD, SVCD, or DVD.
Part of the tovid suite, version 0.18b
Written in 2004 by Eric Pierce
http://tovid.sourceforge.net/
--------------------------------
Adding title: output.mpg as title number 1 of titleset 1
Calculating the duration of the video using the following command:
idvid -terse "output.mpg"
This may take a few minutes, so please be patient...
The duration of the video is 00:21:07
Closing titleset 1 with 1 title(s).
============================================
Done. The resulting XML was written to output.xml.
You can create the DVD filesystem by running the command:
   dvdauthor -x output.xml
Thanks for using makexml!
```

With the XML file created, the next step is use *dvdauthor* to create the DVD filesystem. *dvdauthor* has a number of options you can use to create special DVD filesystems, but since *makexml* has already done the work for us, you can just pass it to *dvdauthor* as an argument. *makexml* also listed the appropriate command to use in its output, so to create a DVD filesystem for our example, type:

```
$ dvdauthor -x output.xml
```

```
DVDAuthor::dvdauthor, version 0.6.11.
Build options: gnugetopt magick iconv freetype fribidi
Send bugs to

INFO: Locale=en_US
INFO: Converting filenames to ISO-8859-1
INFO: dvdauthor creating VTS
STAT: Picking VTS 01

STAT: Processing output.mpg...
STAT: VOBU 3184 at 529MB, 1 PGCS
INFO: Video pts = 0.178 .. 1268.077
INFO: Audio[0] pts = 0.178 .. 1267.506
STAT: VOBU 3194 at 530MB, 1 PGCS
INFO: Generating VTS with the following video attributes:
INFO: MPEG version: mpeg2
INFO: TV standard: ntsc
INFO: Aspect ratio: 4:3
INFO: Resolution: 720x480
INFO: Audio ch 0 format: ac3/2ch, 48khz drc

STAT: fixed 3194 VOBUS
INFO: dvdauthor creating table of contents
INFO: Scanning output/VIDEO_TS/VTS_01_0.IFO
```

dvdauthor will create a directory named *output* and store the *AUDIO_TS* and *VIDEO_TS* DVD filesystem there. If you want to test the DVD before you burn it, you can use *mplayer* to play from the filesystem on the disk with the -dvd-device option:

```
$ mplayer dvd://1 -dvd-device output/
```

This command plays the first title from the DVD filesystem under the *output* directory. If you want to play a different title specify it on the command line.

Now it's time to burn the file structure to DVD. If you use K3b just open it, click File → New Project → New Video DVD Project. Find your DVD filesystem in the top pane and then drag and drop the files inside the *AUDIO_TS* (if any) and *VIDEO_TS* directories into their respective directories on the bottom pane. Then click the Burn button to set the DVD-burning options and, finally, to burn the filesystem to DVD.

If you want to burn the DVD from the command line, you need to install *dvdrtools*, which is a fork of the *cdrecord* utility that is designed to support recordable DVD drives. *dvdrtools* is prepackaged in many newer distributions or, alternatively, you can download the source and build it yourself from the official site at *http://www.nongnu.org/dvdrtools*.

Once *dvdrtools* is installed, the first step is to use the included *mkisofs* utility to create a DVD image out of your file structure:

```
$ mkisofs -dvd-video -udf -o dvd.iso output/
```

With the *dvd.iso* file created, the last step is to use *dvdrecord* to record the *.iso* file to disk. Most of the *dvdrecord* options will mirror the options you would use with *cdrecord*, so reference [Hack #39] for more on *cdrecord* configuration. For my system, I would type:

```
$ dvdrecord -dao speed=2 dev=ATA:1,0,0 dvd.iso
```

With the DVD created, pop it in your DVD player and test your results.

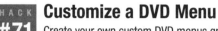

Customize a DVD Menu

#71   Create your own custom DVD menus graphically with DVDStyler.

[Hack #70] covers the basics for converting a video into a DVD-compatible format. Although a DVD that jumps directly into the video can be fine, sometimes you'd like to add menus and other custom touches to your DVD. In the past, if you wanted to do something like this, it meant digging through *dvdauthor*-compatible XML files. Although you can still do it that way (masochist), there are easier options. In this hack I cover how to create your own custom DVD menu using the DVDStyler graphical tool.

DVDStyler is a cross-platform DVD authoring tool that can manage multiple menus, offers drag-and-drop functionality for menus, video, and buttons, and allows you to set chapters for each of your movies. Under Linux it acts as a frontend to the *dvdauthor* tool and creates *dvdauthor*-compatible XML files behind the scenes. While DVD authoring can be a bit advanced, DVDStyler makes it reasonably simple for you to create a basic DVD menu for your movie without much prior know-how.

To get DVDStyler, go to the download page at the official site *http://dvdstyler.sourceforge.net*. Precompiled Debian packages are available there. Otherwise, download and compile the source according to the installation instructions. As I mentioned before, this program acts as a frontend to *dvdauthor* and other DVD creation tools under Linux, so be sure that *dvdauthor*, *mjpegtools*, *mkisofs*, and *growisofs* are installed on your system.

To start DVDStyler, type **dvdstyler** in a terminal. The main window is split into a row of tabs along the left side, then a frame for that tab, and finally a large square window to display your menu or window. Click File → New and choose between NTSC and PAL formats, depending on your television format. DVDStyler will start you off with a single solid black background on which to build your menu.

Add Video Titles

The first step is to add the video or videos you want to this project. DVD-Styler expects DVD-compatible MPEG files, so be sure to follow the steps in [Hack #70] to make your video DVD-compatible. To add a video, click on the Directories tab, find the video file in the directory tree, and drag it to the bottom row of the main window next to the main menu. Repeat for each video you want to add.

DVDStyler treats each video file as a separate title on the DVD, each with its own chapters. By default DVDStyler splits a title into different chapters at fifteen-minute intervals, up to an hour (0, 15, 30, 45, and 60 minutes into a video). To change this, right-click on the video file and choose Properties. In the window that appears (see Figure 3-9) you can change the chapter timings to suit your video. Generally you want to split up the chapters so that they are at similar intervals throughout your video. If you want to get precise, you can even set the chapter intervals to suit specific scenes in the movie. As you'll see later on, you can take advantage of chapter intervals in your main DVD menu to quickly jump to different sections of the video.

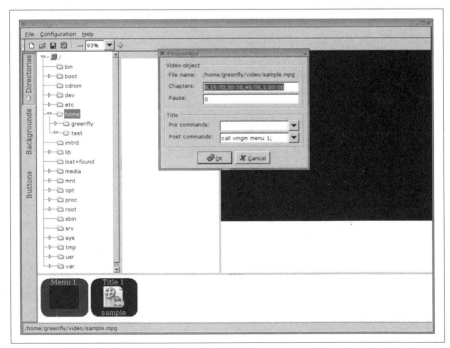

Figure 3-9. DVDStyler video properties

Design the Main Menu

The next step is to design your main DVD menu. Click on Menu 1 in the bottom row of the main window. If you want to set a different solid background color, right-click on the menu display in the main window and change the color settings from properties. If you want to set a background image instead, either click the backgrounds tab and choose one of the predefined backgrounds from there or click on the Directories tab, browse to a background image you want to use, and drag and drop it to the menu. Keep in mind that if the image isn't already in the right proportions, DVDStyler will stretch it to fit the standard NTSC or PAL DVD resolution. I often like to use a screenshot taken from my video as the background since it is already the correct proportion.

> You can add a short MPEG clip to be your background instead. Just create the DVD-compatible MPEG clip beforehand and then drag and drop it from the directories tab to the menu.

Add Buttons

With the background of the menu configured, now it's time to add buttons to the menu. Each button provides a navigation point you can use to play the main video, skip to a different chapter, or skip to a different title, or even skip to a different menu entirely if you set up multiple menus. Click the Button tab and then drag and drop the "button" in the sidebar over to your menu. You can place the button basically anywhere you want on the menu', so organize it to fit best with any background image you might have picked. After you place the button, right-click it and select Properties, and you can configure a number of settings for the button. The first option is which Action to perform when the button is clicked. By default, the button will play the first title of the movie when selected, so the Action is set to jump title 1; but if you want the button to skip ahead to the second chapter in the movie instead, set this to jump title 1 chapter 2; or replace 2 with the number of the chapter you want to skip to.

Next you can configure the text of the button, so pick something that describes what the button will do when pressed. If you don't like the default font, you can also configure that in this window. The next section of the button properties lets you configure what gets highlighted when you press left, right, up, and down on a remote control. The default is set to auto, which lets DVDStyler choose the optimal settings, but you can set this manually as well. Below that you can configure the different colors to use for the button.

Add as many buttons as you need to navigate through the movie, and when you are finished, click File → Save As to save your changes to a *dvdauthor*-compatible XML file. Once everything is set, you are ready to create the DVD.

Create the DVD

To create the DVD, click File → Burn DVD. The window that appears lets you configure where to store temporary files (make sure it's a directory with enough space to store a DVD's worth of content, and that DVDStyler can safely clear out the directory), the location of your DVD drive, and whether to create an *.iso* file or burn a DVD to disc. If the Preview option is selected, DVDStyler will open the newly created DVD directory in *xine* for you to test out before burning to DVD or creating an *.iso*.

As DVDStyler creates the DVD, it will display a progress window so you can see what it is doing every step of the way. When it is finished, be sure to save any final changes, and then click File → Exit to close the program. To resume a project later on, open up DVDStyler and click File → Open.

For more information on how to use the advanced features of DVDStyler, check out the complete manual on the official documentation page, *http://dvdstyler.sourceforge.net/docs.html*.

H A C K   Create Self-Booting Movies
#72   Make a video that will boot and play directly from CD.

I love my son and try to give him what he needs in life. Sometimes I even give him what he wants, too. He has a nice bike that he uses quite a lot, and he is always out and about. Of course he has his own PC, which is online 24/7 while he constantly surfs for sports car images. (For some strange reason, the teachers at his primary school think he's some sort of genius, as he's always telling them that Windows sucks and the TCO is much less when using Linux.) At times I think I let him have too much: I have let him play games on a Windows machine. Then, of course, at age 11 he broke my collarbone, and all I did was lecture him on his propensity for causing "incidents."

However, sometimes I put my foot down. One example involves my DVD collection. I don't trust him with those little discs of plastic and dreams. We sometimes have debates about what he's allowed to watch, and often he wants to take my DVDs to a friend's house, which I absolutely forbid. What's a father to do?

The answer is to make a self-booting CD copy of the DVD that he can watch on any PC. And that is where this hack comes in. It shows you how to reduce a DVD-length movie so it fits on a single CD—and to top it all off, it makes the CD bootable, so when you start a computer with the CD in the drive, it loads a very lightweight Linux OS with just enough software to play the movie on the CD.

Before diving into the guts of the hack, please keep in mind that I'm not suggesting you do anything illegal. I shudder to think that some evil person will impoverish an unassuming multinational corporation by depriving it of the opportunity to make a small profit off a piece of entertainment geared for the unwashed masses. That's why the United States has such wonderful laws protecting companies' rights. (Did I tell you that I live in Canada?) Instead, I implore you to use the following approach only for DVDs unencumbered by licensing issues.

The Tools

Creating a movie involves a few software and hardware considerations:

- The PC that plays the movie must have a CD reader as its primary boot-up device. To play the video without jitters it should have a Pentium III or better CPU.

- The PC used to create the movie must have a DVD reader, a CD burner, and at least 2 GB of free space.

Making these movie backup copies requires several distinct, free utilities, including:

- LAME, the MP3 encoder
- MPlayer, the premier movie player, which can also translate the DVD's native encoding to AVI
- *transcode*, a Linux text-console utility for video streams that includes a utility to break a large AVI file into smaller ones
- *eMoviX*, a mini live Linux OS burned onto a CD, which permits the CD to boot and auto-magically play its files with MPlayer
- *mkisofs*, which of course creates the ISO image
- *cdrecord*, the ubiquitous CD-burning software
- *growisofs*, for those people who have a DVD burner

This list looks pretty daunting, doesn't it? Just look at all those utilities that you need to create your movie.

Actually, you can make things work with very little knowledge by using one more utility that ties all the above together: *K3b* [Hack #62]. K3b is a CD- and DVD-burning application for Linux systems. It is optimized for KDE, but it will run with other desktop environments and provides a comfortable user interface for performing most disc-burning tasks.

The Moviemaking Routine

The basic process for creating this self-booting and playing miracle is:

1. Read the DVD and convert it into an AVI.
2. Break the completed AVI into files small enough to fit onto a CD.
3. Use K3b to create a new eMoviX project/CD for each AVI file.
4. Burn away.

Now let's start putting the pieces together.

Ripping the DVD Using MPlayer. Of all the utilities, MPlayer is not only the most critical but also the trickiest to set up and use correctly. For more information on how to get and use MPlayer, check out [Hack #48].

Ironically, for all MPlayer's complication, you can create your AVI with this simple incantation from the command line:

```
$ mencoder dvd:// -o temp.avi -ovc lavc -lavcopts \
vcodec=mpeg4:vhq:vbitrate=1800 -oac mp3lame -lameopts \
cbr:vol=3 -aid 128
```

Let's break down the above command:

- mencoder specifies the MPlayer command utility used to extract the video information from the DVD.
- dvd:// identifies the device from which the utility reads. You can also add a track number to use a track other than the default, at dvd://1.
- -o temp.avi is the name of the AVI file to create.
- -ovc lavc will use the *libavcodec* codec to compress the video data.
- -lavcopts vcodec=mpeg4:vhq:vbitrate=1800 provides further information to the *libavcodec* codec on constructing the resulting file.

  For the most part, you don't have to worry about this option. However, vbitrate=1800 is crucial to the screen size of the movie. This particular setting, for example, sets the whole screen for a 17-inch monitor. Reducing the number reduces not only the screen size but also the file size! Halving the number means you can fit 2 hours on one CD, rather than 1 hour. [Hack #60] explains *mencoder*'s bitrate settings.
- -oac mp3lame encodes the audio track to the MP3 format.
- -lameopts cbr:vol=3 sets the bitrate method and the volume input for LAME's sound encoding.
- -aid 128 chooses the audio stream (language) to use. DVDs often have more than one language sound track for a given recording. The number 128, for example, is the industry's identification number for the English language.

Normally, you don't need to worry about setting the audio stream because it defaults to English. However, I personally often use 129 for the French language sound track. I add the -alang fr country identification switch, too.

It's a good idea to test the command first, because the encoding process will take several hours. The most common encoding mistake involves recording the sound improperly, and you'll hate to find out you'll have to repeat the wait. Doing a test recording is pretty simple. Add the following switches to the earlier command invocation:

```
-endpos 30 -ss 00:10:00
```

This will cause MPlayer to record for a period of 30 seconds at about 10 minutes into the DVD recording.

There's often more than one track on a DVD. You might want to record something other than the first track. The easiest solution is to simply play the tracks until you find the one you're interested in. For example, **mplayer dvd://** plays the first track by default; **mplayer dvd://1** plays the first track explicitly; and **mplayer dvd://2** plays the second track explicitly.

There's more than one command incantation to create an AVI. It's all a question of experimenting with the different video and audio codecs. For example, you can restate the audio command so the audio stream is directly copied into the AVI without converting it to MP3:

```
$ mencoder dvd://1 -endpos 30 -ss 00:10:00 -o temp.avi -ovc lavc -lavcopts \
vcodec=mpeg4:vhq:vbitrate=1800 -oac copy -aid 128
```

This incantation will normally result in a 1.4 GB AVI.

Play back the ripped recording by running *mplayer*:

```
$ mplayer temp.avi
```

Breaking Up the AVI. The *transcode* suite of utilities is ideal for video-stream processing. That's exactly what we want to use here. For more information on how to install and configure transcode check out [Hack #63]. Once you have installed *transcode*, you can run the *tcprobe* utility on your newly created *temp.avi*:

```
$ tcprobe -i temp.avi
[tcprobe] RIFF data, AVI video
[avilib] V: 29.970 fps, codec=DIVX, frames=135989, width=720, height=480
[avilib] A: 48000 Hz, format=0x2000, bits=16, channels=2, bitrate=448 kbps,
[avilib] 9076 chunks, 254128000 bytes, CBR
[tcprobe] summary for temp.avi, (*) = not default, 0 = not detected
import frame size: -g 720x480 [720x576] (*)
```

```
frame rate: -f 29.970 [25.000] frc=4 (*)
audio track: -a 0 [0] -e 48000,16,2 [48000,16,2] -n 0x2000 [0x2000]
bitrate=448 kbps
length: 135989 frames, frame_time=33 msec, duration=1:15:37.504
```

transcode includes a utility called *avisplit* for splitting AVI files into chunks of a specified maximum size. This example command breaks *temp.avi* into chunks no larger than 640 MB apiece (a perfect size for CDs):

```
$ avisplit -s 640 -i temp.avi
```

In this case, it creates two files, *temp.avi-0000* and *temp.avi-0001*. Remember to check them out by playing little snippets at different points in the movie, say at the beginning and end of each file.

Creating the ISO. At this point you're ready to create the self-booting movie ISO. It'll take several utilities to do this, but using K3b makes it simple.

The first thing to do is to ensure that K3b sees all the requisite utilities, as seen in Figure 3-10. Launch the program, go to the Settings menu item, and click on the Configure option. You won't need all the utilities listed here, but you'll certainly require those listed at the beginning of this hack.

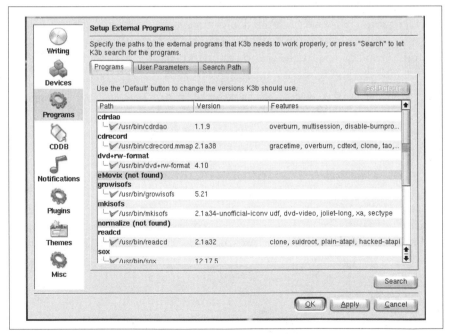

Figure 3-10. K3b external programs window missing eMovix!

Figure 3-11 shows a snapshot of a new eMoviX project. Choose the eMoviX project that suits the medium to which you are burning. You may have a DVD burner, but be sure to select a CD project if the recording medium is a CD-R.

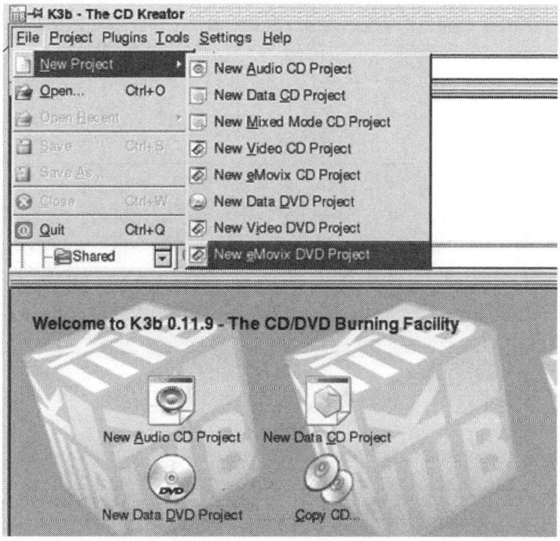

Figure 3-11. Creating a new eMovix project

Using K3b is a fairly intuitive process. When you run the program, you'll first see three panes. The top right one shows the files, defaulting to your home directory. From this pane you can navigate to the AVI files. Now drag and drop the first ISO image into the bottom pane. You can bring up the Burn window by clicking on the Burn icon, selecting Project → Burn from the menu, or pressing Ctrl-B to start the burn process. The Burn window, as shown in Figure 3-12, provides the opportunity to provide the information to include on your CD, as well as indicate how the movie should start and what should happen when it finishes. Take a minute to tab through the options: it's pretty cool what eMoviX can do.

I don't change much of anything except for the volume description and whether I want the system to eject the CD or shut down the system after the movie ends. When you're satisfied with your options, click on the Burn button to begin the burn process.

That's it, folks! Repeat the process for the next images until you have completed burning your CD movie.

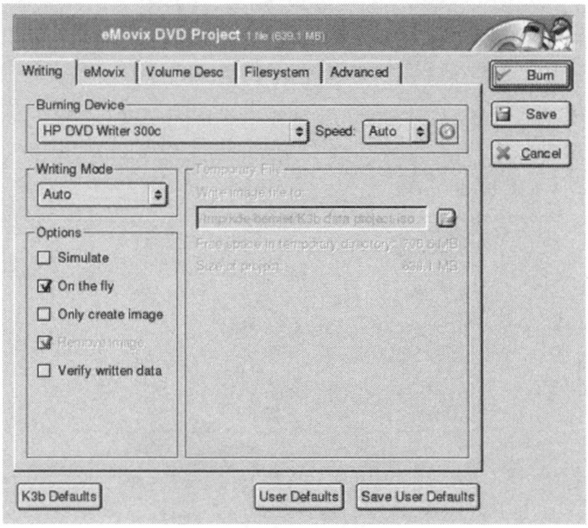

Figure 3-12. The K3b burn window

Using the CDs

Put the first CD in CD drive of any PC and boot the machine. The CD uses ISOLinux to boot a small Linux kernel, run MPlayer, and start up the movie file you have on the CD. When the movie ends on one CD of a multi-CD video, replace it with the next CD, and type **movix** in the console to start the next movie.

One More Trick

I like using an image from the movie as my label for the CD jewel case. I use MPlayer to screen capture an image:

```
$ mplayer dvd:// -ss 00:10:00 -vo jpeg
```

This example command will begin screen capturing several frames per second, beginning 10 minutes into the movie. You will end up with a collection of numbered JPEG images in the directory where you invoked *mplayer*. Press Ctrl-C as soon as you've collected enough images to choose from.

Now load them into your favorite graphics package. I use *display* from the ImageMagick graphics suite because I can load them all with one command:

```
$ display *.jpg
```

Select the one you would like to use, print it, fold the paper, and you're done.

—*Robert Bernier*

## CHAPTER FOUR

Broadcast Media
Hacks 73–88

If you have multimedia content you want to send to a lot of people (and you don't want to spam them) one of the best ways is through a broadcast. Traditionally broadcasts have been thought of in terms of television and radio and required expensive equipment and special expertise to set up and maintain. With the advent of the Internet, however, anyone with a fast enough connection can broadcast multimedia content for others with nothing more than a computer, some free software, and content worth broadcasting. The phenomenon of streaming radio over the Internet and more recently podcasting are examples of how low the bar has become for entry into broadcasting.

This chapter has a number of hacks that cover managing broadcast content using tools available under Linux. Both traditional broadcasting and Internet broadcasting are within your reach under Linux, and this chapter contains hacks to set up TV tuners and watch TV, as well as hacks to manage streaming radio and video broadcast to and from your computer. There is even a series of hacks that unleash the true broadcast management power of Linux by turning it into a full-featured personal video recorder, a la TiVo.

HACK
#73
Install a TV Tuner
Turn your Linux computer into a television set.

So you want to make your own digital video recorder (DVR) under Linux, or maybe you just want to watch TV on your computer. As long as the hardware is Linux-compatible, TV tuner installation under Linux really isn't too difficult for most cards. This hack fills you in on what you need to know to install a TV tuner under Linux.

Installation of the popular Hauppauge WinTV cards is covered in "Create a DVR with MythTV" **[Hack #77]**.

The first step is to identify the chipset and Linux module your tuner card uses. If you have a copy of the Linux kernel source tree on your system, look in its *Documentation/video4linux* directory. Here you will find *CARDLIST. bttv* and *CARDLIST.saa7134* files. Most common TV tuner cards will use the *bttv* driver, but check both lists and see if you can find your card. The *lspci* command can give you a clue about which card you have. For instance, here is the output for a machine with a *bttv*-compatible card:

```
# lspci
. . .
0000:00:0d.0 Multimedia video controller: Brooktree Corporation Bt878
Video Capture (rev 11)
0000:00:0d.1 Multimedia controller: Brooktree Corporation Bt878 Audio
Capture (rev 11)
```

Most modern distributions ship with very modular kernels, so there's a good chance that the *bttv* and *saa7134* modules are already compiled if you are using a stock kernel. If you built your own kernel, go to the Video For Linux section of your kernel config and make sure that Video For Linux support is enabled as a module as well as BT848 Video For Linux, Philips SAA7134 support, or whatever module corresponds to your particular chipset. Then recompile your kernel to create the new modules.

With your TV tuner card installed and Linux booted, load the module that corresponds with your tuner card as root. For this hack I will use the *bttv* module, since that's the most common:

```
# modprobe bttv
```

With the module loaded, type **lsmod** and ensure that the tuner module was loaded and, if not, load that as well:

```
# modprobe tuner
```

In your *dmesg* output, you should see quite a bit of output related to that module being installed:

```
# dmesg
Linux video capture interface: v1.00
i2c-core.o: i2c core module version 2.6.1 (20010830)
i2c-algo-bit.o: i2c bit algorithm module
bttv: driver version 0.7.108 loaded
bttv: using 4 buffers with 2080k (8320k total) for capture
bttv: Host bridge needs ETBF enabled.
bttv: Bt8xx card found (0).
bttv0: Bt878 (rev 17) at 00:0d.0, irq: 17, latency: 32, mmio: 0xdf040000
bttv0: detected: ATI TV Wonder/VE [card=64], PCI subsystem ID is 1002:0003
bttv0: using: ATI TV-Wonder VE [card=64,autodetected]
bttv0: enabling ETBF (430FX/VP3 compatibilty)
i2c-core.o: adapter bt848 #0 registered as adapter 0.
bttv0: using tuner=19
```

```
bttv0: i2c: checking for TDA9875 @ 0xb0... not found
bttv0: i2c: checking for TDA7432 @ 0x8a... not found
i2c-core.o: driver i2c TV tuner driver registered.
tuner: chip found @ 0xc0
tuner: type set to 19 (Temic PAL* auto (4006 FN5))
i2c-core.o: client [Temic PAL* auto (4006 FN5)] registered to adapter [bt848
#0](pos. 0).
bttv0: PLL: 28636363 => 35468950 .. ok
bttv0: registered device video0
bttv0: registered device vbi0
```

In this case, my *bttv* card is using */dev/video0*, and the *bttv* module was able to automatically detect the tuner type (tuner=19). Now add these modules to your */etc/modules* file so that they are loaded each time the system boots. If *bttv* isn't able to discover your tuner or card type, you can force the settings in */etc/modules.conf*. Look through *Documentation/video4linux/CARDLIST.tuner* and *Documentation/video4linux/CARDLIST.bttv* for the card and tuner number that corresponds to your card, and then add the options lines to */etc/modules.conf*:

```
options bttv card=64
options tuner tuner=19
```

> If your TV tuner has a line-out jack, be sure to connect it to the line-in on your sound card, and open your mixer and make sure the line-in isn't muted. Otherwise, you won't be able to hear any sound from the tuner.

Now that the card is installed, check out [Hack #74] for information on configuring it for various *video4linux* frontends.

Watch TV on Your Computer

#74

Choose from a variety of Linux programs to watch TV from your desktop.

Your TV tuner is installed, all the cables are connected, and the card is recognized by Linux, but how do you actually watch TV with it? This hack covers some of the Linux tools you can use to configure your TV tuner and watch TV with it from your Linux desktop.

The most basic program you can use to watch TV under Linux is *xawtv*, which started as an application specifically for the *bttv* driver, but since then has been expanded to work with *video4linux*, so you can use it with a number of tuners. *xawtv* is a good place to start when you want to test your tuner because it has been around for quite a while, so it is not only well tested, it also is likely to be packaged by your distribution. To install it, find the *xawtv* package in your distribution's package manager. If for some reason your distribution doesn't package it, download the latest version of *xawtv* from the official download page at *http://dl.bytesex.org/releases/xawtv* and follow the installation documentation to compile and install it.

With *xawtv* installed, you could just immediately launch it; however, no channel frequencies for your particular tuner have been configured yet, so you won't be able to tune into a channel. It's possible to configure everything by hand, but *xawtv* includes a utility called *scantv* that scans the tuner for available channels (much like the scan function on many car stereos) and generates a configuration file for *xawtv*. Open up a terminal and type:

```
$ scantv -o ~/.xawtv

please select your TV norm
0: PAL
    1: NTSC
    2: SECAM
    3: PAL-Nc
    4: PAL-M
    5: PAL-N
    6: NTSC-JP
    7: PAL-60
nr ? 1

please select a frequency table
    0: us-bcast
    1: us-cable
    2: us-cable-hrc
    3: japan-bcast
    4: japan-cable
    5: europe-west
    6: europe-east
    7: italy
    8: newzealand
 9: australia
   10: ireland
   11: france
   12: china-bcast
13: southafrica
   14: argentina
   15: australia-optus
   16: russia
nr ? 1

scanning channel list us-cable...
1    ( 73.25 MHz): no station
  . . .
```

Since I'm in the United States, I selected NTSC for the TV norm and us-cable as the frequency table. *scantv* then scans through every channel at that frequency table for valid channels and makes a note of any it detects. It then outputs everything into ~/.xawtv. Now start *xawtv*:

```
$ xawtv
```

There isn't much to the interface by default—just a basic window with no extra buttons. Table 4-1 lists keyboard shortcuts you can use to navigate through *xawtv*. Use the up and down arrows to move through the channels, and left and right keys to fine-tune the frequency of a channel if it's a bit off.

Table 4-1. xawtv key bindings

Key	Function
up/down	Tune up/down one channel.
left/right	Fine-tune.
pgup, spacebar / pgdown, backspace	Change the stations in the config file up/down.
Ctrl-up	Scan for the next station.
F5–F12	Adjust bright/hue/contrast/color.
Esc, q	Quit.
+/- (keypad)	Volume up/down.
Enter (keypad)	Mute.
f	Toggle full screen.
g	Grab screenshot (full-size *ppm*).
j	Grab screenshot (full-size *jpg*).
o	Options window.
c	Channels window.
r	AVI recording window.

To configure *xawtv*, right-click on the window and choose from the number of configuration options in the menu that appears. If you didn't run *scantv*, you can change the frequency table and TV norm from this menu instead. Remember to save your changes before you close *xawtv* so they will be there the next time you start.

Zapping

xawtv works fine, but it doesn't have much of a GUI. *Zapping* is a TV viewing program designed for the GNOME environment, but it will work on either GNOME or KDE. Zapping is already packaged for a number of distributions, so check with your package installation tool first, and if it isn't there, download and compile Zapping from the source package at *http:// zapping.sourceforge.net/cgi-bin/view/Main/Download*.

To start Zapping, launch it from your desktop menu or type **zapping** in a terminal window. Zapping will automatically scan for valid *video4linux* devices and connect to the first one found. You must initially configure which video standard to use, so click Channels → Video standards and choose your standard from the list (I'm in the United States, so I would choose NTSC). If you have more than one *video4linux* device in your computer, click Edit → Preferences to open the preferences window, and then click Devices → Video. You can change the video device to use from this window, and click Devices → Audio to change your audio device. One nice feature of Zapping is that it supports OSS as well as ESD and aRts audio output. The preferences window also lets you configure a lot of other general options such as keyboard shortcuts and on-screen display settings.

Next you need to configure the channels for your tuner device. Click Edit → Channels to bring up the channel configuration window. Choose your region from the region drop-down menu, and then click "Automatic station search" to let Zapping search for channels for you. Alternatively you can have Zapping load the channel information from a *xawtv* configuration file. In this window, you can also assign names for each of the channels and a key binding so you can quickly switch to a certain channel.

You can change channels in the main interface either with the buttons on the toolbar, or by pressing PgUp and PgDown. The + and - keys control the volume. You can even take a quick screenshot with the s key.

HACK #75 Output to a TV with NVIDIA Cards

Use two different methods to output your video to a TV. One method uses NVIDIA's special drivers and the other doesn't.

A general-purpose Linux computer has incredible potential for playing videos. You can play not only DVDs, VCDs, and SVCDs, but also any *.avi*, *.mpg*, or even Ogg Theora videos on your hard drive. Of course, sometimes your furniture isn't exactly arranged to watch movies on the computer, particularly with friends. In these cases it would nice to be able to output your computer display to your TV where you can more comfortably seat a group of people. Often support for TV-out under Linux is spotty, depending on the manufacturer, but with an NVIDIA card, you can pretty easily set up a cloned display on your television with either NVIDIA's drivers or output to TV with the *nvtv* utility. This hack covers how to set up both methods for TV out on modern NVIDIA video cards.

nvtv

nvtv is a program designed to talk to NVIDIA cards directly to enable their TV out modes. It doesn't require any special video drivers or kernel support, so it is a good choice if you don't wish to install NVIDIA's Linux drivers.

nvtv is packaged by most major distributions, so you can find and install it with your standard distribution package tool. If your distribution doesn't package it, download the precompiled binary tarball from the official *nvtv* page at *http://sourceforge.net/projects/nv-tv-out*. Since the files are already compiled, you can extract them from the package and copy them directly to a *bin* directory in your path. To do this, use the following command as root:

```
root@moses:~# tar xvzf nvtv-0.4.7-bin.tar.gz
root@moses:~# cd nvtv-0.4.7-bin
root@moses:~/nvtv-0.4.7-bin# cp nvtv nvtvd /usr/local/sbin/
```

Since *nvtv* directly accesses the video card, you will need to run the program as the root user (one reason to put it in an *sbin/* directory). Become root and type **nvtv** in a terminal to start the program. The main window has a number of tabs along the far left side that organize the different configuration options. The *nvtv* tab opens to the Mode page. *nvtv* defaults to the PAL TV system, so if you live in the United States, be sure to change modes to NTSC. Then choose which resolution to output to the TV, and which size. Try the Normal size first and see if it fully fits your TV screen; if not, try Small, Huge, or the other modes and see what fits the screen best. You can also tweak the position of the output on the TV screen from the Position page. The Mode page also allows you to output only a particular window instead of the full screen, so you can click X Select and then click on the window you want to display.

Once you have configured the *nvtv* window to suit your environment, click Apply and then click TV On (or hit F1) to output to the TV. Click TV Off (or hit F2) to toggle back to the desktop display.

NVIDIA X Drivers

If you have NVIDIA's proprietary drivers installed on your system, you might find that their method of TV output will work better for you. Installing and configuring NVIDIA's X drivers is outside the scope of this hack, but NVIDIA's documentation on the subject is thorough, so go to the official NVIDIA Linux driver page at *http://www.nvidia.com/object/unix.html*, click on the link to the latest driver, and then click on the link to the text README file from that page.

To add TV-out support to your NVIDIA driver, open your */etc/X11/XF86Config-4* or */etc/X11/xorg.conf* file and go to the Device section of the file where your NVIDIA card is configured, which will look something like the following:

```
Section "Device"
    Identifier     "Geforce2MX"
VendorName    "Unknown"
    BoardName     "Unknown"
    Driver     "nvidia"
    Option     "NvAGP" "1"
    Option     "NoLogo" "1"
    Option     "CursorShadow" "On"
EndSection
```

Don't worry if your configuration is somewhat different from this one; the main thing is that you are configuring the Device section for your current NVIDIA card. NVIDIA calls their particular multiple display support Twinview. While this is like Xinerama support under X, and even supports Xinerama extensions, it isn't Xinerama. To turn on this support add a few extra options to this configuration to turn on Twinview and Cloning support, and to tell the driver to output to the TV:

```
Option    "TwinView"
Option    "TwinViewOrientation" "Clone"
Option    "MetaModes" "1024x768,640x480"
Option    "ConnectedMonitor" "CRT, TV"
Option    "TVStandard" "NTSC-M"
Option    "SecondMonitorHorizSync" "30-50"
Option    "SecondMonitorVertRefresh" "60"
```

This config sets my CRT to 1024×768 while the TV is set to 640×480. You might want to set both displays to be the same resolution, particularly if you plan to run a program full-screen. In addition, I set the TVStandard option to NTSC-M, but refer to NVIDIA's documentation for all of the different PAL modes that are supported. Finally I set up the horizontal and vertical rates for my TV. Be sure to use conservative settings like these unless you know for sure that your TV can support higher frequencies. After all the additions have been made, the Device section should look like the following:

```
Section "Device"
     Identifier      "Geforce2MX"
VendorName     "Unknown"
     BoardName      "Unknown"
     Driver    "nvidia"
     Option    "NvAGP" "1"
     Option    "NoLogo" "1"
     Option    "CursorShadow" "On"
     Option    "TwinView"
     Option    "TwinViewOrientation" "Clone"
     Option    "MetaModes" "1024x768,640x480"
     Option    "ConnectedMonitor" "CRT, TV"
     Option    "TVStandard" "NTSC-M"
     Option    "SecondMonitorHorizSync" "30-50"
     Option    "SecondMonitorVertRefresh" "60"
EndSection
```

Now save your changes, log out of your desktop environment, and restart the X server either through GDM/KDM/XDM or by hitting Ctrl-Alt-backspace. X will start up with the display cloned on both your monitor and your television. If, for some reason, X doesn't start or isn't outputting to TV, check for clues at */var/log/XFree86.0.log* or */var/log/xorg.0.log*.

Cut Commercials

Use avidemux to quickly and easily cut commercials out of your recorded TV shows.

So you have set up MythTV [Hack #77], retrieved shows from your TiVo, or otherwise have some sort of television show in digital form on your computer. One nice feature of a VCR, TiVo, or other video recorder is the ability to quickly skip commercials in TV shows you have recorded. If you have recorded a show in digital format, you can certainly just fast-forward each time a commercial appears, but that requires extra work each time you watch the show. Also, with some time-based recording methods you end up getting a bit of the previous show and perhaps a bit of the next show in your recording in case your clock differs from the TV station's clock. If you plan to archive the show and watch it multiple times, you probably want to crop out all those commercials and bits from other shows. This is especially true if you plan on converting the video to VCD, SVCD, or DVD format, as discussed in [Hacks #69 and #70].

Now, before you get visions of sitting behind a huge sound board or in front of three monitors full of advanced video-editing software, let me say that cropping out commercials is *not* very difficult or time-consuming if you use the proper tools. After all, if it takes more work to crop the commercials than to watch them, what's the point? With the *avidemux* video-editing software, and particularly with its "Scan for black frames" feature, you can locate and remove commercials from your videos quickly and without much effort.

The first step is to download and install the *avidemux* software. This step will vary based on your distribution, but visit the *avidemux* download page at *http://fixounet.free.fr/avidemux/download.html* and find the precompiled package for your distribution. If there is no precompiled version, then download the *.tar.gz* source from the site and follow the installation documentation at *http://fixounet.free.fr/avidemux/doc/en/install.xml.html* to install the software. There are very few definite required libraries for *avidemux*, it mostly requires *GTK+* and *glib2.x*, *libmad*, *libxml2*, and *nasm*—all software that should be readily available on any major Linux distribution. Apart from that, other libraries are optional and only serve to increase *avidemux*'s support for various video and audio formats. Use [Hack #53] to find and install various extra codecs and libraries for your computer.

 avidemux also has been ported to OSX and Windows so you can crop commercials from those environments as well. Just download those binaries from the same download page.

Once *avidemux* is installed, launch it from a menu or type **avidemux** from a console. The default interface has a lot of different options but for your purposes you only need to use a few of them. First click File → Open and choose the video you wish to edit from the dialog box. A large number of video formats are supported, including DivX, Xvid, MPEG1 and MPEG2, Nuppelvideo, DV, and a number of other formats (a full list is available at *http://fixounet.free.fr/avidemux/doc/en/input.xml.html*). *avidemux* shows you the first frame in the main section of the window, and if you want you can even start playback from this interface.

The key to removing commercials in broadcast content is identifying black frames. Broadcasters usually use one or more black frames to separate commercials from the actual show or from each other, so if you can identify these frames you can use them as guide points for where to cut.

The simplest way to remove commercials from a program is chronologically. The following method also takes into account the fact that a commercial break might contain multiple sets of black frames in between individual commercials. Since your show probably doesn't have any black frames, it's easiest to move to different sections of the show, then move forward or backward to find black frames that signal new commercials.

The first step in the commercial removal process is to remove any commercials or other content from the beginning of the video so your video starts with the beginning of the show. This step is a bit easier than removing commercials from the middle of the video, so it's a good place to start. If your recording already starts at the beginning of the show you can skip this particular step. With the video you wish to edit open but paused, drag the bar along the bottom with your mouse to skip ahead until you find the beginning of your show. Now click Play → Search Previous Black Frame (or click the corresponding button on the bottom toolbar) and *avidemux* will scan backwards through the video for a black frame. Once it finds the black frame, click Edit → Set Marker B or press]. This sets the end marker for where to cut. Now move the slider to the very beginning of the video and click Edit → Set Marker A or press [. This sets the beginning marker for where to cut. Now hit the Delete key and *avidemux* will delete all the frames in between the two markers, leaving you at the beginning of your show.

Now you are ready to remove any commercials that are within the show. Skip ahead a few frames in the show so you are definitely on a non-black frame, then click Play → Search Next Black Frame. *avidemux* will skip through the program and find the next black frame. Set the opening marker (Edit → Set Marker A) and then drag the slider to skip ahead through the commercials. While you could just skip to the next black frame, often there are black frames between commercials so this is a timesaver. Skip through the commercials with the slider until you see your show again. Now click Play → Search Previous Black Frame to find the end of the commercials, then set the closing marker (Edit → Set Marker B), and press Delete to remove all of the frames between the markers.

Repeat the previous step until you reach the end of the show. If there is commercial content past the end of the credits, just seek to the black frame, set an opening marker, then skip to the end of the video, set the closing marker, and delete. After your video is all edited, click File → Save → Save Video to save your changes. Once you get some practice, you'll find you can remove commercials from your shows rather quickly.

HACK #77 Create a DVR with MythTV

Turn any reasonably modern computer it into an open-source digital video recorder that rivals and even surpasses a TiVo in features.

People are busy and can't always be at home when their favorite show comes on. You could rearrange your life so you'll always be at home during the primetime broadcasting hours, but why bother? You've heard of a TiVo right? That magical appliance known as a DVR that digitally records all of your television shows and is much easier to figure out than a VCR. Well, now you can create your own TiVo using a computer and the free software program called MythTV. Although the instructions in this hack apply specifically to Fedora Core 4, a Linux user with just a modest amount of experience should be able to adapt these instructions to install and configure MythTV on most any distribution.

The Hardware

One of the most frequent questions asked by people wanting to build their own DVR is what hardware they'll need. Most people assume there is a magic bullet combination of hardware that is vastly superior to all others, but that simply isn't true. The hardware you need for your MythTV system really depends on your budget, your needs, and your own personal sense of taste. To find out about hardware other people have used to build their systems, visit the PVR hardware list found at *http://pvrhw.goldfish.org/tiki-pvrhwdb.php*.

The following list gives you a few more specific guidelines:

Processor
> Your processor needs to be fast enough to decode the video playback stream. This usually means a Pentium III or better processor that is 500 MHz or faster. Either AMD or Intel processors are just fine, even in 64-bit form, but you would be wise to avoid the VIA processor family,

because it generally lacks the oomph necessary for the task. The faster your processor, the better the playback and the more actions your MythTV system can perform at a time. For example, if you are using a *bttv*-based capture card as explained in [Hack #73], you will need at least a 1 GHz processor if you expect to watch live TV and timeshift. However, if you use a Hauppauge WinTV card, as suggested in this hack, you can use a slower processor because the Hauppauge card performs the video encoding work for you, thus freeing your processor for other tasks, such as decoding for playback. Also, a fast processor will compress video more quickly (this includes compressing ripped DVDs and CDs) and finish scanning for commercial breaks within minutes of when the recording stops.

Memory

MythTV is not a memory-intensive program, and there is little to be gained having more than 256 MB, but additional memory could be useful if you are running multiple encoders.

Hard drives

You don't need the fastest hard drive with the largest cache, but you probably do want one with a high storage capacity. Any P-ATA or S-ATA 5,400 rpm drive or better should be up to the task. The amount of space taken by a recording varies depending upon the capture card, the resolution and bitrate of your recording, and the encoding scheme, but don't be surprised to see file sizes of 1 GB or more per hour of recording. If you are using an HDTV capture card (not covered in this book) you may see rates as high as 7 GB per hour of recorded video! Many people set up their video recording directory on a Linux Volume Manager partition so they can add more drive space at a later date. Also, many people favor Seagate and Hitachi drives as they are known to be quieter than other offerings.

Video card

Since you'll be sending your output to your TV, you need a video card with TV-out capability. Many people favor the NVIDIA cards that are fully covered in [Hack #75]. You may be tempted to get an ATI All-in-Wonder card, which has a video-capture ability as well as TV-out, but all the features of these cards are not yet well supported in Linux so I don't recommend it.

Capture card

As explained in "Install a TV Tuner" [Hack #73], a capture card is the device that enables you to tune into TV broadcasts and capture the stream into a format useable by your computer. In this hack I suggest you use a Hauppauge WinTV capture card of the 150/250/350 or 500 series. These cards have a built-in encoder ability, which converts the raw broadcast into

MPEG2, thus relieving your processor of the duty of encoding the video. These cards come with a decent remote, and are well supported in MythTV—and the 500 series card even comes with two tuners! If you want to capture HDTV broadcasts you need to use a card which supports HDTV, such as those found at *http://www.pchdtv.com*.

Motherboard

Your choice of motherboard is usually determined by the processor brand and model you are using, the size your case will support, and the number of PCI slots you need to fit your capture cards. This means that if you want the ability to record three shows at a time but you only have single-tuner capture cards, you'll need at least three PCI slots. Though this requirement is easily met with an ATX motherboard, it might be difficult to meet with a micro-ATX ina slim form factor case.

Case

The case you choose for your MythTV project is your chance to make a style statement. Some people opt for basic tower cases that are hidden away behind the TV or in another room. Other people prefer stylish cases that can be placed on the A/V rack and look at home with the receiver and VCR. The Silverstone and Ahanix cases are quite popular.

Sound

Pretty much any sound card supported by the ALSA project will work well with MythTV. You can output your sound, analog or digital, to your receiver and have that device interface with your speakers. One reason the Hauppauge capture cards are better than most is they have integrated audio capabilities, which eliminates the need to have a sound card matched to each tuner.

You can purchase your computer hardware most anywhere, but two popular sites are *http://www.pcalchemy.com* and *http://www.newegg.com*.

The hardware used in this hack is a reasonably powerful 933 MHz Pentium III system with 256 MB of RAM, a GeForce 4 MX video card, a Hauppauge WinTV PVR-250 tuner card with remote control, and a 120 GB hard drive.

The Basic Steps

Before launching into the details of how to set up your MythTV system, here's a basic rundown of the steps involved:

1. Assemble your computer. This is obviously needed and I'm not going to cover this in the hack itself.

2. Install a Linux distribution with a minimal feature set. This hack uses Fedora Core 4, but other distributions could certainly be used.

3. Install MythTV and related software. If you use a different distribution, you'll need to use its package management tools to install the needed software, but configuration of the system should basically be the same as outlined here.

4. Configure your hardware, particularly your capture, sound, and video cards. You can optionally configure your remote at this time, but it is really a step that can be visited whenever you want.

5. Create the MythTV database.

6. Create a Zap2It account so you can retrieve program-listing data.

7. Run the MythTV setup program and configure it for your capture card and cable or broadcast network.

8. Populate the database with your program guide data.

9. Set up your system to output to a TV instead of a monitor.

10. Do the final tweaks to MythTV and your system to ensure smooth, minimal maintenance operation.

Without further ado, here are the specific steps you need to set up MythTV.

Install Fedora Linux

To start, you need to install Linux on the computer. While MythTV packages exist for multiple distributions, for this example, I'm using Red Hat's latest community release, Fedora Core 4. Note that for successful completion of this task, you'll also need an Internet connection, and the faster the better, because there's a fair amount to download. Start out with your system hooked to a regular monitor, but with the intention of connecting it to an analog television set when you've got everything all set up.

> A lot of the instructions for setting up MythTV that you find on the Internet show you how to configure it for different desktop environments and window managers. Traditionally, MythTV was run with KDE, but in this hack, we'll set it up with GNOME.

You can obtain disc images for Fedora Core 4 from your friendly neighborhood Red Hat download mirror, which you can find by visiting *http:// fedora.redhat.com/download/mirrors.html*. For simplicity's sake, perform a clean installation of a simple Personal Desktop install (which requires only the first two of the four FC4 CD images), but when you get to the partitioning section, select custom partitioning scheme "Manually partition with Disk Druid" so you can carve out a sizable dedicated partition for MythTV's video storage. On the example system above, I created a 100

MB */boot* partition, a 256 MB swap partition, a 10 GB / partition, and allocated all remaining space to a */video* partition, which is where I'll tell MythTV to place all recordings.

 Later in the install, you'll have the option to customize your "to be" installed package selection. This is a good chance to remove any extra desktop packages you really don't think you'll need, such as Evolution or OpenOffice.org.

Your choice of filesystem does make a difference with MythTV, and you will most likely want to choose a journaled filesystem. ext2 is non-journaled, so in the event of a system crash and subsequent reboot, it will scan through all of the files on your */video* partition to verify their integrity. Considering that most files will be in the gigabyte range, this can take a very long time on large partitions. Your best choice is to pick either ext3, XFS or JFS. ext3 is not as good a performer when it comes time to deleting files as other filesystems—XFS and JFS are very good at deleting multi-gigabyte files, but ext3 will most likely have better support from your distribution. XFS and JFS may not even be install-time options for you. In the example above, you may need to leave the final 100 GB */video* partition unformatted until after your system has been installed, at which point additional tools such as *xfsutils* and *jfsutils* will be available for you to complete the task.

Many users opt to manage their */video* partition with LVM, which will later allow them to expand the partition over multiple disks without the need to reformat the original */video* partition.

I highly recommend that you configure a static IP address to your MythTV box, since changing addresses on the fly can have bad side effects, especially if you intend to have multiple MythTV boxes running as a cohesive system at some point. I also recommend disabling both the firewall and SELinux, at least for your first try, to minimize possible problems that might hinder your progress. Finally, you'll want to make sure to properly set the time zone for your machine, so that your programming guide data will match up with reality (otherwise, you'll end up recording the wrong programs). Now allow the installation to complete, and then restart your machine.

Configure Fedora

Upon restarting your machine, you'll be greeted by Fedora's *firstboot* utility. The first page of importance to your setup is the Date and Time page. You've already set the time zone, but now you need to set your clock to synchronize with an Internet time server.

This step is important to ensure clock accuracy. If you don't set this up, your system clock might drift, and you could quickly start to see recordings ending before the crucial final minutes of your favorite shows! Try to set the time as accurately as possible on the Date and Time tab, and then click over to the Network Time Protocol tab. On that tab, click the Enable Network Time Protocol checkbox. The provided time servers should be sufficient for your needs.

Continuing on, *firstboot* will now ask you to set up your display. Just opt for 1024×768 for the moment. At this point the resolution isn't a big deal, since you're only running on this display temporarily—you'll reconfigure everything for your TV later. Next, *firstboot* prompts you to create a normal user account. Create a user named mythtv, which you'll use to run MythTV. You'll also be prompted to test your sound card, so go ahead and make sure that's working. Click the rest of the way through *firstboot*, and then watch as your system finishes starting up.

Once you've been greeted by the Fedora Core login screen, log in to the system as the user mythtv. You'll make heavy use of your terminal application for much of the setup process, so click Applications menu → System Tools → Terminal to launch it.

Update Fedora

Generally, you ought to start out by applying all released errata updates. You can short-circuit this step if you want to save a bit of time by not downloading and applying all available updates to your system. However, if you've got the time and bandwidth, it's definitely a good idea. You can use either the *up2date* utility (click the flashing red circle with the exclamation mark in your tool bar), or the command-line *yum* utility. You'll make a lot of use of *yum* to install MythTV components, so you might as well get familiar with it. Become root, then type:

```
# yum upgrade
```

After some dependency processing, you'll be informed of the upgraded packages to be installed and asked if you want to continue. Hit **y** and Enter, and then go get something to snack on. The further away from the initial release of Core 4, the more packages that need updates. Take special note of whether or not a new kernel package was installed, as you'll want to be running the latest available errata kernel for both security reasons and availability of third-party kernel modules, which you'll need to complete your MythTV setup. Assuming a new kernel was installed, go ahead and restart one more time so you're running on that new kernel.

Configure a Third-Party MythTV Repository

Now, you'll need to configure *yum* to be able to access a third-party RPM package repository, where you'll obtain all the necessary MythTV bits and their dependencies. Everything you need can be found in Axel Thimm's ATrpms repository, at *http://atrpms.net/*. First, install the ATrpms package-signing key as root to verify the authenticity of the packages you'll be installing:

```
# rpm -import http://atrpms.net/RPM-GPG-KEY.atrpms
```

Now, add a *yum* configuration file called *atrpms.repo* in the */etc/yum.repos.d* directory containing the following information:

```
[atrpms]
name=ATrpms for Fedora Core $releasever stable
baseurl=http://apt.atrpms.net/fedora/$releasever/en/$basearch/at-stable
gpgcheck=1
enabled=1
```

Install MythTV

At this point, you are ready to pull down all the MythTV packages. Through the beauty of automatic dependency resolution and installation tools like *yum*, doing so is simply a matter of issuing a one-line command as root, and then sitting back and watching it execute:

```
# yum install mythtv-frontend mythtv-backend mythtv-themes
```

This is all it takes to pull down and install the core MythTV packages, themes, and any and all dependencies required. Depending on the speed of your Internet connection, this might be a good time to go get something to drink or maybe even take a nap if you're on dial-up!

If you're curious what all it is that you're NOT having to do manually by using the ATrpms packages, give the official MythTV documentation, written by Robert Kulagowski, a read-through at *http://mythtv.org/docs/mythtv-HOWTO.html*. By using a third-party repository, you avoid having to compile anything or worry about dependencies, but for those who prefer to go straight to the source (code), Robert's guide is your ticket to compile.

After the intermission for all those packages to download and install, you'll still need to install a few more bits and pieces. You need a few kernel modules that aren't available in the main kernel tree. ATrpms provides these kernel modules in pre-packaged, easy to swallow pills. For your NVIDIA video card, you'll need the ATrpms *nvidia-graphics* kernel module packages; for your WinTV PVR capture card, you'll need the *ivtv* kernel module; and for its remote, the *lirc* kernel module.

Run the following command as root to retrieve all of these (the use of `uname -r` in these commands is to ensure you grab the appropriate module for your kernel):

```
# yum install nvidia-graphics7174-kmdl-`uname -r` \
nvidia-graphics7174 ivtv-kmdl-`uname -r` \
ivtv lirc-kmdl-`uname -r` lirc
```

Now you have all the software you need installed on your system, so now you are ready to configure it for MythTV.

Configure System Modules

You'll need to make some modifications to *etc/modprobe.conf* to tell the system about some of your hardware and which drivers to use with it. For the PVR-250, its remote, and your video card, you should have the following additions: (the nvidia portions may have been inserted already when the nvidia-graphics packages were installed):

```
# ivtv
alias char-major-81 videodev
alias char-major-81-0 ivtv
alias tveeprom tveeprom-ivtv
alias msp3400 msp3400-ivtv
alias tuner tuner-ivtv
# lirc
alias char-major-61 lirc_i2c
install lirc_i2c /sbin/modprobe ivtv; /sbin/modprobe --ignore-install lirc_
i2c
# nvidia kernel module
alias char-major-195 nvidia-1_0-7174
alias nvidia nvidia-1_0-7174
```

After making these changes, rebuild your module dependencies:

```
# /sbin/depmod -ae
```

Setting up your NVIDIA card. Next, swap your X configuration and switch over to the nvidia driver (up to this point, you've been using the open source nv driver, which doesn't perform nearly as well as NVIDIA's own binary driver in key areas like video decoding). The ATrpms package actually created an appropriate configuration file based on your existing configuration, so switching drivers is a relatively painless process. As root, make a backup of your current configuration for good measure, then swap the *xorg.conf.nvidia* configuration into place:

```
# cd /etc/X11
# mv xorg.conf xorg.conf.nv
# mv xorg.conf.nvidia xorg.conf
```

Now all that's left is to restart X. All open programs are going to terminate when you restart X, so save any unfinished business, then hit Control-Alt-backspace. Soon you will see the NVIDIA splash screen and then be taken back to a login prompt. Log back in and continue on with loading and testing the drivers for the PVR-250.

Setting up your capture card. To get the PVR-250 prepped and ready for MythTV to use, you need to load the *ivtv* driver via a quick *modprobe*:

```
# /sbin/modprobe ivtv
```

If you want to troubleshoot what's going on during this process, check out the */var/log/messages* file. The *ivtv* driver has matured to the point where any PVR-250 on the market *should* be recognized and auto-configured correctly. Connect an antenna or cable feed to the coaxial input on the PVR-250, and then test the functionality of the capture card with *cat* and *mplayer*:

```
$ cat /dev/video0 > testfile.mpg
(hit ctrl-c to stop capture after a few seconds)
$ mplayer testfile.mpg
```

 If you don't get good audio and video in the test capture above, launch the *ptune-ui.pl* utility to tweak the video settings, while having MPlayer play video straight from */dev/video0*, so you can change channels and other parameters in search of a viable signal:

```
$ /usr/lib/ivtv/ptune-ui.pl &
$ mplayer /dev/video0
```

Also, note that we're using *mplayer* to test the card; the output produced by the *ivtv* driver is a standard MPEG2 stream, not raw video, so programs such as *xawtv* and *zapping* will not work.

Setting up your remote control. Once you're happy with the video from your tuner card, load up the necessary *lirc* modules and test out the functionality of your remote.

```
# /sbin/modprobe lirc_i2c
# wget http://wilsonet.com/mythtv/lircd-g3.conf.txt
# mv lircd-g3.conf.txt /etc/lircd.conf
# /sbin/chkconfig lircd on
# /sbin/service lircd start
```

Note that there are actually three different remotes that have come with PVR-250 cards over time, and the previous code is for the newest version. For the two older versions, you can find appropriate configuration files for them in */usr/share/doc/ivtv-*/*. Now launch the *irw* program, point your remote at the PVR-250's IR receiver and press some buttons. *irw* should output some text corresponding to the button presses it's seeing.

```
$ /usr/bin/irw
00000000000017e1 00 CH- hauppaugegrey
00000000000017e1 00 CH- hauppaugegrey
00000000000017d0 00 VOL+ hauppaugegrey
00000000000017d0 00 VOL+ hauppaugegrey
(control-c to stop)
```

If the output from this test looks good, you can drop a button-to-function mapping file for *lirc* to control MythTV into place:

```
$ wget http://wilsonet.com/mythtv/lircrc-haupgrey-g3.txt
$ mkdir ~/.mythtv
$ mv lircrc-haupgrey-g3.txt ~/.mythtv/lircrc
$ ln -s ~/.mythtv/lircrc ~/.lircrc
```

The last line symlinks the configuration file to the location *xine* and *mplayer* expect to find a *lirc* button mapping file. The file also contains settings for those programs, and some MythTV plug-ins also use the file to perform duties that'll be covered later on.

Appropriate *lircrc* files for the two earlier Hauppauge remotes are also available. A second-generation config file is located at *http://wilsonet.com/mythtv/lircrc-haupgrey.txt*.

The second-generation file should also work for most of the black first generation remotes, but users with these remotes may have to search the Internet (or ask the *lirc* mailing list) for a full configuration file.

Create the MythTV Database

The next step in the process is to actually configure MythTV itself. The bulk of MythTV's configuration settings and data are stored in a MySQL database backend, so you'll need to prepare a database before you can start configuring MythTV.

Fedora Core's stock MySQL configuration parameters cause it to perform sub-optimally with MythTV. To increase performance, there are a few parameters you should configure before you start up MySQL. To do this, edit */etc/my.cnf* and add the following configuration options under the [mysqld] section in the file:

```
key_buffer = 16M
table_cache - 128
sort_buffer_size = 2M
myisam_sort_buffer_size = 8M
query_cache_size = 16M
```

With those changes in place, you now need to set MySQL to load at startup, and then start it.

```
# /sbin/chkconfig mysqld on
# /sbin/service mysqld start
```

Set the mysqlroot password, replacing ROOT_PWD with a password of your choosing:

```
# mysql -u root mysql
mysql> UPDATE user SET Password=PASSWORD('ROOT_PWD') WHERE user='root';
mysql> FLUSH PRIVILEGES;
mysql> quit
```

Now create and populate the MythTV database (called mythconverg) with some initial data:

```
$ mysql -u root -p < /usr/share/doc/mythtv-*/database/mc.sql
(enter the password you just set above when prompted)
```

Configure Zap2it Data Direct

A Personal Video Recorder without some means of knowing which programs are on which channels and at what time is nothing but a glorified VCR. A PVR with a good data source becomes much more powerful, since it is able to automatically adjust the scheduled program list.

If you give it some thought, it's pretty obvious that a PVR will need that data source. But how can it get it in a computer-readable format? Prior to April 2004, MythTV used a project called *xmltv* (*http://xmltv.org*) which implemented a number of programs called grabbers and an XML format to describe the details of a program, such as the start and end times, the name, channel, and so on. The grabbers worked in various ways to obtain raw data and place it into XML format. The grabber for the United States would execute the following basic algorithm:

> Connect to *http://www.zap2it.com* and request a one-page listing of all programs for day *x* on channel *y*. Repeat for all channels in your zip code and for days 1 to 13.

As you can deduce, this is very inefficient. Zap2it had to generate a dynamic web page for each request, so in a typical cable TV lineup of 50 channels multiplied by 13 days, they had to create 650 web pages for each user. Typically, users would update their listings once a day, so that would be another 50 to 200 web pages to obtain updated listings for today, tomorrow, and any new days that had been added.

If you then multiply that by the popularity of MythTV in the United States, you can see what a server load MythTV was placing on Zap2it.com, especially between midnight and 5 A.M.

So, when Zap2it offered a means for non-commercial users to obtain listing data (Data Direct) in an XML format that didn't require dynamic web page generation on the Zap2it end or the error prone process of "screen scraping" on the user side, it was a win-win situation all around.

Zap2it gets demographic data on users, and users get greatly expanded, high-quality guide data listings. Zap2it offers detailed subtitles and episode descriptions, which were not available through the screen-scrape method.

Users who are not in the United States will need to use a XMLTV grabber. See the XMLTV web page for a list of supported countries.

Create your Zap2it account prior to configuring MythTV. Go to site *http://labs.zap2it.com* and click on "New User? Sign Up." Fill out the information requested, and for Certificate Code use **ZIYN-DQZO-SBUT**. Your account should be activated immediately and will expire in three to four months. MythTV will indicate in various status screens when your account will expire. Zap2it.com will send you an email approximately one week before your account expires; when you re-subscribe they'll ask some additional survey questions. Zap2it states that they have no intention of charging non-commercial users for access to the guide data.

Once you've entered your Zip Code and configured your channel lineup you may exit the Zap2it web page.

If you don't receive a particular channel, make sure that your Zap2it account reflects that, since MythTV will be using this information to schedule programs.

Configure MythTV

Now that you have somewhere to store your settings and you've configured your Zap2it account, start up the MythTV backend server configuration utility:

```
$ mythtv-setup
```

The first time you run *mythtv-setup* you will be asked for your preferred language, then whether you want to clear out any existing configurations for your capture cards and your channel lineup information. On this first launch go ahead and answer yes to both of those questions (but not for any subsequent runs, unless you have good reason to, or you'll have to reconfigure both your capture cards and channel lineups).

After these initial questions you'll be presented with five choices:

- General
- Capture cards
- Video sources
- Input connections
- Channel editor

You can use the arrow keys to move about the interface, and the space bar to select items. You'll want to go through these steps in order, as some later steps depend on earlier steps.

 MythTV does not have mouse support—it is designed on the premise that you are going to be using a remote control.

Since you only have one system running MythTV at the moment, you can leave the IP and port settings on the front page at their default values of 127.0.0.1. If you are aiming to have multiple MythTV systems (either multiple backends or a backend and some remote frontends), you want to put the IP address of the machine's Ethernet interface into both of these slots.

The next settings page lets you set the directory paths where MythTV will store recorded programs and what partition should be used for the live TV buffer. You need to double-check that these paths exist and that your MythTV user login has read/write permissions on them, or bad things will happen (well, MythTV just plain won't work). The defaults for Live TV buffer and Minimum free Live TV buffer should be suitable, and leave the "Save original files after transcoding" option off, as the topic of transcoding is one for another day.

The Global Backend Setup page is where you'll specify your TV format, which should be self-explanatory. Leave VBI format set to None for now, as VBI (a.k.a. teletext or closed captioning) support isn't yet very well supported by the *ivtv* driver. The channel frequency table should also be fairly evident, but you can try a few different ones if you aren't certain which one is right for your locale. Start out without any time offset for your XMLTV listings and the last two options on this page unchecked.

Leave the Shutdown/Wakeup Options page at all of its default values for now, as configuration of these settings can get quite involved. It may be possible to set up your MythTV box such that it'll hibernate when not in use, but save that for another day and just get basic functionality working first. Similarly, options on each of the last few pages under the General heading should suit you fine for your initial setup.

Under section 2, Capture cards, set up a new capture card, of card type MPEG2 Encoder card (if your card has an MPEG2 encoder; otherwise, choose a setting that matches your card), a video device of */dev/video0*, and Tuner 0 for your default input.

In section 3, Video sources, configure your channel listings lineup. Start by giving it a descriptive name, and then select the XMLTV listings grabber for your location. Assuming you're in North America, you'll use the DataDirect grabber. Enter your Zap2it username and password in mythtv-setup. For those outside North America, you'll find some helpful details on the matter in the official MythTV documentation, specifically on this page: *http://mythtv.org/docs/mythtv-HOWTO-9.html*.

Continuing on, in section 4, Input Connections, assign your channel lineup to an input on your capture card. Specifically, assign the channel lineup you just created to the Tuner 0 input of your PVR-250. Highlight "[MPEG: /dev/video0](Tuner 0) → (None)" and hit the space bar, then assign the video source accordingly. The only other setting you should touch is the starting channel. Set it to a known working channel (so you can have your tuner fall back to that channel by restarting the backend if anything goes haywire).

The last section, the Channel Editor, isn't something you'll need to touch at this time. For starters, there's no data in it until you've successfully run a *mythfilldatabase* operation, which you'll do once you've exited *mythtv-setup*.

Running MythTV for the First Time

Now exit *mythtv-setup*, start up the backend server for the first time, and run *mythfilldatabase* as the exit message on the console suggests you do:

```
$ mythbackend &
$ mythfilldatabase
```

The *mythfilldatabase* step can be a time-consuming process, depending on how many channels are in your channel lineup, the speed of your Internet connection, and the efficiency of your listings grabber. The North American DataDirect grabber is extremely quick, as zap2it provides an XML feed, while other grabbers have to rely on screen-scraping web pages of listings to gather guide data. The moral of the story here is: be patient!

You should already have the *mythbackend* server running in your existing terminal window, so open up another one in which you'll type the following, to launch the *mythfrontend* application:

```
$ mythfrontend
```

The benefit of running the frontend and backend from different windows initially is that you can tell what messages are being output to the console by which component—so if something goes wrong, you might have a clue why.

A nice easy test to see if the primary functionality is operational is to simply try watching Live TV. Also thumb around with the remote control a bit to verify its functionality. The top menu item of the very first screen you're presented with when starting up the *mythfrontend* is Watch TV. Pressing either the Play button or the OK button on the remote should start up Live TV mode. The channel up and channel down buttons should allow you to move from channel to channel, just like your "normal" TV, while buttons such as Pause, FF, and Rew will allow you to do things that a normal TV almost certainly cannot do.

Assuming that Live TV and the remote work as expected, you can be pretty confident everything else will fall into place, so its now time to configure the *mythbackend* server process to start automatically at system boot time, and then make some additional preparations to hook your system to the television. Set the *mythbackend* to run at system startup by issuing the command:

```
# /sbin/chkconfig mythbackend on
```

Automatically Log In and Start MythTV

To have the *mythfrontend* automatically start when your mythtv user logs in, click Desktop → Preferences → More Preferences → Sessions. Then, on the Startup Programs tab, add *mythfrontend*. That takes care of starting MythTV once you've logged on to GNOME, but ideally you'd take it one step further, which is to have a default user (namely, mythtv), automatically logged into the desktop environment.

To have your mythtv user automatically logged in when the system boots, you'll make some changes to the GNOME Display Manager (GDM). Launch the *gdmsetup* utility from a root prompt:

```
# gdmsetup
```

Within *gdmsetup*, on the first tab, called "General," you should see a section titled "Automatic login." Check the box for "Login a user automatically on first bootup" and select your mythtv user from the pop-up menu.

Alternatively, if you are not very comfortable with Linux just yet, and you suspect there may be occasions where you've mucked something up to the point that an auto-login will lock up the computer, you might not want to use Automatic Login. Instead, you might opt to use the "Timed Login" option, to log in the mythtv user a few seconds after the login screen first appears. This way, you can circumvent the mythtv user logging in, and log in as root to (hopefully) correct whatever you've broken.

Connect to TV

At this point, you should have your system configured far enough that
you're ready to hook it up to your television and control it from the couch
with your remote control (and/or wireless keyboard). You just have to make
a few little changes to your X configuration to let the video card know you're
going to be hooking up to a television now, instead of a computer monitor.
Add the following options to the Device section in */etc/X11/xorg.conf*
(assuming an S-Video connection and NTSC-M below):

```
# TV Out Setup
Option      "TVStandard" "NTSC-M"
Option      "TVOutFormat" "SVIDEO"
Option      "ConnectedMonitor" "TV"
```

Adjust accordingly for your location and connection type, per Appendix J of
NVIDIA's README for driver, available online at *ftp://download.nvidia.
com/XFree86/Linux-x86/1.0-7174/README.txt*. Now shut your machine
down, hook it up to the television, and you should be in business!

> NVIDIA creates new versions of the Linux driver frequently,
> so ensure that you've downloaded the correct version of the
> documentation for the driver you're running.

There are a few more adjustments to make now that you've got your system
hooked up to your television. First, you'll want to launch the *nvidia-settings*
utility from a terminal window:

```
$ nvidia-settings
```

With *nvidia-settings*, you can adjust your computer output to the visible area
of your television screen. I also recommend adjusting the flicker filter setting. Turn it up a little ways to eliminate some of the flicker inherent with
outputting a computer's display, which is intended for a progressive-scan
computer monitor, on an interlaced display. Once you're happy with your
settings, simply exit out of the *nvidia-settings* utility. To get these settings to
be applied the next time you restart your machine (you shouldn't have to
very often), go back into Sessions utility you used earlier to auto-start
mythfrontend and add a line:

```
nvidia-settings --load-config-only
```

Final MythTV Tweaks

Now go into the Utilities/Setup → Setup section of *mythfrontend* to adjust a
few other settings. On the third page under the General section, you can
adjust default audio volume levels to taste. On the last page of that section,

you'll want to enable the "Automatically run mythfilldatabase" setting, so that your guide data gets refreshed on a nightly basis.

Under the Appearance section, you can choose different themes for the *mythfrontend* user interface (G.A.N.T. for me), pick different Qt styles (different button and menu styles—I prefer Keramik here), font sizes, a few different menu layouts, and other settings.

Under TV Settings → General, you can adjust some recording parameters, such as setting an amount of time before a show is supposed to start and/or after it is supposed to end that also gets recorded.

Under TV Settings → Playback, you can enable a deinterlace filter if video playback seems to be full of jagged lines in high-motion scenes, adjust your automatic commercial skipping behavior, your seeking behavior, overscan of the TV picture if necessary, and alter your on-screen display theme and font (Isthmus with FreeSans is my personal preference).

The last little section of note at the moment is TV Settings → Recording Profiles, where you can adjust the bitrate and resolution at which your recordings are made (and even have them transcoded, if you so desire). A lower bitrate means less storage will be used per recording, so you might want to tweak these settings to get an optimal combination of storage usage and visual quality.

The *keys.txt* file will specify which commands are associated with each button on the keyboard.

Schedule Recordings

The first order of business to attend to now that you have things set up to your liking is to schedule some recordings. From *mythfrontend* click Manage → Schedule to find yourself at a menu listing where you can schedule a show to record by paging through the electronic programming guide (Guide), browsing an alphabetical listing of all known shows (Finder), by any number of search methods (Search), or by manually specifying a time and channel to record (Custom Record).

Of course, when choosing a program to record, you can choose to record only that showing or pick from any number of repeating algorithms, ranging from "record only in this timeslot on this channel on this day of the week" to "record this show any time it comes on any channel." The MythTV scheduler is very powerful, and because most grabbers will give you from 12 to 14 days of program listings, sometimes it may be best to give the scheduler more leeway in deciding when to record something. Rather than thinking "I have to record channel 'X' at time 'Y' in order to watch program 'foo'," you should consider that what you really want to do is to record program 'foo' and allow the scheduler figure out how to make that happen. This is especially useful when two or more programs you'd like to watch are on at the same time. Hopefully, at least one program will have a repeat; if not, and you are continually running into scheduling conflicts, the simplest solution may be to purchase additional capture cards.

With the Hauppuage PVR-500 card (which has two separate MPEG2 encoders on the card) and an Intel D865G motherboard (6 PCI slots) you could potentially record 12 programs at the same time, which should be enough to satisfy most people. If 12 programs aren't enough, simply set up an additional MythTV backend and configure it as a slave. The MythTV scheduler will then deconflict as many programs as possible.

Your MythTV system should now be happily recording your favorite TV shows for viewing (without having to watch commercials) when you get around to it. Once you have one or more programs recorded, simply navigate from the main page into the Media Library section and then into Watch Recordings. Just thumb through the recordings library and pick one to view at your leisure.

Conclusion

By no means was this a complete or authoritative look at all that MythTV has to offer and the myriad of options and features, but hopefully, it's a good start to your MythTV journey. A wealth of information can be found in the official MythTV HOWTO (*http://mythtv.org/docs/mythtv-HOWTO. html*), and the preceding is a somewhat abridged (and altered) version of the web site I maintain, dedicated to running MythTV on Fedora Core, which can be found at *http://wilsonet.com/mythtv/fcmyth.php*.

The MythTV community is a very active, on both the developer and user sides, with lively mailing lists (*http://mythtv.org/modules.php?name=MythInfo*) and IRC channels (#mythtv and #mythtv-users on FreeNode), as well as a number of community-run forums and wikis. If you have any problems or questions, there's bound to be someone out there who can help you on your way to MythTV nirvana.

—Jarod Wilson

MythTV as a Digital Hub

MythTV can do more than just show TV—it can be a complete digital hub for your home. Learn about MythTV's various plug-ins that extend its capabilities.

As alluded to in "Create a DVR with MythTV" [Hack #77], there's much more to MythTV than just recording and time-shifting TV. MythTV has a plug-in architecture that allows you to add an array of modules to extend the capabilities your MythTV system and make it a true digital media hub for your home.

All these plug-ins are available individually, or you can grab all of them (and all dependencies) in one fell swoop if you have configured *yum* per [Hack #77] Just type:

```
# yum install mythplugins
```

Most other distributions provide the plug-ins via the package manager, but if yours doesn't, you can always grab the source code from the Download page at *http://www.mythtv.org*.

After installation, fire up the MythTV frontend, and you should find numerous additional buttons throughout the UI, grouped in (hopefully) logical places—for example, MythWeather and MythNews are accessed under the Information Center menu on the main MythTV frontend menu. Most plug-ins are configured within the Setup section of the MythTV frontend. A quick hit list of the most popular plug-ins with brief descriptions follows.

MythVideo

Got a large collection of DVDs you've painstakingly converted into video files that your computer can play? Maybe a large library of digitized home movies? Wouldn't it be nice to have it all cataloged and ready to browse, complete with a description of the plot, MPAA rating, run-time, and a movie poster for every Hollywood flick in your collection? MythVideo gives you just that. Just fire up MythVideo's setup utility, which searches your movie storage directory for new files, and then let MythVideo search for your movie on the Internet Movie Database (*http://www.imdb.org/*) and pull down all that information for you. Now you can thumb through your movies like you were at the video store, select a movie, and start watching it, all without leaving your couch.

MythVideo makes use of a backend video player such as MPlayer or xine. If you don't like the features offered in the default (MPlayer) you can easily make a switch by installing the alternative player and then going to Utilities/ Setup → Setup → Media Settings → Video Settings → Player Settings. You'll be required to enter a command-line argument to run your video player. Here is sample line for xine:

```
xine -pfhq --no-splash %s
```

MythDVD

The plug-in enables you to watch your DVD and VideoCD movies as you would with any off-the-shelf DVD player. Because video playback is handled by software, your DVD experience may actually improve as the software is upgraded. For example, early hardware DVD players did not have progressive scan playback, a feature that enhances the quality of the video sent to the TV, and those people who have these players still lack that feature. However, a software DVD player that lacked progressive scanning may receive the feature during its next program update. Thus, your MythDVD system is more versatile than a hardware DVD.

Most packages have MythDVD set up to use MPlayer as the DVD playback tool, but since MPlayer lacks the ability to display DVD menus, it is not a very good choice if you want to access more content than the main feature. The following command, placed in the DVD Player Command Field located in Utilities/Setup → Setup → Media Settings → DVD Settings → Play Settings, will enable playback with the xine backend, which can display the DVD movies:

```
xine -pfhq --no-splash dvd://
```

MythDVD also gives you the ability to rip your DVDs to the hard drive. Many people may find this feature more user friendly than following the steps found in "Rip a DVD" [Hack #59]. The rip settings are controlled using the same path I just gave you for the player settings, except you'll choose Rip Settings instead. Ripping a DVD shouldn't take more than a few minutes, but encoding it into a smaller file format will take several hours.

MythMusic

What digital hub would be complete without a way to interface with your entire music library, be it digitized audio files or your prized CD collection? You can listen to your CDs, rip them to digital audio files on your Myth box, play them back, build playlists, randomly play your entire library, and display an assortment of visualizations full screen on your television, pulsating in time to the music. Coming soon (as of this writing) is support for remote playlists shared out by iTunes.

MythGallery

Everyone loves a good slideshow of the kids or your vacation to the tropics, don't they? With actual slides and slide projectors having pretty much gone the way of the dinosaur and the rampant use of digital cameras, many of us never see our captured memories outside a computer monitor. Well, how 'bout putting them up on that big screen TV? MythGallery lets you set up folders full of pictures to display slideshow style on your television, complete with slide-to-slide transition effects (plus background music support planned).

MythGame

Long before touching their first Linux box, many of today's Linux enthusiasts were video game junkies—ranging from the old Commodore and Atari systems, up through all that Nintendo, Sega, Sony, and Microsoft have to offer. MythGame provides a coherent interface between a library of game images and a number of today's popular video game system emulators, currently including those for Nintendo, Super Nintendo, and the multi-arcade machine emulator (MAME), with additional emulator support in development.

MythWeather

The Weather Channel for your Myth box, it is always tuned to your local conditions. MythWeather fetches forecasts, current conditions, and radar imaging off the Internet for your location, available for your perusal on demand, no waiting for the meteorologist to get to the part you care about.

MythPhone

With the rising popularity of Vonage and similar digital voice services from the major telcos, its pretty clear Voice over IP (VoIP) will play a dominant role in the future of telecom. The future is already here and then some with MythPhone, which goes above and beyond, providing both voice and video over IP. You can turn your television into a video phone with the right hardware and VoIP service provider.

MythNews

Nearly every major news site, and even most minor ones have an RSS (really simple syndication) newsfeed available for consumption. MythNews provides you with an RSS feed aggregator to let you read all the day's top stories from all the sources you care about with just a quick glance at your television.

MythBrowser

Just want to sit back on the couch and surf the Web on your big screen? MythBrowser is a web browser tuned for use on a television screen, with nothing but a remote control (but you can use a keyboard too).

MythWeb

When combined with the ubiquitous Apache web server and PHP, Myth-Web gives you a web interface into your entire MythTV system. Browse your program guide and current recordings, schedule, delete, and download recordings, adjust preferences, key bindings, and much more. Imagine you're away from home and suddenly realize there's a special on that afternoon that you wanted to see. With an appropriately configure setup, you can schedule that recording from anywhere on the Internet. Several plug-ins are also configurable or useable to some extent via MythWeb as well—with support for more on the way.

The plug-ins mentioned above are all officially sanctioned and supported by the MythTV project, and are maintained in MythTV's source code repositories. Additional plug-ins can be found in the wild—use 'em at your own risk!

—*Jarod Wilson*

HACK #79 Take (Remote) Control

A keyboard and a mouse aren't the only way to control your computer.

While the geek in you probably doesn't mind having a wireless keyboard and mouse to control your multimedia powerhouse computer, it can be a bit cumbersome, especially if you have to share control. Here comes the Linux Infrared Remote Control (LIRC) project to the rescue (*http://www.lirc.org*).

The LIRC project has the simple goal of letting you use the remote of your choice to control your Linux system. LIRC supports a wide range of infrared receivers, ranging from home-made serial port versions and dongles on TV tuner cards to even Microsoft Windows XP Media Center USB receivers, along with many different remotes ranging from those bundled with some of the above-mentioned receivers to a wide range of universal and programmable remotes. Check out the LIRC web site for further details on supported hardware.

To install LIRC, you can obtain a source tarball from the site, but since it is already available as a package on several platforms check your package manager and your distribution's third party repositories first. For instance, Axel Thimm's ATrpms package repository at *http://atrpms.net* carries packaged

LIRC binaries for all recent Red Hat and Fedora Core releases, installable using your favorite automatic dependency resolution program with the ATrpms repository enabled. The quick version of how to do this with a recent Fedora Core release and the Fedora-provided *yum* utility is to first install the ATrpms package-signing key

```
# rpm -import http://atrpms.net/RPM-GPG-KEY.atrpms
```

Then create a *yum* config file at */etc/yum.repos.d/atrpms.repo* for ATrpms:

```
[atrpms]
name=ATrpms for Fedora Core $releasever stable
baseurl=http://apt.atrpms.net/fedora/$releasever/en/$basearch/at-stable
gpgcheck=1
enabled=1
```

With that done, you can now install the necessary LIRC components, with the command:

```
# yum install lirc-kmdl-`uname -r` lirc
```

Note that those are back-ticks, not single-quotes, and you'll need to be running the latest errata kernel, as ATrpms only actively maintains packages for the latest errata kernel.

The ATrpms packages are built with support for as many different LIRC drivers as possible, covering all standard/popular interfaces, so unless you have some oddball receiver, you should be covered. The following example shows the necessary additions to */etc/modprobe.conf* for the IR dongle on a Hauppauge WinTV PVR-250 (assuming you already have the *ivtv* driver configured for the card):

```
# lirc
alias char-major-61 lirc_i2c
install lirc_i2c /sbin/modprobe ivtv; /sbin/modprobe --ignore-install lirc_
i2c
```

For a serial port IR receiver on COM1, the following should do the trick:

```
# lirc
alias char-major-61 lirc_serial
options lirc_serial irq=4 io=0x3f8
install lirc_serial /bin/setserial /dev/ttyS0 uart none ; \
    /sbin/modprobe --ignore-install lirc_serial
```

Other receivers require fewer options, needing only an alias line for their specific lirc_* driver. A little poking around the LIRC web site and some Googling should turn up information on just about any receiver.

With your *modprobe.conf* entries in place, load up your driver, substituting i2c, serial, and so on for <your driver>:

```
# /sbin/modprobe lirc_<your driver>
```

The next step is to set up a configuration file for the LIRC daemon, *lircd*, that'll map IR codes for your particular remote to their corresponding buttons, so you can later assign buttons to functions, rather than IR codes to functions. This configuration file exists as */etc/lircd.conf*. Distributed with LIRC are a myriad of configuration files for remotes, contributed by the LIRC user community. You can find them on your system in the directories under */usr/share/doc/lirc-*/remotes*. If you don't find one in there for your remote, do a bit of Googling and you may come up with one (if not, check out the man page for *irrecord*, and you can generate your own).

With the proper *lircd.conf* file in place, start up *lircd*, via the command:

```
# /sbin/service lircd start
```

Now fire up the *irw* tool, distributed by the LIRC folks, to verify basic functionality. When you press a button on your remote, *irw* will output the button label associated with the IR code *lircd* picked up from your receiver, per your *lircd.conf*.

```
$ /usr/bin/irw
(control-c to stop)
```

If the output looks correct, all that remains is to configure your applications to receive commands from *lircd*. The majority of Linux multimedia applications have support for LIRC, and details on how to configure LIRC to work with them can typically be found the respective applications' documentation. [Hack #77] includes some tidbits on configuring LIRC to work with MythTV, MPlayer and xine.

—Jarod Wilson

H A C K
#80   Browse Streaming Radio Stations

Install streamtuner and browse through a large directory of public streaming radio stations.

A complaint you might often hear among music fans is "there's nothing good on the radio." While the truth of that statement is largely a matter of musical taste, it is true that the further your tastes stray from the mainstream, the less likely they will be served by mainstream radio stations. Streaming radio over the Internet is one solution to the problem. Because it's very easy for someone to set up their own streaming music radio station, there are thousands of such stations available, which means you have a very good chance of finding one or more that appeals to your eclectic tastes. (Find information on making your own radio stream in [Hack #84]). Now that you know the perfect song for you is out there somewhere, how do you find it without some sort of stream station directory listing? Use *streamtuner*, a Linux program that lists and organizes various streaming radio stations and makes it easy for you to filter through them to find streams that match your taste.

To install *streamtuner*, first check with your distribution's packaging tool and see whether it has already been packaged. If not, visit the official *streamtuner* page at *http://www.nongnu.org/streamtuner* and either download one of the unofficial packages for your distribution, or download and compile the source code according to the installation instructions. After it is installed, launch it from your panel menu or type **streamtuner** in a console.

The initial GUI has a toolbar with a number of common actions and below it a row of tabs (see Figure 4-1). These tabs organize each of the different networks of streaming audio servers into their own tabs along with your bookmarks and any local streams. *streamtuner* provides plug-ins for streaming networks such as SHOUTcast, Live365, Xiph, basic.ch, and a number of others. Each of these streaming networks host (often large) numbers of streams organized by genre.

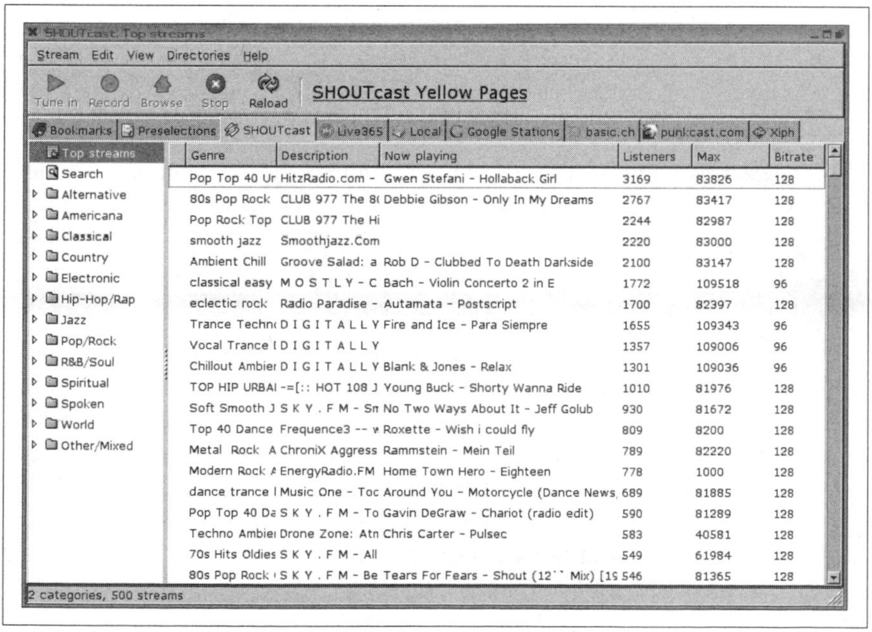

Figure 4-1. streamtuner main window

While all of these networks stream audio, they sometimes do so in different ways. Click the corresponding tab for a network and for most networks *streamtuner* will download the latest list of streams and display a list of genres on the left and a list of streams for that genre on the right. Since some streaming networks don't offer a direct feed in this way, they may not show all of this information and may instead offer links to web pages that contain further information about a stream. Click the Update button in the toolbar to refresh the list of streams for a network. For some networks (such as *punkcast.com*) *streamtuner* will only display links to the particular stream's web site. Click on the link and *streamtuner* will open it in your configured web browser.

> Some of the tabs will provide columns that list artist, album, and other information about the particular stream. Right-click on one of the columns (such as Description) and choose Stream Columns to configure which of the columns to show and which to hide.

By default, *streamtuner* is configured to use *xmms* as its media player. To use a different application for your streams, click Edit → Preferences and choose Applications from the preferences window. This window allows you to configure the default commands that *streamtuner* will run to listen to a stream, a playlist, open a web page, and a number of other options. Most Linux media players that support streaming audio will support a stream passed as an argument on the command line, so to change *xmms* to your media player, just replace *xmms* in the preferences window with the command-line name of your application.

The preferences window also lets you configure other *streamtuner* options. Click Network to configure a proxy server if your network uses one, or click Plugins to set specific options for the installed *streamtuner* plug-ins. These preferences vary for each plug-in but often allow you to configure settings such as how many streams to load per category.

With *streamtuner* configured for your music player, choose one of the network tabs, select a stream from the list, and click Tune In to start listening to the stream (or just double-click on a stream name). If the Browse button in the toolbar is enabled, you can click on that button to visit the stream's web page in your browser. Select a different stream and click Tune In to switch to the new stream. When you find a stream that you like, right-click the stream and select Add Bookmark to add the stream to the Bookmark tab so you can easily find the stream at a later date.

> *streamtuner* can also act as a frontend to your local music collection. Point *streamtuner* to the directory where you store your music files in the preferences window, and then click the Local tab. *streamtuner* will list all of the directories and files within your music directory and allow you to tune into one or multiple files.

streamtuner also provides a frontend to the *streamripper* program. If the Record button is enabled and *streamripper* is installed, you can actually record the streaming audio directly to MP3 files. The exact *streamripper* command-line arguments can be configured in *streamtuner's* preferences window, but by default it will open *streamripper* in your default terminal and save the files in your home directory (or the directory you launched *streamtuner* from). To find out more about how to configure streamripper, check out [Hack #81].

Rip Streaming Audio

Streamripper lets you rip the live streaming audio station of your choice directly to MP3 for later listening.

Streaming audio has allowed a number of people to easily broadcast not only their favorite music tracks, but also other types of radio shows. Instead of being broadcast all day long, some shows are broadcast only at certain times of the day. If you aren't at your computer when the show is broadcast you'll miss out—unless you have *streamripper*.

streamripper is a simple but powerful command-line application that allows you to record streaming audio directly to local MP3 files. To install *streamripper*, see if your distribution has already packaged it, otherwise download the source from the official page at *http://streamripper. sourceforge.net* and compile and install it according to the installation instructions.

To use *streamripper*, simply pass it the URL to your streaming audio station in a console window:

```
$ streamripper http://69.56.219.92:8072
```

By default, *streamripper* will create a directory named after the stream in the current directory and then start storing the streaming content as MP3s within an incoming directory. When a file is complete, *streamripper* will move it up from the incoming directory to the stream's main directory. Each file is named after the artist and track metadata that *streamripper* grabs from the audio stream. You can leave *streamripper* running as long as you wish (provided you have enough hard drive space), and it will continue to grab and store MP3s in the stream's directory. Provided you have enough band-width, you can even launch multiple instances of *streamripper* and simultaneously capture multiple streams.

The *streamripper* defaults are suitable for standard uses, but *streamripper* also allows you to configure everything through command-line options. For instance, the -d argument tells *streamripper* to rip files into the specified directory instead of the current working directory. The -s argument tells *streamripper* not to create a directory for each stream, and instead to save all of the MP3s into a single directory.

By default, MP3s that *streamripper* saves are titled after the artist and track name only. For some audio streams you might want to store the files in the order they were played on the stream. The -q option will cause *streamripper* to add a sequence number to the beginning of each filename starting from 001. In addition the -P prefix argument will let you add a particular string to the beginning of each file. Use the -a filename argument, and *streamripper* will store the entire stream to a single large file in addition to multiple files. Add the -A argument, and *streamripper* will only store to the single file and won't create the individual files.

 streamripper requires that the URL always be the first argument you pass it, so if you use other arguments, be sure that the URL is always first.

Schedule Recordings

Due to its command-line nature, *streamripper* is ideal for scheduling recordings with *at* or *cron*. The -l argument lets you configure a number of seconds for *streamripper* to record before it automatically exits. Combine this with the -q and -P options and you can easily create an archive of your favorite radio show. For instance, one stream I like to listen to only plays between noon and 6:00 P.M. PST Thursday through Saturday. I created the following script called *streams* to record it:

```
#!/bin/sh

# rips from Punk FM (http://punkfm.co.uk)
# this stream is broadcast from noon to 6pm PST Thu-Sat

URL='http://69.56.219.92:8072'
DAY=`date +%F-`

streamripper $URL -d /mnt/audio/mp3/streams -q -P $DAY -l 21720 --quiet &
```

This script rips the URL into my */mnt/audio/mp3/streams* directory, makes sure that the tracks are named sequentially with the -q argument, prepends the current day's timestamp with the -P option, and tells *streamtuner* to run for six hours and two minutes with the -l option (I added the extra two minutes in case my clock is out of sync with the streaming computer's clock). The --quiet option disables all normal output so that my *cron* job doesn't fire off an email to me each time the script runs. I then added the following line to my user's *crontab*:

```
59 11 * * 4-6 /home/greenfly/bin/streams
```

This line will execute the script at 11:59 A.M. on Thursday, Friday, and Saturday. Read the *crontab* manpage (**man 5 crontab**) for more information on how to schedule programs with *cron*.

Listen to Streams as They Are Ripped

Another nice feature of *streamripper* is the ability to create a relay server for streams as they are being ripped. The -r option tells *streamripper* to create a relay server on port 8000, or you can specify a different port to use as an argument. If port 8000 isn't available, *streamripper* will try to use higher and higher ports until it finds one it can use. Then you can point your music player at port 8000 (or the port you configured) on that machine either from the same computer (*http://localhost:8000*) or over the network (*http://ip_address:8000*). By default *streamripper* will only allow a single connection to this relay server, but you can pass the -R number argument to it to allow a specified number of clients to connect. If you set the argument to zero, *streamripper* will allow an unlimited number of clients to connect (well, limited by your bandwidth and processor speed). So, to rip and relay a stream and allow three clients to connect to it, type:

```
$ streamripper URL -r -R 3
```

If I wanted to allow three clients to connect to the stream my bash script recorded, I would change the command to the following:

```
streamripper $URL -d /mnt/audio/mp3/streams -q -P $DAY -l 21720 --quiet -r -R 3 &
```

Track Detection

streamripper automatically splits tracks in the stream based on the silence it detects when tracks change. This method isn't perfect however, and depending on the stream (such as streams that use cross-fading) you might end up with tracks that contain a few seconds of the previous song at the beginning, or a few seconds of the next song at the end. *streamripper* provides a series of --xs arguments that let you configure this algorithm for tricky streams. For instance, if each track begins with three seconds of the previous track, the following will tell *streamripper* to offset the track splitting by an extra three seconds (expressed as milliseconds):

```
$ streamripper URL --xs_offset=3000
```

Alternatively, if a track has three seconds of the next track at the end, you can set the offset to a negative amount:

```
$ streamripper URL --xs_offset=-3000
```

If you notice that *streamripper* contains a various amount of previous or following tracks, but it isn't a constant value, you can also have it create a number of seconds of padding around each track so that you can go back later and edit the MP3 by hand. For instance, to add two seconds of padding before the split point and three seconds after each split point, type:

```
$ streamripper URL --xs_padding=2000:3000
```

You can also combine the following two options. If for instance, each track contains a number of seconds of the previous track, but it varies between two and six seconds, you can set the split offset in the middle of the variation, or four seconds, and then create a padding of two seconds before and after the split:

```
$ streamripper URL --xs_offset=4000 --xs_padding=2000:2000
```

HACK #82 Rip Streaming Video

Use MPlayer to rip streaming video feeds directly to a file for later viewing.

With broadband connections becoming more and more the norm, many web sites are providing not just streaming audio but even streaming video content. Like with streaming audio, sometimes you would like to save a streaming video feed to a file for later (possibly offline) viewing. [Hack #81] discusses how to use *streamripper* to rip audio feeds, which it does well, but to rip video feeds you need to use a tool such as Mplayer.

MPlayer is an incredibly flexible video and audio player (for more information on MPlayer check out [Hack #48]). MPlayer supports a wide variety of audio and video formats including streaming audio and video and can also dump the raw video and audio streams directly to a file.

The first step to rip a stream is to get the URL for the streaming video. In some cases this is as easy as right-clicking a link on the web page and selecting Copy Link. Some video streams are embedded in a web page, so you might have to view the page's source code to find the direct link to the stream (many Quicktime feeds are like this). After you have found the URL, the next step is to play a bit of the stream to confirm that MPlayer can, in fact, access it:

```
$ mplayer http://movies.sample.com/example.mov
```

Replace the URL with the path to the video stream you want to play. After MPlayer does some initial caching of the streaming content, you will see the video playback in a window. If the video doesn't play, check the error output in the console for some reasons why. MPlayer might not have all of the codecs it needs to play the video, so check out [Hack #53] to make sure you have all of the codecs you need.

After MPlayer has successfully played part of the video, hit Ctrl-C to stop playback, then add two extra options to rip the stream:

```
$ mplayer URL -dumpstream -dumpfile filename
```

This command sets MPlayer in a special mode to dump the streaming content directly to the file you specify with the -dumpfile argument. Replace filename with the name of the output file you wish to use. Keep in mind that this is a raw output file directly from the stream, so to play it back in other video players you may need to convert it to a more universal format. For more information on converting video files between formats check out [Hack #63].

HACK #83 Command-Line Streaming MP3 Player

Use basic command-line tools to create your own streaming MP3 player.

When setting up Obsequeium (*http://obsbox.sf.net*) or Jinzora (*http://jinzora. org*) web jukeboxes [Hack #84], I've found it helpful to set up a dedicated streaming player so I can listen to my net jukebox constantly while testing. Preferably the MP3 stream should never stop and, should something happen to the playback, it should pause for a moment and try the stream again. It may seem the *mpg123/mpg321* command-line players are perfect for this task, but they have a habit of locking up and not exiting or retrying when something goes wrong with the stream. This makes them unsuitable for use as dedicated streaming players.

You can build a robust command-line streaming player with one command if you have *madplay* and *wget* installed. *wget* and *madplay* are both popular programs and should be prepackaged by your Linux distribution. Use your distribution's software installation tool to install these programs. If for some reason you don't have these tools prepackaged, download the tarballs from *http://www.underbit.com/products/mad/* and *http://www.gnu.org/software/ wget/wget.html*, compile, and install them according to the included installation instructions.

With *wget* and *madplay* installed, the following command will play the stream from *http://example.com/mystream*:

```
$ wget -q -O - http://example.com/mystream | madplay -Q --no-tty-control -
```

wget reads the MP3 stream and quietly writes it to stdout which gets piped to *madplay's* stdin. From there, *madplay* decodes the stream and writes it to the default sound device. The -Q and --no-tty-control options tell *madplay* to play the music without any text output and places the process in the background so it won't take over the terminal.

There is one more gotcha to overcome before our robust streaming MP3 player can run for days on end. MP3 streams that run for days have this nasty habit of dying right as you're grooving to your favorite track. To prevent this from happening, call the streaming player in a simple shell script loop:

```
#!/bin/sh
while [ 1 ]
do
    wget -q -O - http://example.com/mystream | madplay -Q --no-tty-control -
sleep 5
done
```

Should something happen with the stream and the player exits, it will pause for five seconds and then restart the stream again. The five-second pause prevents the player from pummeling your streaming server with connection requests in case something happens with the server.

Finally, to ensure the robustness of the command-line player, I recommend killing the player once a day at a slack time to restart the stream and make sure that it doesn't die in the middle of your favorite track. Use *cron* to accomplish this by adding this line to your *crontab* (edit your *crontab* with **crontab** –e):

```
0 4 * * * killall -9 madplay
```

This causes *cron* to kill *madplay* each day at 4 A.M. Pick a time when you expect the least number of people to listen, because listeners will need to sit through five seconds of silence.

That completes our hassle-free robust streaming MP3 player. This player configuration has played music for me for nearly two years without requiring human attention.

—Robert Kaye

H A C K   **Build a Linux Jukebox with Jinzora**
#84   Sharing your music collection with friends has never been easier.

If you've ever wished that you could share your entire audio collection with others and build a communal MP3 collection that your friends can tap into, then this hack has a perfect solution in store for you. Until recently, Linux users had the choice between two leading networked jukeboxes: Netjuke and Jinzora. But now Netjuke has merged into Jinzora and now two development teams work toward one common goal. This means that you can expect the development pace for Jinzora to pick up quite a bit, which seems slightly ironic for an application package already overflowing with features.

Jinzora's (*http://www.jinzora.org*) impressive feature list includes:

- Fully web based, so there are no client-side tools to install
- Complete music collection browsing (by artist, album, or genre) and searching

- Media management support for retagging and massaging your music collection via the web interface
- Download lyrics, cover art, and metadata over the net
- Suggest related artists from your own collection
- Stream from the server via m3u playlists
- Support for multiple users and themes

Since Jinzora uses the web interface for everything, the only software required by the client machine is an MP3 player, which makes Jinzora particularly useful in mixed OS environments. Jinzora also supports user accounts, which gives you control over who can view, play, and manipulate the music collection. All of these features make it perfect for an office environment or a large home environment where multiple users want to share one music collection. Figure 4-2 shows a typical artist browse screen in Jinzora.

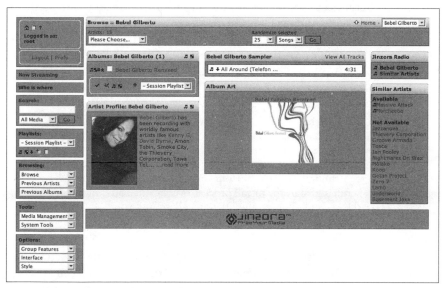

Figure 4-2. Snapshot of Jinzora artist browse screen

Even though Jinzora requires a lot of packages to run, the installation process proves quite simple. To install it, you'll need a web server capable of running PHP scripts, which should be prepackaged by your Linux distribution of choice. Use your distributions software installation tool to install these programs. If for some reason you don't have these tools prepackaged, download the tarballs from *http://httpd.apache.org* and *http://php.net*, compile, and install them according to the included installation instructions.

Once you have Apache set up, download the latest Jinzora tarball and untar it into the DocumentRoot of your Apache web server. Apache serves its files from this location, and the exact location of this directory depends on how you installed the web server. If you're not sure, locate Apache's configuration file *httpd.conf* and search for DocumentRoot. After untarring the Jinzora tarball, change to the *jinzora2* directory and run:

```
$ sh configure.sh
```

This sets up the permissions so that the install can proceed. After this, switch to your web browser and load the install pages with this URL: *http://myserver.com/jinzora2/index.php*. Replace myserver.com with the URL for your own Apache installation. This brings up the excellent Jinzora web-based installer—from here you'll need to follow the instructions on the web pages to finish the setup of Jinzora. During the first install step, Jinzora checks for prerequisite software and verifies the permissions on the files and directories that it needs to use. If you need to install more software modules (e.g., required PHP modules) during this step, make sure to restart your Apache server after you've installed the new modules to ensure that the new modules get loaded into Apache.

> The installer does seem to have one flaw—once you've made a selection, Jinzora remembers your selection and doesn't give you the option to change it later in the install process. Rather than going in and hand-editing the configuration files to change the configuration files to your liking, it may be easier for you to wipe out the existing installation. This way you can simply untar the Jinzora tarball, re-run the *configure.sh* script and start the install process over again. You'll find that the second time around the install script, you'll fly right though it.

In the last step of the install, you're prompted for your media directories to import existing MP3s into your new Jinzora setup. Point Jinzora to your MP3 collection and have it import all your music. Once Jinzora completes the import, it will launch Jinzora and prompt you to remove the *install* directory that contains unsafe installation files (for security reasons). Now you're ready to explore Jinzora and invite your friends to help you build and enjoy the MP3 collection.

—Robert Kaye

Stream Video with VLC

HACK
#85
VLC provides the ability to stream video to and from any platform it runs on.

There are many different commercial streaming video servers out on the Internet, but if you have installed VLC [Hack #56], not only can you view videos, but you can also stream them across the network. This hack describes how to use the VLC streaming video wizard to stream your video content across the network.

There are a number of reasons you might want to stream video using VLC besides just "because you can." Streaming video across the network puts the primary load of encoding video onto the server. This means you can play back video on systems that might be too slow to play the video otherwise because the viewing application only needs to perform one task—decoding the video rather than the two tasks of encoding and simultaneously decoding. Or you might store your video files on a fileserver and want to play them on your laptop over the wireless network, but the wireless link is a bit too slow to play it directly over the network. Or, you might just want to play the same video on multiple computers at the same time. Whatever the reason, VLC provides a wizard that takes most of the guesswork out of configuring a streaming server.

To set up the streaming video server, first launch VLC and click File → Wizard. Select "Stream to Network" in the window that appears and click Next. The next window lets you choose the input stream to use. You may choose to input using a local file, in which case you click Choose to select one or more files from your file system. Alternatively you can click "Existing playlist" to select one or more files from your current playlist. Click Next once you have selected input to stream.

The next window lets you choose your streaming method. If you plan to stream to only one computer, select UDP Unicast and enter the client's IP address in the text box below. UDP Multicast lets you stream to multiple computers using multicast. If you have a multicast network, enter the IP address of the multicast group in the text box (between 224.0.0.0 and 239. 255.255.255). If you aren't sure what multicast is, you probably want to choose either UDP Unicast or HTTP. Click HTTP and VLC will stream over HTTP. You may either enter an IP address and port that VLC will listen for incoming connections. A better move is to just leave it blank and have VLC default to listening to connections for your IP address on port 8080. Click Next after you have made your choices.

The next window allows you to choose how to encapsulate the video. What you choose here depends largely on the speed of the streaming server and the speed of the client. If your client is fast, you might want to stick with the default format that VLC chooses for the video. For slower clients you might want to choose MPEG S (MPEG transport stream format) to stream MPEG video, which slower computers will have an easier time playing. The next window lets you configure the Time-To-Live setting for UDP Unicast methods. Generally leave this value alone so VLC will use the default. Click Finish and VLC will start streaming the video.

Once the video begins streaming, you can pause or stop playback from the VLC controls just like with any video. On the client side, launch VLC (or any other video player like MPlayer that can handle VLC streams) click File → Open Network Stream and choose either UDP/RTP, UDP/RTP Multicast, or HTTP to match the VLC server settings. Click OK, and VLC will start playback of the streaming video in progress.

HACK #86　Grab Podcasts from the Command Line

A simple shell script is all it takes to pull down your favorite podcasts from the command line.

While streaming audio on the Internet has been around for a number of years, one problem is that since it is a live stream, you have to tune in to the stream at a certain time or you miss the broadcast. [Hack #81] discusses one method for saving streaming broadcasts, but a number of people have come up with another solution—podcasting. Podcasting is a way to publish files (most often audio files) on the Internet using RSS feeds. There are three basic steps to podcasting:

1. A podcaster records a broadcast in some audio format and then makes it available on her web site.

2. The podcast RSS feed gets updated with the link to the new content and people who have subscribed to the RSS feed then get the notification of the new content.

3. Subscribers download the podcast and listen to it on their computers or portable music players.

There are a number of programs out there for various platforms that aggregate podcast feeds and keep track of and download new feeds when they appear. Many of them even synchronize the new feeds with portable audio players such as an iPod so you can listen to the broadcast at your leisure (this is where the "pod" in podcasting came from). Under Linux, one such program is Bashpodder.

Bashpodder is impressive in its pure simplicity. Bashpodder is comprised of a forty-or-so-line shell script, a small stylesheet, and a config file that simply contains links to RSS feeds you want to subscribe to. To install Bashpodder, download *bashpodder.shell*, *parse_enclosure,xsl*, and *bp.conf* files from the official site at *http://linc.homeunix.org:8080/scripts/bashpodder* and put them in a special directory (such as *~/bashpodder*). Then make the *bashpodder.shell* script executable. Here are the commands necessary to set up Bashpodder:

```
greenfly@moses:~/$ mkdir ~/bashpodder
greenfly@moses:~/$ cd bashpodder
greenfly@moses:~/bashpodder$ wget http://linc.homeunix.org:8080/scripts/
bashpodder/bashpodder.shell
greenfly@moses:~/bashpodder$ wget http://linc.homeunix.org:8080/scripts/
bashpodder/parse_enclosure.xsl
greenfly@moses:~/bashpodder$ wget http://linc.homeunix.org:8080/scripts/
bashpodder/bp.conf
greenfly@moses:~/bashpodder$ chmod a+x bashpodder.shell
```

The next step is to configure Bashpodder with the feeds you wish to subscribe to. Open *bp.conf* in a text editor and add the URL to your RSS feed to the file, one feed per line. By default *bp.conf* contains some sample feeds the Bashpodder author likes, so you can use those as examples.

After *bp.conf* is configured with your feeds, you are ready to grab the latest podcasts. Run the Bashpodder shell from the command line:

```
greenfly@moses$ ~/bashpodder/bashpodder.shell
grep: podcast.log: No such file or directory
. . .
```

The first time you run Bashpodder, it will basically download all of the podcasts linked to inside your config file, which might take some time. Don't worry about the grep: podcast.log: No such file or directory error. Bashpodder creates that file after the first run so it can keep track of what it has already downloaded. Again, since it is downloading every single file linked to in the feeds, it will take some time to complete. Bashpodder puts each of the files it grabs in a directory named after the current date so you can look inside that directory to keep track of the progress.

 If you don't want to download every single item in a podcast the first time through, create your own *podcast.log* file and add direct links to each of the MP3s you want Bashpodder to ignore. Then run *bashpodder.shell* and it will skip over those files.

Since Bashpodder is just a shell script, it lends itself very well to running within a *cron* job. This way, you can synchronize your podcasts daily, weekly, or whenever you want. For example, to run Bashpodder every day at 4:30 A. M., edit your user's *crontab* (type **crontab -e**) and add the following line:

```
03 4    * * *   /home/username/bashpodder/bashpodder.shell
```

Replace the above path with the path to your *bashpodder.shell* file.

The nice thing about the simplicity of Bashpodder is that with minimal shell scripting ability you can customize it to your needs. You could add a shell command to synchronize the downloaded files with your portable audio player, or you could change how it names the directory it stores the podcasts in, or any number of other things. The Bashpodder site contains some of the customizations other users have made already.

Get Podcasts with a GUI

#87

Use Monopod to pull down podcasts with a simple GUI interface.

A big attraction of podcasting is convenience: downloading voice or music shows from the Web for later listening on your computer or music player. Convenience is something that Monopod, a podcast client for the GNOME desktop, does well. Instead of presenting a baffling plethora of configurable options, it is designed to let you subscribe to podcast feeds, go do something more interesting, and then listen at your leisure.

Install

To install Monopod, visit *http://downloads.usefulinc.com/monopod*. From there you will find up-to-date instructions on how to get started. Ready-to-use packages can be found for some Linux distributions, while some other users will have to compile Monopod themselves.

Run Monopod

Start Monopod from its entry in the GNOME menu, or by running *monopod* from the command line. A black circular icon shows up in the system notification area (if you don't have a notification area, add one to the GNOME panel first by right-clicking on the panel and choosing "Add to Panel").

Monopod's various actions can be used by right-clicking on the notification area icon, as shown in Figure 4-3.

Figure 4-3. Monopod's main menu

To control which podcast feeds you are subscribed to, choose the Subscriptions menu item. You will see a window similar to that shown in Figure 4-4.

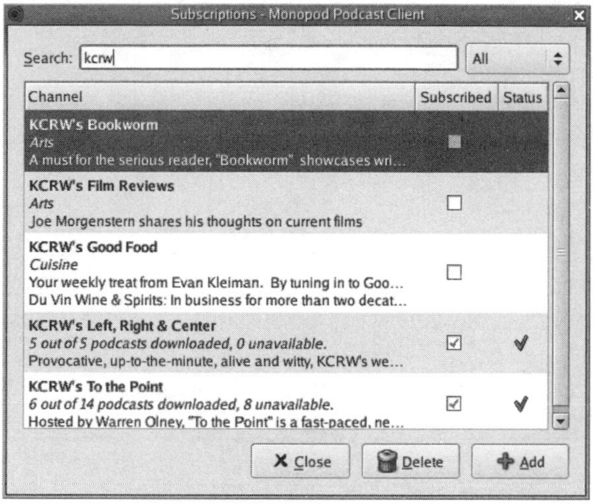

Figure 4-4. Monopod subscriptions window

The subscriptions window will be filled initially with some default channels, which you can use to experiment with. Check the box in the Subscribed column to make Monopod retrieve podcasts for a channel. The download status of the channel is shown in the subscriptions window. Each channel is checked once a day for new content, and the new audio is downloaded automatically onto your hard drive.

To add channels not in the default list, click the Add button and enter the URL of the podcast channel. Various directories of podcasts can be found easily on the Web by searching for podcast directory. One such popular directory is at *http://www.podcast.net*.

Once you've found a channel you want to subscribe to, copy the URL for a podcast channel's RSS feed into the Add Channel window. Alternatively, drag and drop the link from your web browser into the Subscriptions window.

Listening to Podcasts

Once Monopod has started downloading podcasts, you want to listen to them. Select Show Podcasts from Monopod's main menu, and you will see the folder to which your music has been downloaded, similar to that in Figure 4-5.

Monopod creates a folder per channel. Inside each folder are the audio files for the podcast, along with a *playlist.m3u* file. This playlist file can be loaded by media players such as XMMS and Totem, and will play each podcast episode in turn from the channel.

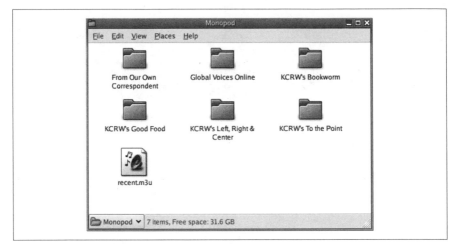

Figure 4-5. Downloaded podcast folder

In addition, Monopod creates a *recent.m3u* playlist in the top-level folder, which is simply a playlist of the most recent podcasts downloaded.

Synchronizing with an iPod

Monopod provides some basic iPod synchronization facilities. Plug in your iPod, select the Update iPod menu item from the main menu, and you see a window similar to that in Figure 4-6.

Figure 4-6. Monopod's iPod window

The Update iPod window gives you a choice between different iPods attached to the system: some lucky folks have more than one! Click the Update button to synchronize with the iPod. This removes any listened-to podcasts from the iPod and adds in any new ones. Monopod creates a "Recent podcasts" playlist on the iPod, giving easy access to the podcast audio programs.

—Edd Dumbill

Broadcast Sound to AM with a Monitor

HACK #88

Use the TEMPEST surveillance technology to broadcast sound from your monitor to an AM radio.

If you hang around tinfoil hat–wearing paranoid types much, you might have heard about van Eck scanning or TEMPEST. TEMPEST (an acronym for Transient Electromagnetic Pulse Emanation Standard) is a term used to describe techniques used to prevent sensitive information from being leaked from computer equipment via electromagnetic emanation. In general, electronic equipment sends out electromagnetic waves when it's powered on. A common illustration of this fact is the interference you might get on your television when various electronic devices are turned on around it. Your computer monitor (CRTs especially, but also LCDs to a lesser degree) also sends out electromagnetic waves when it is powered on. Methods exist to pick up these signals from a distance and, using special equipment, reconstruct what is displayed on the monitor without actually seeing it.

While there are a number of practical uses for this type of technology, especially for surveillance, for this hack, I cover one of the less practical and more fun applications. Since you can control what signals emanate from your screen, you can conceivably send out messages using just your computer monitor. A special piece of Linux software, *tempest_for_eliza*, uses this principle to actually broadcast sound from a monitor that can be picked up with an AM radio.

The first step is to download and build the *tempest_for_eliza* software. Download the latest version from the official page at *http://www.erikyyy.de/tempest*. This software requires that SDL libraries be installed to compile, but most distributions package this for you; just use your package manager and install the SDL (or possibly libSDL) and SDL-devel (or possibly libSDL-dev) packages. Then extract the source from the tarball, configure, and compile *tempest_for_eliza*:

```
greenfly@moses:~$ tar xfvz tempest_for_eliza-1.0.5.tar.gz
greenfly@moses:~$ cd tempest_for_eliza
greenfly@moses:~/tempest_for_eliza$ ./configure
greenfly@moses:~/tempest_for_eliza$ ./make
```

Now that the program is compiled, you need to make sure that X is set up appropriately. This method works best if X11 is at a low color depth, so use your X configuration tool to change the default color depth to 8 bits per pixel (bpp). Alternatively, edit */etc/X11/XF86Config-4* or */etc/X11/xorg.conf*, find the Screen section in the file, and change DefaultDepth to 8. Also make sure that there is a Display subsection there for the 8 bpp color depth. Once X is configured, restart X so you go into the new color depth.

Now that X has restarted, open a terminal and type **xvidtune** to start the *xvidtune* program. Write down the HDisplay, VDisplay, HTotal, VTotal, and Pixel Clock values. Now go get an AM radio and find a frequency where there isn't much noise. For this example I will use 750 kHz. Change to your *tempest_for_eliza* directory and execute the *tempest_for_eliza* program inside with the pixel-clock (multiplied by one million), HDisplay, VDisplay, HTotal, and radio frequency values, followed by the file to play. To play the sample "Fur Elise" by Beethoven that is included with the program, type:

```
greenfly@moses:~/tempest_for_eliza$ ./tempest_for_eliza 56300000 800 600 \
1046 750000 songs/forelise
```

In this example my pixel clock was 56.3 (56.3 * 1,000,000 = 56,300,000), my resolution was 800×600, my HTotal value was 1,046, and I wanted to broadcast on 750 kHz (750,000). You probably will need to change most if not all of these variables to suit the values *xvidtune* displays on your monitor.

Once you start the program, your monitor will display lots of what appears to be random static. Get your AM radio and slowly tune it to the broadcast frequency search around that frequency until you find the (possibly faint) tune. It is easier to sync it up, I've found, if you search for the periods where the monitor turns black (for silence) and listen for that bit of silence on the radio. It might take some experimenting with different frequencies before you find one that comes through clearly.

Of course, this program doesn't actually play sound files. The file it plays is a text file that lists particular notes to play in order. Check out the different files in the songs directory to see how to construct a sound file of your own.

Also included with this software is the *tempest_for_mp3* program, which will let you broadcast MP3 files using the same method. I've noticed this method is trickier to get working, so you will probably have to experiment a bit before you find the right combination of frequencies that work for you. The first step is to run the *tempest_for_mp3* program and point it at a nonexistent file. The *tempest_for_mp3* program has a few extra options, and again order matters, so pass the following settings in order: pixel clock, HDisplay, VDisplay, HTotal, VTotal, radio frequency, play mode (use 0), amplification (use 20), and the filename. Here's an example:

```
greenfly@moses:~/tempest_for_eliza$ ./tempest_for_mp3 56300000 800 600 1046\
631 750000 0 20 foo.raw
```

Notice that most of these options are the same as before, only I added the VTotal setting (631), the play mode (0) and the amplification (20). Run this with a nonexistent file so that *tempest_for_mp3* will pass the audio file frequency to use with those settings in its output so you can create a special raw audio file with that frequency. Look for a line in the output that says something like:

```
audio file frequency should be 13519.890261 Hz
```

Then run the included *mksong.sh* script to convert your MP3 to the raw audio file *tempest_for_mp3* needs:

```
greenfly@moses:~/tempest_for_eliza$ ./mksong.sh 13519 example.mp3 output.raw
```

Notice that I listed the audio frequency in Hz. This script requires that both *sox* and *amp* be installed, but if you want, you can replace *amp* with another program that can convert MP3s to WAV files provided you change the *mksong.sh* script as well. Now that you have the *output.raw* file, run *tempest_for_mp3* again, specifying the new file:

```
greenfly@moses:~/tempest_for_eliza$ ./tempest_for_mp3 56300000 800 600 1046
631 750000 0 20 output.raw
```

You will notice that the monitor displays even more interesting static this time around. Slowly tune into the appropriate frequency until you hear the audio. Again, experiment with different frequencies until you find one that works for you.

Web

Hacks 89–100

The Web is a place where all types of media come out to play. While the Web was originally a text-only media, nowadays it's not uncommon for pages to make use of text, images, sound, and video to display information. Historically, a lot of these features didn't play well with Linux-based browsers, which caused some members of the Linux community to dismiss web-based multimedia, take their ball, and go home. These days even Linux users can be part of the game. Someone browsing the Web with Linux can access most, if not all, the multimedia content on their favorite sites, from movies to PDFs to Flash pages.

This chapter highlights some handy tools Linux has available to use multimedia content on the Web, such as plug-ins that help you watch video inside your browser, manage PDFs, and grab color profiles from web sites. You can also generate and host your own web images with a webcam and image gallery software. Follow the steps in these hacks to get the most from your Web experience.

HACK #89 Install the Macromedia Plug-in in a Flash

Add Flash and Shockwave support to Mozilla-based browsers and Konqueror.

Flash and Shockwave plug-ins have a rather mixed reputation among Internet users. Some people think that Flash and Shockwave are overused on web sites and, as the name itself suggests, offer more flash than substance. Others enjoy the ability to view interactive content on the Web like games and animated cartoons. Whichever side of this debate you rest on, if you want to view Flash- or Shockwave-based content on the Web under Linux, you need to install the Flash Player web browser plug-in.

Certain distributions have prepackaged installers to automate Flash player installation, but for the purposes of this hack, I'll describe the all-purpose, all-distribution method. The first step is to download the Flash Player package from *http://www.macromedia.com/shockwave/download/alternates*. Scroll down to the Other Operating Systems table, choose the newest Flash Player package listed for Linux x86, and save it to your hard drive.

Next, open a terminal and extract the tarball you have downloaded:

```
$ tar xvzf flash_player_7_linux.tar.gz
```

There is a shell script installer you can run; however, it's just as easy to copy the two plug-in files to your Mozilla plug-in directory. Change to the extracted directory and copy the following two files to your Mozilla plug-in directory as root (change the *plugins* directory to match your Mozilla plug-ins directory):

```
[root@localhost ~]# cd install_flash_player_7_linux
[root@localhost install_flash_player_7_linux]# cp libflashplayer.so \
flashplayer.xpt /usr/lib/mozilla/plugins
```

At this point, restart any browser you have open. If you use Mozilla-based browsers, you can go straight to testing the plug-in. If you use Konqueror, you may need to first scan for the new plug-in. To do this, launch Konqueror and click Settings → Configure Konqueror. In the window that appears, scroll down and select the Plugins option from the list on the left. Make sure the directory where you added the plug-ins exists and then click Scan for New Plugins. The Shockwave plug-in should appear in the list of plug-ins shown in the Plugins tab in that window. Click OK to close the settings window.

To test the plug-in, visit *http://www.shockwave.com* and make sure that all of the content on the page is visible (if it isn't, you will see blank sections on the screen and your browser might prompt you to install a plug-in). If the plug-in isn't working, confirm that you have copied the two plug-in files to the Mozilla plug-ins directory and that they are readable by all users.

Use the Real RealPlayer
HACK #90

Install the official RealPlayer to enable streaming multimedia apps from your Mozilla-based or Konqueror browser.

It used to be that the Web was mostly a text-based medium. Along came images and sounds, and finally video content. It's nice to read a review of a movie, or a description of a keynote speech, but it's even better to be able to watch a movie preview and a live keynote speech directly from a browser. There are a number of different streaming audio and video formats that are popular on the Web, including the Real audio and video formats.

Recently, Real has decided to base their commercial player on their open source Helix player (*https://player.helixcommunity.org*). While Real has released Linux-compatible players and plug-ins for some time, this move helps ensure future Linux compatibility in the player and format.

To install the RealPlayer application and plug-ins, visit *http://www.real.com* and click on the Download RealPlayer link on the main page. The download will be in the form of a single executable file named something like *RealPlayer10GOLD.bin* (the site detects that you are running Linux, so it provides the correct file automatically). After the file is downloaded, open a terminal and change to the directory storing the file. Give the file executable permissions and then run it from the terminal:

```
$ chmod a+x RealPlayer10GOLD.bin
$ ./RealPlayer10GOLD.bin
```

The RealPlayer install script extracts temporary files into the current directory and prompts you for a directory to use to install the program. Since you are installing this as a user, pick a directory such as */home/username/ RealPlayer*. The installer will extract all the RealPlayer files into that directory and set up the Mozilla plug-ins, but not the actual media player. Once the installer is finished, run the *realplay* program to perform the initial setup process for the player itself.

```
$ ~/RealPlayer/realplay
```

Now the plug-in should be ready to use. If you use Konqueror, you might need to first scan for the new plug-in. To do this, launch Konqueror and click Settings → Configure Konqueror. In the window that appears, scroll down and select the Plugins option from the list on the left and then click Scan for New Plugins. Click OK to close the settings window.

Now when you click on any Real Audio or Video content, your browser will prompt you to open it using *realplay*. Then RealPlayer will open in a separate window and start playback.

Watch Videos Within Firefox

HACK #91

Use mplayerplug-*in* to view video embedded into web pages.

If you chat with a group of geeks for any extended period of time, the conversation inevitably steers into talks of the "good old days" of computing, when geeks were geeks and you edited your files with a magnet and a magnifying glass. Let me be the first to break rank and say that the good old days of watching embedded web video under Linux were anything but. In the case of QuickTime video (such as movie trailers), once Linux was able to play them, you still couldn't watch them in a browser: instead you had to put on your detective hat and often dig around in the web page source for the URL you needed to download the video. That of course was only if you could find the right URL.

MPlayer's support of streaming URLs from the command line improved things a bit, but considering the steps Windows users had to take to watch video streams on the Web, it was still pretty troublesome. A breakthrough came with the creation of the *mplayerplug-in*—a plug-in for Mozilla-based browsers (Konqueror is not currently supported) that embedded MPlayer into web pages offering streaming video. Now every video that MPlayer can play outside of the browser you can play embedded inside the browser so the experience is more or less the same as browsing under Windows.

Since *mplayerplug-in* uses MPlayer for all the video playback, you will need MPlayer version 0.92 or higher installed on your system. ([Hack #48] explains how to install and use MPlayer.)

The downloads page for *mplayerplug-in* at *http://mplayerplug-in.sourceforge. net* offers links to precompiled packages for a number of Linux distributions, so installation is simple: download the package that matches your distribution and install it using your distribution's package manager. If you use a Debian-based distribution, the package is called *mozilla-mplayer* and is a part of the Debian "unstable contrib" repository. Add the following line to your */etc/apt/sources.list*, run **apt-get update**, and then install the package:

```
deb ftp://ftp.nerim.net/debian-marillat/ unstable main
```

If there isn't a package for your particular distribution, just download the source code from the project page and follow the installation instructions at *http:// mplayerplug-in.sourceforge.net/install.php* to compile and install the software.

After the software is installed, open Firefox or another Mozilla-based browser and browse to your favorite movie-trailer site. When you open a page that has embedded video, *mplayerplug-in* should display in the video's space. By default *mplayerplug-in* caches 25% of the video before it plays, and it shows the current cache status as it is downloading. When the cache limit of 25% is reached the video begins. You can control playback with the buttons along the bottom of the interface. There is also a button to the far right of the controls that will toggle full-screen mode for the video.

mplayerplug-in chooses sane defaults, but it also provides a number of options for you to tweak. Configuration tweaks that affect all users can be done in */etc/mplayerplug-in.conf*. Or you can put a configuration that just affects your user in *~/.mplayer/mplayerplug-in.conf*. This file contains all *mplayerplug-in* options, set to their defaults and commented out. This way you can see your options and their normal behaviors. The *mplayerplug-in* documentation at *http://mplayerplug-in.sourceforge.net/config.php* describes the purposes of all the options, but a few bear mentioning here. Table 5-1 lists a number of interesting *mplayerplug-in* options and their functions.

Table 5-1. mplayerplug-in options

Option	Function
vo=[xv,x11...etc.]	Override the default MPlayer video output settings.
ao=[arts,esd,oss...etc.]	Override the default MPlayer audio output settings.
qtspeed=[low|medium|high]	Set the QT speed, low for dialup, medium for DSL, and high for higher-speed connections.
noembed=[0|1]	If set to 1, will force video to be displayed in its own window instead of embedded in the browser.
keep-download=[0|1]	If set to 1, videos you view will be automatically saved to the directory specified in *dload-dir*.
dload-dir=*/path/to/directory*	Where to store movies that *mplayerplug-in* downloads.

H A C K   Kaffeinate Konqueror
#92   Use the Kaffeine video player to watch videos embedded into the Konqueror browser.

If you are a Konqueror user and read "Watch Videos Within Firefox" **[Hack #91]**, you might feel a bit left out. The *mplayerplug-in* is all fine and good, but you want an embedded video player that fits in with KDE and its Swiss Army knife browser Konqueror. There are a few options to embed video inside Konqueror, and this hack focuses on how to use the Kaffeine video player from within the web browser.

Kaffeine is one of a few graphical video players designed for KDE (although it works with GNOME or other desktop environments as well), so from the start it integrates well with KDE's general look and feel. Kaffeine uses *xine-lib* behind the scenes to manage video playback and, as such, can play basically any type of media xine can.

To install Kaffeine, visit the official page at *http://kaffeine.sourceforge.net* and download the package for your Linux distribution from their download page. If your distribution doesn't have a prepackaged Kaffeine binary, download and compile the source according to the installation instructions.

Once installed, Kaffeine automatically integrates with your Konqueror browser. This means that if you don't already have an embedded video player configured, Kaffeine will assume that role for most embedded video content. Visit a streaming video page such as *http://quicktime.apple.com* and try out one of the videos. Kaffeine will load the video inside the web page and start playback. Right-click on the video to pause, stop, play, and skip through the video. This embedded plug-in will work with default settings even if you haven't started up the full Kaffeine application yet.

> The Kaffeine embedded player won't show up as a plug-in for Konqueror, so don't worry if you don't see it there.

If Kaffeine doesn't automatically start up when you visit a page with streaming video, or it starts in a window of its own, you need to modify Konqueror's file associations. Click Settings → Configure Konqueror, and select File Associations from the left side of the window that appears. Next click on the video part of the file association tree and make sure that it is set to embed video by default. Also open up the video tree and find the particular video stream type from the list and make sure that it is set to play embedded in Konqueror and that Kaffeine is the first application on the list to try.

Install the Acrobat Reader Plug-in

HACK #93

View PDFs within your web browser with the official Acrobat Reader plug-in.

While there is still quite a ways to go, commercial support for the Linux platform has come a long way, particularly in the multimedia realm. One good example of this is Adobe's Acrobat Reader program. While there are a number of other open source alternatives under Linux for reading PDF files, they neither seem to quite have as nice a user interface nor render PDFs as nicely as Acrobat Reader. In this hack, I describe the steps needed to install and configure Acrobat Reader and its associated browser plug-in.

Adobe's Acrobat Reader software is proprietary, so most major distributions don't package it out of the box. This means that the standard methods you might use to install software automatically under Linux won't work, so you must install Acrobat Reader the old-fashioned Windows way—go to the official web site, download the software from there, and install it.

> A number of third-party or non-free repositories exist for different distributions that have packaged Acrobat Reader, or at least a script that automates the process of downloading and installing it. The method and package name to use will vary depending on your distribution, but *acroread* is a common name for the package, with *acroread-plugin* and *mozilla-acroread* being popular names for the Mozilla plug-in.

First, visit the official Acrobat Reader page at *http://www.adobe.com/products/acrobat/readermain.html*. Click the Get Acrobat Reader graphic. This page lets you choose language, connection speed, and platform options. If you use an RPM-based distribution, choose Linux (*.rpm*) as your platform. Otherwise choose Linux (*.tar.gz*) and submit your information. Click the download link on the next page and download the *.rpm* or *.tar.gz* file to your home directory.

If you chose the *.rpm* file, use your standard package installation tool to install the RPM or become root and type:

```
# rpm -Uvh AdobeReader_enu-7.0.0-2.i386.rpm
```

If you chose the *.tar.gz* file, extract the file and then execute the install script inside as root:

```
# tar xzf AdbeRdr70_linux_enu.tar.gz
# ./AdobeReader/INSTALL
```

For either method, all of the Acrobat Reader files will be installed under */usr/local/Adobe* and a symlink to */usr/local/Adobe/bin/acroread* will be placed under */usr/bin*. You can type **acroread** from the command line to launch the full Acrobat Reader at this point.

One final step is involved to install the Acrobat Reader plug-in for Mozilla. Adobe includes a basic install script that automates the process. As root, type:

```
# /usr/local/Adobe/Acrobat7.0/Browser/install_browser_plugin
```

When prompted, tell the script to perform a global installation, and then point it to your browser install directory (usually */usr/lib/mozilla*). The plug-in is copied to the plug-ins directory. Restart your browser if it is running and then browse to a PDF on the Web. If you use Konqueror, you might need to first scan for the new plug-in. To do this, launch Konqueror and click Settings → Configure Konqueror. In the window that appears, scroll down and select the Plugins option from the list on the left and then click "Scan for New Plugins." Click OK to close the settings window. When you open a PDF from your browser window, Adobe Acrobat will launch inside the browser pane just like on Windows and Mac OS X.

HACK #94 Control Your Media Player with Firefox

Use the FoxyTunes plug-in as a remote control for your media player without leaving Firefox.

If you are like me, you spend a good deal of the day looking at a web browser window. I like to keep my web browser window almost completely maximized when I can, which means that other apps, such as my media player, end up being minimized or rolled up to some degree. To switch tracks you need to set up key bindings, or you are left unshading or unmini-mizing the media player just to skip a track. With the FoxyTunes Firefox plug-in, this is no longer the case—you can control your media player directly from your Firefox window.

To get FoxyTunes, click Tools → Extensions in your Firefox window to go to the extensions manager. Then click on Get More Extensions to go to the main Firefox extensions page. From there you can search for FoxyTunes—

although I often find it is directly linked to on the main page. The Foxy-Tunes extensions page will provide an install link. Click on the link to install the FoxyTunes plug-in and then restart Firefox.

When Firefox restarts, you will see a new set of controls in the bottom right-hand corner of the screen (see Figure 5-1). Most of the buttons have the familiar audio control icons for play, pause, and so on and each has a description that will pop up if you hover over the button. The first button, which looks like two music notes, is of immediate interest because this is where you configure FoxyTunes for your player. FoxyTunes supports a wide range of media players on multiple platforms, so you can use this on Windows or Mac OS X as well. Click the music notes button, click Player → Select, and choose your media player from the list. Under Linux, Foxy-Tunes supports amaroK, Beep, Juk, Music Player Daemon, Noatun, Rhythmbox, and XMMS.

Figure 5-1. FoxyTunes toolbar

After your media player is selected, click the Play button to launch the player if it isn't loaded yet or to tell it to start playing. While a file is playing, hover your mouse over the single music note icon to display track information. If you would prefer FoxyTunes to be in a different location on your Firefox window, click one of the corners of the interface and drag it to a different location. If you want to hide most of the interface, click the triangle on the far right of the controls. Click the triangle on the far left side to toggle the track display on or off.

 FoxyTunes supports a number of skins as well. Click Main Menu → Configuration → Skins to go to the main Foxy-Tunes skins page, where you can view screenshots and install new skins.

HACK #95 Grab Color Profiles from Other Web Sites

Use the ColorZilla Firefox extension to sample colors from any web site you visit with a simple eyedropper interface.

They say that a good artist borrows and a great artist steals. Sometimes when you browse the Web you run across a site and think "Man, those colors would look perfect on my page." What you might do then is either view the source code for the page to find color settings for fonts or backgrounds, or you might even open up one of the images on the site in an image manipulation tool such as the GIMP so you can analyze it with the eyedropper. If you ever find yourself in this kind of situation, ColorZilla is for you.

ColorZilla is a Mozilla Firefox extension that allows you to scan any web page for individual pixel colors. Once installed, you can enable ColorZilla, and the mouse becomes an eyedropper tool. Click a location on the page and the color settings will be displayed along the bottom.

ColorZilla is relatively easy to install. Open Firefox and click Tools → Extensions and then "Get New Extensions" to load the Firefox extensions page. ColorZilla is located under the Miscellaneous extensions category, or you can visit the official page directly at *http://www.iosart.com/firefox/colorzilla*. Click on the link to the ColorZilla *.xpi* file to install the extension into Firefox. Newer versions of ColorZilla claim you aren't required to restart Firefox once it is installed, but you might want to restart in any case.

After the extension is installed, you will notice a new eyedropper icon along the bottom left-hand corner of the Firefox window (Figure 5-2). To get a color profile, click the eyedropper and then move your mouse around the web page. The color stats for your current mouse position will appear along the bottom. When you have found a color you want to save, click the mouse to set that color. Alternatively, click the eyedropper to toggle out of eyedropper mode. If you have saved a color, you can either jot it down, or right-click on the eyedropper to be presented with the color in a number of formats. Click one of these formats to copy it to your clipboard so you can paste it elsewhere.

	#FFFF80 | ΔX: 3, ΔY: 158 | a.navigation-link | 58x16 | X: 22, Y: 8

Figure 5-2. ColorZilla toolbar

On some web sites, you might find that it's difficult to hone in on exactly the color you want just because there are so many other colors surrounding it. Luckily, ColorZilla provides a zoom tool as well. Right-click on the eyedropper and choose your level of zoom from the Zoom menu. If you selected a higher percentage of zoom, the web page becomes more pixelated so you can more easily find the exact pixel you want.

 You can use ColorZilla to set up your own color profiles. Right-click the eyedropper and choose Color Picker. A new window appears with a palette you can adjust to find just the right color.

Browse Graphical Sites from an xterm

Install the w3m-img extension and view web sites and their images from within a regular xterm.

This book talks a lot about the different types of multimedia on the Web. Generally speaking you want to use a standard web browser to access all of this content, but sometimes it can be useful to test your site against a text-based browser to see how your code holds up. Maybe you just like to browse the Web from a text browser for the sheer geek factor. Whatever the reason, text-based web browsers generally make you miss out on all of the multimedia content on the Web—even the images. In this hack I tell you how to use the *w3m* browser to look at web sites and their images from an xterm.

When you think about text-based web browsers, usually you think of a browser like *lynx* or *links*. Over the past few years, a new text-based web browser called w3m has started to get more use due to its support for complicated layouts, its *vi*-style navigation, and now, its support for in-line images. With this feature, w3m displays the web page and renders the images within the terminal itself.

It used to be that image rendering was a separate extension to w3m. Nowadays it is part of the full w3m project; however many distributions package the binary with image support in a separate package, so those who don't want the image support can download a smaller binary. w3m is a popular project and has been around for a number of years, so your distribution should have packages available for it. Look specifically for a package labeled *w3m-img* or something similar, as that will contain the binary with image support. Alternatively you can download and compile the latest version of w3m yourself from the official site at *http://w3m.sourceforge.net*.

After you have installed w3m with image support, it will automatically load images as it renders a page. Just pass the URL to w3m on the command line, or if w3m is already loaded type **U** and enter a new URL. For instance, to load Google inside w3m from the command line, type:

```
$ w3m http://www.google.com
```

Figure 5-3 shows the default Google page as loaded through w3m. One nice thing about w3m is the fact that you can use the arrow keys to move a cursor around in the web page itself, instead of moving from hyperlink to hyperlink, making it faster to get to the links you want to use. Table 5-2 shows a list of common w3m key bindings.

Figure 5-3. w3m with Google loaded

Table 5-2. Common w3m key bindings

Key	Function
Spacebar	Forward page.
b	Backward page.
l, right arrow	Cursor right.
h, left arrow	Cursor left.
j, down arrow	Cursor down.
k, up arrow	Cursor up.
J	Roll up one line.
K	Roll down one line.
>	Shift screen right.
<	Shift screen left.
.	Shift screen one column right.
,	Shift screen one column left.
Tab	Move to the next hyperlink.
Enter	Follow hyperlink.
a	Save link to file.
U	Open URL.
Esc-b	Load bookmark.
Esc-a	Add current to bookmark.
/	Search forward.
?	Search backward.
H	Help.
a	Quit.

Most web pages assume the default background is white, but most terminals default to a black background. When using w3m you might want to launch a terminal with a white background and a dark foreground. To launch an xterm with a white background and a black foreground type:

```
$ xterm -fg black -bg white
```

HACK #97 Star in Your Own Reality TV Show

Install and use common USB webcams under Linux.

Webcams have a variety of uses, from video conferencing to surveillance to just showing your friends what you are doing at the moment. Linux support for webcams, particularly USB webcams, is pretty good, provided you know where to look. Once the webcam is installed, there are a lot of programs available to take quick snapshots, automatically upload images to a server periodically, and even turn your webcam into a motion detector. In this hack, I cover the general steps you need to install a webcam under Linux, and highlight some of the popular Linux webcam applications.

Install the Webcam

The first and most difficult step to installing a webcam is figuring out which Linux module it uses. There are a number of webcam modules built into the standard kernel series, but there are also quite a few that aren't, so the sort of detective work you need to do will vary depending upon your webcam. Before you do too much detective work though, just plug in your webcam and check the output of *dmesg* to see if your system automatically recognizes your webcam. Here is some sample *dmesg* output showing a webcam being recognized.

```
$ dmesg
. . .
usb 1-1: new full speed USB device using uhci_hcd and address 3
Linux video capture interface: v1.00
/home/greenfly/src/spca5xx-20050701/drivers/usb/spca5xx.c: USB SPCA5xx
camera found. Type Labtec Webcam (unknown CCD)
/home/greenfly/src/spca5xx-20050701/drivers/usb/spca5xx.c: [spca5xx_probe:
8652] Camera type GBGR
usbcore: registered new driver spca5xx
/home/greenfly/src/spca5xx-20050701/drivers/usb/spca5xx.c: spca5xx driver
00.57.00 registered
/home/greenfly/src/spca5xx-20050701/drivers/usb/spca5xx.c: VIDIOCMCAPTURE:
invalid format (7)
```

In my case, the above message didn't appear automatically because I wasn't lucky enough to have support for my webcam directly in the kernel. If your system doesn't automatically find your webcam, you will have some work to do.

The steps vary depending on the driver, but the basic steps are to locate your style of webcam, download the module for your device, extract the source code, and build the module according to the instructions. The Webcam HOWTO at *http://www.tldp.org/HOWTO/Webcam-HOWTO* provides a pretty thorough listing of webcam drivers and the devices they support, so go there first and find your device in the list. You will need kernel headers to build this module, so if you didn't build your own kernel you will need to install the kernel headers package for your distribution's kernel.

After the webcam module is installed, plug in your webcam if it wasn't plugged in already, and check *dmesg* again to see if it was recognized. You might need to manually load your webcam module as root before it gets recognized. In the case of my spca5xx webcam module I would type:

```
# modprobe spca5xx
```

Webcams use the video4linux support in the kernel and will register with a */dev/videoX* device starting with */dev/video0*, so if you plug in more than one webcam or have more than one video4linux device installed either look through *dmesg* for information on which device was assigned to which webcam or use a tool like *xawtv* to scan for the device:

```
$ xawtv -hwscan
This is xawtv-3.94, running on Linux/i686 (2.6.10)
looking for available devices
port 56-56
    type : Xvideo, image scaler
    name : Intel(R) 830M/845G/852GM/855GM/865G Video Overlay

/dev/video0: OK                         [ -device /dev/video0 ]
type : v4l
    name : Labtec Webcam
    flags:  capture
```

Because webcams use */dev/video*, just as with TV Tuners and general frame grabbers, you can also use webcam software with a camcorder that is attached to your hardware frame grabber.

Use Your Webcam

With the webcam installed, it's time to actually test and use it. One of the easiest GUI webcam tools to use is *gqcam*, which is probably already packaged by your Linux distribution, so look for it in your package installation tool. If not, download it from the official page at *http://cse.unl.edu/~cluening/gqcam* and compile and install it according to the installation instructions.

Start Gqcam from your desktop menu or type **gqcam** in a terminal. Gqcam opens and displays video it gets from the first video device. The interface is pretty basic and provides you with the general controls that you need to adjust brightness, contrast, hue, and other video settings. You can also control whether the video is full sized or a fraction of the highest resolution. To grab a frame from the webcam, click Snap Picture, and enter a filename to save the image. Click Freeze Picture to stop at the current video frame.

A popular application for webcams is to periodically snap pictures and upload them to a site. Although you could do this manually, the appropriately named *webcam* program seeks to automate the task. *webcam* is part of the *xawtv* package **[Hack #74]** discusses. *webcam*'s design makes it easy to run from a cron job. It takes no arguments on the command line other than an optional configuration file to load, otherwise all configuration is done in the *~/.webcamrc* file.

The *.webcamrc* file is split into two sections, grab and ftp. The grab section has all of the settings for image capture. Here is a sample grab section from a *.webcamrc* file:

```
[grab]
device = /dev/video0
text = "webcam %Y-%m-%d %H:%M:%S"
fg_red = 255
fg_green = 255
fg_blue = 255
width = 320
height = 240
delay = 3
wait = 0
rotate = 0
top = 0
left = 0
bottom = -1
right = -1
quality = 75
trigger = 0
once = 0
```

The configuration file options are pretty self-explanatory and are documented completely in the man page, but here are a few interesting options. The text parameter defines what text will be overlaid onto the image. In this case each image would say the word "webcam" followed by the timestamp. The fg_red, fg_green, and fg_blue options control the colors for the text overlay (in this example, white). The delay option specifies the delay in seconds between image grabs, so adjust this value depending on how often you want to take pictures. If the trigger option is set to something other than zero, *webcam* will compare the current image with the last uploaded image and only upload the new image if the difference is greater than the value of trigger.

The ftp section of *.webcamrc* contains all of the settings for the upload server. Here is a sample ftp section:

```
[ftp]
host = www.example.com
user = username
pass = password
dir  = public_html/images
file = webcam.jpeg
tmp  = uploading.jpeg
passive = 1
debug = 0
auto = 0
local = 0
ssh = 0
```

These options are also pretty self-explanatory. Enter the account information for the ftp account on your server. *webcam* also supports SSH uploads as an alternative, provided you already have passwordless SSH keys set up, just set *ssh* equal to 1.

To test *webcam* locally, set the local variable to 1. You might want to modify the dir variable as well, so that it will copy the image to an existing local directory. Then start *webcam*. Here's example output from *webcam* set to put files under */tmp* for testing:

```
$ webcam
reading config file: /home/greenfly/.webcamrc
video4linux webcam v1.5 - (c) 1998-2002 Gerd Knorr
grabber config:
  size 320x240 [24 bit TrueColor (LE: bgr)]
  input (null), norm (null), jpeg quality 75
  rotate=0, top=0, left=0, bottom=240, right=320
write config [ftp]:
  local transfer /tmp//uploading.jpeg => /tmp//webcam.jpeg
```

Once you have confirmed *webcam* is grabbing images correctly, change the local and dir variables back to their original settings and restart *webcam* so it will start uploading images to the remote server.

One easy way to constantly take webcam images is through *cron*. Since you only want *webcam* to be run once, set the once variable in *.webcamrc* to 1 and then edit your user's *crontab* with:

```
$ crontab -e
```

Here's an example *crontab* entry to run *webcam* every two minutes:

```
*/2 *   * * *   webcam > /dev/null
```

Make Internet Phone Calls with Skype

HACK #98

Use the cross-platform Skype tool to call friends and family over your Internet connection.

VoIP (Voice over IP), or placing phone calls over the Internet, has gotten a lot of hype recently. After all, why pay long distance or even local telephone fees if you can make the same phone call using the Internet connection you already have? There are a number of different methods for placing computer-to-computer calls over the Internet, but lately the Skype software, which blends voice chat with regular instant messaging, has become increasingly popular. Skype offers Windows and Mac clients, but it also offers a Linux client, so with a little configuration, you can talk to your friends and family regardless of which OS they use. This hack covers how to install and configure Skype for voice chat.

To learn more about VoIP, check out the O'Reilly books *Skype Hacks* and *VoIP Hacks*.

The first step is to download and install Skype for Linux. Skype is a commercial product and although the software can be downloaded for free, it is not Open Source software. To get Skype, visit the official Skype Linux download page at *http://www.skype.com/products/skype/linux*. This page provides precompiled packages for a variety of distributions including SUSE, Fedora, Mandrake, and Debian. If your distribution isn't represented, you can download the precompiled software in tarball form and extract it wherever you want to store it. Otherwise use your distribution's package manager to install the precompiled package.

After Skype is installed, type **skype** in a console window, or type the full path to the *skype* executable if you installed it somewhere other than in your path. The first time that Skype launches, it will prompt you to create a new Skype account. If you have a previously created account you may enter it here, otherwise think of a username and password for yourself. After the account has been created, you can also enter in other personal information, although this step is optional. This personal information can be used so that your friends (or I suppose your enemies too) can search for you without knowing your exact username.

The next step is to add contacts to your contact list. Click Tools → Add a Contact and type the contact's username, or click the search icon to search for someone if you aren't sure of his exact username. As the contact list gets populated, you will notice that each contact has a status icon so you can see whether they are online, and if so, whether they are available to talk.

To place a call, right-click on the contact you wish to call and select Call this Contact or click the phone receiver icon that will be highlighted on the bottom of the window. Make sure that the volume levels for the speaker and microphone are set to a reasonably high setting in your mixer program. You can call more than one person at a time and place them all on the same line, and you can click Call → Hold to put someone on hold. When you are finished with a call, click Call → Hangup. When someone calls you, Skype will make a ringing sound (which can be rather startling, particularly if you have headphones on) and prompt you so you can choose to accept or reject the call.

The default configuration for Skype works well for the average user. Click File → Options if you want to configure the settings. The configuration window is split into the following tabs:

General tab
> This tab lets you configure basic settings such as the default behavior when you double-click a contact.

Privacy tab
> This tab lets you configure whom you allow calls and chats from and lets you manage a list of blocked users.

Hand/Headsets tab
> This tab is used to configure which audio device Skype will use. By default it uses */dev/dsp* but you can direct it to */dev/dsp1*, */dev/dsp2*, or another audio device.

Call Alerts and Chat Alerts tabs
> These tabs allow you to control what happens when someone initiates a call or chat with you. Settings you can configure include whether or not to play a ring tone and whether to display a notification in the system tray.

Advanced tab
> This tab lets you change which port Skype uses for incoming connections, so you can adjust it according to any firewall you may have in place.

 If your sound card does not natively support multiplexing (see "Play Multiple Sounds at the Same Time" **[Hack #15]**) be sure no other devices are accessing the sound card while you start Skype so it will have access to */dev/dsp*. **[Hacks #33 and #45]** provide tips on using microphones under Linux.

Skype also offers two pay services that link Skype with standard phone lines. SkypeOut allows you to call standard telephones from your Skype program. After you sign up for the plan, the Start tab will display your current account balance. Click the Dial tab in the main window, and then dial the number you wish to call on the number pad in that window. You can hang up or hold the call like with computer-to-computer Skype calls. In addition, Skype offers a plan called SkypeIn that lets you set up a phone number people can call from a regular phone that will ring your Skype program.

HACK #99 Turn Your Linux Box into a PBX

Install and test the Asterisk open source telephony server on your Linux PC.

Asterisk is open source software to turn a Linux computer into a Voice over IP Private Branch Exchange (PBX). As a PBX it can be the backbone server to provide telephone service to hundreds of office telephones or a call router and voicemail server for an especially geeky individual— like you. As VoIP is the future of telephony, playing around with an Asterisk server is a good way to get your toes wet in this exciting new field, and this hack shows you how to get it installed.

Some RPM packages are available to simplify Asterisk's installation, but manual compilation is relatively easy. So I'm going to show you how to download, compile, and install Asterisk the "old-fashioned" way. The development branch you'll download from is stable, though once you get comfortable with Asterisk you'll want to jump out on the bleeding edge and try the developer releases, too. Each release tends to introduce something new and worthwhile, even if it's not in the stable branch yet.

The easiest place to download the Asterisk software is the CVS repository at Digium, the company responsible for Asterisk and some of the hardware components that work with it. To access the CVS repository, you'll need to be logged into your Linux computer at a shell prompt as root. Type these commands to run the CVS check-out routine and download the source code:

```
# cd /usr/src
# export CVSROOT=:pserver:anoncvs@cvs.digium.com:/usr/cvsroot
# cvs login
# cvs checkout zaptel libpri asterisk
```

Alternatively, you can specify a particular version of Asterisk:

```
# cvs checkout -r v1-2 zaptel libpri asterisk
```

When prompted, use **anoncvs** as a password. If you don't use /usr/src as the local location for compiling programs, substitute the appropriate path. The CVS client you're running here will create the /usr/src/asterisk directory that contains all the Asterisk source code. Once the download completes, you are ready to begin compiling.

Asterisk consists of several software components for Linux. Not all of these packages are required, as some of them are drivers for Digium's interface cards. If you aren't planning to use Digium's cards, you'll need to build only the last of the three, *asterisk*:

libpri

> A driver module that supports Zaptel-compliant interface cards so that ISDN and PRI trunks can be interfaced with Asterisk.

zaptel

> A driver module that allows legacy telephone line interfaces cards that provide FXO, FXS, and T1/E1 signaling to be used with Asterisk.

asterisk

> A modular software daemon that provides telephony, management, and call-accounting features, including voicemail, Session Initiation Protocol (SIP) telephone support, dial plan, and so on; in a nutshell, Asterisk is an all-software PBX.

If you're wondering about these technical terms, don't worry. As you experiment with Asterisk and learn more about VoIP, they'll become very familiar. For now, just compile and install all three of them.

Since you ran the CVS download, the source code for each Asterisk software component is sitting in its respective directory in */usr/src*. Let's compile each software component by issuing the following commands. Again, you need to compile *zaptel* and *libpri* only if you're planning on using legacy or Digium interface cards. Many of the examples in this book use legacy devices, so it's probably a good idea to compile them all right now. Here is the sequence of commands:

```
# cd zaptel
# make clean ; make install
# cd ../libpri
# make clean ; make install
# cd ../asterisk
# make clean ; make install
```

It should take 20 minutes at most to complete the whole build on an average PC. Once built, Asterisk is ready to use. But you can't race this Ferrari without a training lap on the test track, and you can't really use Asterisk until you understand the basics of configuring it. So it's time for driving school. To get started, run this command in the Asterisk source directory:

```
# make samples
```

This creates a basic sample set of Asterisk configuration files and places them in */etc/asterisk*. You might want to peruse these files—especially *extensions.conf* and *sip.conf*, where you'll likely be spending a lot of time.

If you've used an RPM package or some other precompiled Asterisk distribution (or if you've obtained a Linux distribution with Asterisk already installed), you can still obtain the source distribution files from Digium's CVS repository and issue only the make samples command. This will give you the sample configuration files without actually rebuilding Asterisk on your PC.

Start and Stop the Asterisk Server

The Asterisk program has two modes of operation: *server* mode and *client* mode. The server is the instance of Asterisk that stays running all the time, handling calls, recording voicemails, greeting callers while users are away, and so on. The client is the instance of Asterisk that allows you to monitor and manipulate the server while it runs. The mode the program uses depends on how Asterisk is invoked at the command prompt or within a shell script.

To launch Asterisk in server mode, execute this command:

```
# asterisk -vvv &
```

The more *v*'s, the more verbose Asterisk's console output will be.

To connect Asterisk in client mode on the local machine already running in server mode, execute this command:

```
# asterisk -r
```

Once the Asterisk client is connected to the Asterisk server, you can use Asterisk's command-line interface to issue queries and commands about the telephony server. These include listing calls in progress, listing used and unused channels, and stopping the Asterisk server.

You can shut down the server using one of several Asterisk CLI commands:

- *restart now*
- *restart when convenient*
- *stop now*
- *stop when convenient*

The *restart* commands stop and then restart the Asterisk server process, which can be helpful in situations where the server's configuration has changed significantly and needs to be restarted. The *stop* commands just shut down the Asterisk server process. You'll have to execute the Asterisk program in server mode to get it running again.

The *now* and *when convenient* arguments tell Asterisk how quickly to shut down or restart. If you want to interrupt the current calls and tasks in progress on the server, *now* is appropriate. If you want Asterisk to wait until all the calls and tasks are finished and there is no call activity at all, *when convenient* is appropriate. Generally, especially if you're planning to have any callers besides yourself on the system, get in the habit of using *when convenient*.

> All these commands ultimately shut down Asterisk. If you make a configuration change that doesn't require a complete restart, such as a change to a certain phone extension, you can just use *reload* at the Asterisk prompt.

Linux-Specific Start and Stop Scripts

Depending on your particular flavor of Linux, be it Fedora, Debian, SuSE, or something else, you'll find your system's normal startup scripts in a place that's unique to each flavor. Fortunately, Asterisk's makefile has an option that lets you automatically generate start and stop scripts that are specific to your flavor of Linux. In your Asterisk *src* directory, just issue the command make config, and the scripts will be installed. These scripts start and stop not only Asterisk, but also the Zaptel drivers, if you've compiled them.

As it stands at this point, your Asterisk server won't be especially useful. You'll be able to explore the Asterisk command prompt with asterisk -r, but the truly fun stuff, like hooking up phone lines and phones, is still to come. To try out Asterisk's cool demonstration routines—like interactive voice response (IVR) and an Internet-based VoIP call—you've got to configure a phone of one sort or another to access the Asterisk server. I explain how to do this in my book *VoIP Hacks* (O'Reilly), but if you want to get started quickly and don't have a VoIP hardphone (a physical phone), then you should try connecting to your server with the X-Lite softphone, available at *http://www.counterpath.com*, or any one of several other softphones. Unfortunately, because Skype uses a proprietary protocol, you won't be able to connect to your Asterisk server using this popular cross-platform VoIP program.

—*Ted Wallingford*

HACK   **Host a Photo Gallery**

#100   Use Gallery to easily thumbnail, label, and organize your photos into galleries— all from a web interface.

Photo albums have a long tradition of reminding us of special family moments as well as embarrassing a family member in front of their significant other. As nice as they are, photo albums have some problems. For one, photos degrade over time. For another, if a family is spread out geographically, it can be difficult to share photos without making multiple prints.

Of course, in the age of the Internet and digital cameras, you can simply move your photos away from a physical album into a digital one stored on the Web. This way you can share photos with family and friends no matter where they are, plus they can flip through the album at their leisure and download copies of the photos all on their own. There are a number of tools out there, both commercial and free, to help you manage your digital photo album, but one particularly nice project for Linux, Gallery, makes managing a number of photo galleries simple to set up, simple to administer, and simple for everyone to view.

The Gallery project home is located at *http://gallery.menalto.com*. The site itself is a great resource, with extensive documentation and a number of sample sites so you can see how others have used Gallery. To install Gallery, you must first meet a few requirements:

Web server
> Gallery is a web-based application and as such it requires a web server to host it. Apache is the preferred web server for Gallery, although it is also known to run under Microsoft's IIS web server. This might be a web server that you personally host, or you might make use of a paid hosting service (some ISPs offer a certain amount of space for free) provided these services include PHP and an image-processing library.

PHP
> Gallery is written in PHP, so the web server that hosts it needs to support PHP code.

Image-processing library
> To perform basic image manipulation, Gallery needs either NetPBM or ImageMagick installed. If you don't already have these libraries installed (or your web host doesn't), download precompiled binaries at *http://sourceforge.net/project/showfiles.php?group_id=7130&package_id=14464*.

There are also a number of optional libraries that Gallery can utilize if they are installed including *mod_rewrite* (so Gallery can create shorter URLs for albums), *jhead* (allows Gallery to extract EXIF data from images), *zipinfo* (so Gallery can unzip *zip* archives containing multiple photos), and *jpegtran* (provides Gallery with the ability to losslessly rotate JPEG images).

After you have met Gallery's requirements, you are ready to download and install the Gallery package. Go to the official page and click the Download Now link on the left side bar. There you will see links to download sites for the Gallery package itself as well as links to optional libraries. Click the link for the latest stable release and download the newest *gallery*.tar.gz* file you see.

Extract the tarball in a directory on your machine, create two blank files called *.htaccess* and *config.php* in the new *gallery* directory, and then make them world-writeable:

```
greenfly@napoleon:~$ tar xvzf gallery-1.5.tar.gz
greenfly@napoleon:~$ cd gallery
greenfly@napoleon:~/gallery$ touch config.php .htaccess
greenfly@napoleon:~/gallery$ chmod 0777 config.php .htaccess
```

Now create a directory to hold all of the different albums and make it world-writeable. This directory just needs to be accessible somewhere in your web directory, but you might as well put it in your *gallery* directory so everything is together:

```
greenfly@napoleon:~/gallery$ mkdir albums
greenfly@napoleon:~/gallery$ chmod 0777 albums
```

 Yes, all these world-writeable files and directories seem like a bad security measure. Don't worry, you will lock down the permissions after the basic configuration tests have been done.

Now copy the *gallery* directory to your web server. The method you use for this will be different depending on whether you are using hosted web space (in which case you will likely FTP the entire directory up) or your own web server (in which case you will copy it however you wish). You don't necessarily need to put *gallery* in the root of your web directory, but for the purposes of these examples that is where the *gallery* directory will be.

With the *gallery* directory copied up, open a web browser and go to *http://www.example.com/gallery/setup/index.php* replacing `www.example.com` with the URL to your web space. This page is the gallery configuration wizard, and it will perform some tests to ensure that all of its requirements are met. If all the checks come up green, then you are ready to move on to the next step. If any checks come up red, the test failed and you will need to fix the listed problem on your web server. Some tests might fail with a yellow warning, in which case you might want to remedy the problem, but you don't necessarily have to for Gallery to function.

After Gallery finds no serious errors, you may move on to the second page, which will walk you through settings to apply to the entire site. The third page lets you configure the default settings for a new album. The fourth and final page displays the actual *config.php* configuration file. If everything is set the way you want it, click Save Config.

With the configuration saved, you can now lock down the file permissions. If you have shell access to the *gallery* directory, execute the *secure.sh* script inside the main *gallery* directory. If you have FTP access you can use *chmod* directly:

```
ftp> cd gallery
ftp> chmod 644 .htaccess
ftp> chmod 644 config.php
ftp> chmod 400 setup
```

At this point Gallery is configured and ready to accept your first album. Go to your main Gallery page, click on the login link, and log in with your administrator username and password. After you have logged in, you will notice new options along the top of the screen. Click the new album link to create a new album. After the screen refreshes, click the main link to your new untitled album to go inside. Gallery supports both single albums with photos and nested albums. Nested albums are basically albums inside of albums, and can be useful if you want to separate multiple days of a vacation or otherwise organize a particular album into subcategories. Click "add photos" to add new photos to the current album or click new nested album to create a new album within the current one (see Figure 5-4).

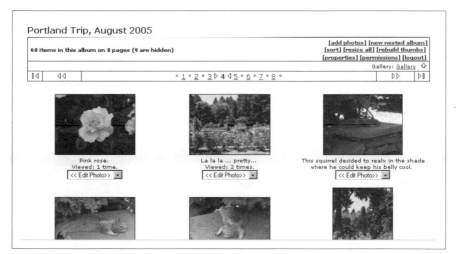

Figure 5-4. Default gallery page with a few thumbnails

When you click the add photos link, a new window will appear with a few different options for file uploading. The first option is to click the various Browse buttons on the screen and find individual photos that you want to upload. Alternatively, you can FTP or otherwise copy the files to the web server, and then type in the full path to that directory. After the file path or paths are configured, click Submit. A new window will appear and show you which files gallery is about to process. Approve the list and gallery will begin uploading (if the files were loaded locally) and processing the files.

Depending on the speed of your network and the speed of your processor this might take some time for a large number of images since Gallery makes different thumbnail sizes for each photo. Once it is finished processing the files, close the window and go back to the window for your album. The page should refresh to show you the new photos you have added.

Gallery provides you with a number of options for photos in an album. You can add individual captions to each album and photo, rotate the photo, hide it so that regular visitors won't see it, move it to another gallery, or set it as the highlight photo. A highlight photo is the photo that will be used as the main photo for a particular album. Once you are finished editing your photos, go back to the main page for the album and rename the title and add a description to the album. Then log out if you wish and email your friends and family with the URL of your new album.

Index

\ (backslash), indicating line breaks, 4

Numbers

3D control (surround sound), 36

A

AAlib library, 156
acidrip utility, 169–172
Acrobat Reader, 271
album art, 60
   adding to ID3 tags, 78
Album Cover Art Downloader
      program, 78
album name, changing with id3v2, 77
ALSA sound system, 34
   alsamixer, 36
      configuring for surround
         sound, 39
   aplay player, testing surround
      sound, 40
   Intel8x0 Alsa driver, 39
   output plug-in for XMMS, 49
   volume controls, additional, 36
   volume controls, basic, 35
AM radio, broadcasting sound to from
      computer monitor, 263–265
amaroK, 56–63
   configuring, 58
   display styles, 57
   downloading and installing, 57
   main window, 57
   sidebar, 59–62

Collections pane, 61
Context pane, 60
Files pane, 62
Media Device pane, 62
Playlist pane, 61
storing data in MySQL database, 62
amp utility, 265
Analog Real-Time Synthesizer (see aRts)
animate tool (ImageMagick), 6, 29, 32
animation, screen capture movie, 27–32
Apache web server
   preferred for Gallery, 287
   using with Jinzora, 255
Apple HFS+ file system, 119
aRts (Analog Real-Time Synthesizer), 42
   configuring, 43
   legacy compatibility, 44
   use by amaroK, 59
artsdsp program, 44
ASCII art, converting movies to, 156
aspect ratios supported by tovid, 195,
      199
Asterisk, 283–286
   downloading from CVS repository at
      Digium, 283
   Linux-specific start and stop
      scripts, 286
   software components for Linux, 284
   starting and stopping server, 285
asterisk (modular software
      daemon), 284
at command, scheduling
      recordings, 250

We'd like to hear your suggestions for improving our indexes. Send email to *index@oreilly.com*.

Colophon

Our look is the result of reader comments, our own experimentation, and feedback from distribution channels. Distinctive covers complement our distinctive approach to technical topics, breathing personality and life into potentially dry subjects.

The tool on the cover of *Linux Multimedia Hacks* is a stereoscope. By independently presenting slightly different images, together called a stereopair, to each eye, stereoscopes simulate the depth perception humans experience in real life. The first known stereoscopes were developed around 1833, predating the invention of photography, and used drawings for the stereopairs. In the early days of photography, stereopods and travel photographs were very popular, due to their vivid presentation of faraway places.

Jamie Peppard was the production editor and proofreader for *Linux Multimedia Hacks*. Nancy Reinhardt was the copyeditor. Reba Libby and Claire Cloutier provided quality control, and Lydia Onofrei provided production assistance. Ellen Troutman Zaig wrote the index.

Marcia Friedman designed the cover of this book, based on a series design by Edie Freedman. The cover image is from fotosearch.com. Linda Palo produced the cover layout with Adobe InDesign CS using Adobe's Helvetica Neue and ITC Garamond fonts.

David Futato designed the interior layout. This book was converted by Keith Fahlgren to FrameMaker 5.5.6. The text font is Linotype Birka; the heading font is Adobe Helvetica Neue Condensed; and the code font is LucasFont's TheSans Mono Condensed. The illustrations that appear in the book were produced by Robert Romano, Jessamyn Read, and Lesley Borash using Macromedia FreeHand MX and Adobe Photoshop CS. This colophon was written by Jamie Peppard.

Related Titles from O'Reilly

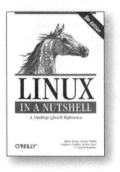

Linux

Building Embedded Linux Systems

Building Secure Servers with Linux

The Complete FreeBSD, *4th Edition*

Even Grues Get Full

Exploring the JDS Linux Desktop

Extreme Programming Pocket Guide

GDB Pocket Reference

Knoppix Hacks

Knoppix Pocket Guide

Learning Red Hat Enterprise Linux and Fedora, *4th Edition*

Linux Cookbook

Linux Desktop Hacks

Linux Device Drivers, *3rd Edition*

Linux in a Nutshell, *5th Edition*

Linux in a Windows World

Linux iptables Pocket Reference

Linux Network Administrator's Guide, *3rd Edition*

Linux Pocket Guide

Linux Security Cookbook

Linux Server Hacks

Linux Unwired

Linux Web Server CD Bookshelf, *Version 2.0*

LPI Linux Certification in a Nutshell

Managing RAID on Linux

More Linux Server Hacks

OpenOffice.org Writer

Programming with Qt, *2nd Edition*

Root of all Evil

Running Linux, *5th Edition*

Samba Pocket Reference, *2nd Edition*

Test Driving Linux

Understanding the Linux Kernel, *3rd Edition*

Understanding Open Source & Free Software Licensing

User Friendly

Using Samba, *2nd Edition*

Version Control with Subversion

O'REILLY®

Our books are available at most retail and online bookstores.

To order direct: 1-800-998-9938 • *order@oreilly.com* • *www.oreilly.com*

Online editions of most O'Reilly titles are available by subscription at *safari.oreilly.com*

Keep in touch with O'Reilly

Download examples from our books

To find example files from a book, go to: *www.oreilly.com/catalog* select the book, and follow the "Examples" link.

Register your O'Reilly books

Register your book at *register.oreilly.com* Why register your books? Once you've registered your O'Reilly books you can:

- Win O'Reilly books, T-shirts or discount coupons in our monthly drawing.
- Get special offers available only to registered O'Reilly customers.
- Get catalogs announcing new books (US and UK only).
- Get email notification of new editions of the O'Reilly books you own.

Join our email lists

Sign up to get topic-specific email announcements of new books and conferences, special offers, and O'Reilly Network technology newsletters at:

elists.oreilly.com

It's easy to customize your free elists subscription so you'll get exactly the O'Reilly news you want.

Get the latest news, tips, and tools

www.oreilly.com

- "Top 100 Sites on the Web"—PC Magazine
- CIO Magazine's Web Business 50 Awards

Our web site contains a library of comprehensive product information (including book excerpts and tables of contents), downloadable software, background articles, interviews with technology leaders, links to relevant sites, book cover art, and more.

Work for O'Reilly

Check out our web site for current employment opportunities:

jobs.oreilly.com

Contact us

O'Reilly Media, Inc.
1005 Gravenstein Hwy North
Sebastopol, CA 95472 USA
Tel: 707-827-7000 or 800-998-9938
    (6am to 5pm PST)
Fax: 707-829-0104

Contact us by email

For answers to problems regarding your order or our products:
order@oreilly.com

To request a copy of our latest catalog:
catalog@oreilly.com

For book content technical questions or corrections: **booktech@oreilly.com**

For educational, library, government, and corporate sales: **corporate@oreilly.com**

To submit new book proposals to our editors and product managers:
proposals@oreilly.com

For information about our international distributors or translation queries:
international@oreilly.com

For information about academic use of O'Reilly books:
adoption@oreilly.com
or visit:
academic.oreilly.com

For a list of our distributors outside of North America check out:
international.oreilly.com/distributors.html

Order a book online

www.oreilly.com/order_new